Paul's Necessary Sin

The Experience of Liberation

TIMOTHY ASHWORTH
Woodbrooke Quaker Study Centre, UK

ASHGATE

© Timothy Ashworth 2006

Published by
Ashgate Publishing Limited
Gower House
Croft Road
Aldershot
Hampshire GU11 3HR
England

Ashgate Publishing Company
Suite 420
101 Cherry Street
Burlington, VT 05401-4405
USA

Ashgate website: http://www.ashgate.com

British Library Cataloguing in Publication Data
Ashworth, Timothy
  Paul's necessary sin : the experience of liberation
  1.Paul, the Apostle, Saint 2.Bible. N.T. Epistles of Paul - Theology
  I.Title
  227'.06

Library of Congress Cataloging-in-Publication Data
Ashworth, Timothy, 1954-
  Paul's necessary sin : the experience of liberation / Timothy Ashworth.
      p. cm.
  Includes bibliographical references and index.
  ISBN 0-7546-5499-0 (hardcover : alk. paper)
  1. Bible. N.T. Epistles of Paul–Theology. 2. Liberation–Religious aspects–Christianity–Biblical teaching. I. Title.
  BS2655.L5A84 2006
  227'.06–dc22

                                                                                    2005030617

ISBN-13: 978-0-7546-5499-5
ISBN-10: 0-7546-5499-0

Printed and bound in Great Britain by MPG Books Ltd. Bodmin, Cornwall.

Contents

Acknowledgements

Three inspirational teachers nourished the early stages of this work: C. T. R. Hayward, Robert Morgan and James D. G. Dunn. Colleagues and students at Woodbrooke Quaker Study Centre provided creative support as the work progressed. Clare and family at home constantly reminded me that there is much more to life than Paul. Richard Bevan, Rachel Muers, Ian J. H. Parker and Paula Gooder provided practical help with the content at crucial stages. The team at Ashgate, Sarah Lloyd, Ann Newell, Tom Bertram and Robert Rowinski, have been a pleasure to work with. Ben Pink Dandelion, having caught something of my own excitement for this material ten years ago, has offered his clear-thinking and colleagueship with extraordinary generosity. It is a joy to publicly thank all of them.

Given that this work has been so long coming, it is a particular pleasure to be able to dedicate it to my father on his 78th birthday, with thanks for his faith and trust, challenge and guidance.

Woodbrooke Quaker Study Centre
Birmingham
29 August 2006

Bibliographical Information

Bibles

The Scripture quotations contained herein (except where noted) are from *The New Revised Standard Version of the Bible*, Anglicized Edition, copyright © 1989, 1955 by the Division of Christian Education of the National Council of Churches of Christ in the United States of America, and are used with permission. All rights reserved.

NRSV   New Revised Standard Version

Other versions used:

AV	Authorized Version = King James Version
JB	Jerusalem Bible
NEB	New English Bible
NIV	New International Version
NJB	New Jerusalem Bible
REB	Revised English Bible
RSV	Revised Standard Version
RV	Revised Version
TEV	Today's English Version = Good News Bible

Greek text	Aland, Black, Martini, Metzger, Wikgren (1975), *The Greek New Testament*, 3rd edition, United Bible Societies.

Works referred to in the main text

Unless indicated otherwise the quotations of Dunn, Sanders and Ziesler are from:

Dunn, James D. G. (1998), *The Theology of Paul the Apostle*, Edinburgh: T&T Clark/Grand Rapids, Michigan: Wm. B. Eerdmans.

Sanders, E. P. (2001), *Paul: A Very Short Introduction*, Oxford: Oxford University Press, = Sanders, E. P. (1991), *Paul* (Past Masters series), Oxford: Oxford University Press. Page numbers are given for both editions.

Ziesler, John (1990), *Pauline Christianity*, Oxford: Oxford University Press.

Other works referred to are:

Dunn, James D. G. (1988), *Romans*, 2 volumes, Word Biblical Commentary 38, Dallas: Word.

Dunn, James D. G. (1993), *The Epistle to the Galatians*, London: A&C Black/ Peabody: Hendrickson.

Hays, Richard B. (2002) [1983], *The Faith of Jesus Christ: the narrative substructure of Galatians 3:1 – 4:11*, Grand Rapids, Michigan/Cambridge: Wm. B. Eerdmans.

Sanders, E. P. (1977), *Paul and Palestinian Judaism*, London: SCM/Philadelphia: Fortress = *PPJ*.

Sanders, E. P. (1983), *Paul, the Law and the Jewish People*, London: SCM/ Philadelphia: Fortress = *PLJP*.

Ziesler, John (1989), *Paul's Letter to the Romans*, London: SCM/Valley Forge, PA: TPI.

Ziesler, John Ziesler (1992), *The Epistle to the Galatians*, London: Epworth.

Reference works

BAGD   Bauer, W. (1979), *A Greek-English Lexicon of the New Testament and Other Early Christian Literature*, ed. W. F. Arndt and F. W. Gingrich; 2nd edition, ed. F. W. Gingrich and F. W. Danker, University of Chicago.

SOED   Onions, C. T. (ed.) (1972), *Shorter Oxford English Dictionary*, Oxford University Press.

TDNT   Kittel, G. and Friedrich, G. (1964-76), *Theological Dictionary of the New Testament*, 10 volumes, Grand Rapids: Eerdmans.

All used with permission.

Introduction

This book offers a radical and original interpretation of the theology of Paul that opens up a fresh understanding of early Christianity. It explores the nature of transformation among early Christians showing how a new way of living is bound together with a new perception of how the old life had been a kind of slavery which had not been perceived as such. It shows too how Paul uses the universal image of the movement from childhood to adulthood to illuminate his transformed sense of how God acts. No longer was God perceived by Paul as the source of power and authority outside of him, guiding him through written religious law, but Paul claimed to have come to an inward knowledge of God characterised by a sense of maturity and liberation. Such was the overwhelmingly good quality of his own experience that it brought with it a complete conviction that this was something given by the same God who had given the law to Moses. Major sections of Paul's writings are concerned with the questions this experience raises for Paul and others: how could God who gave the law now be demanding a different way of relating to the divine? Was the law a failure on the part of God? Or is God simply inconsistent? To make sense of his experience and defend before his fellow Jews his complete confidence that it is God-given, Paul interprets what happens to him not just as a personal transformation but as a new and universal act of God bringing the same possibility of a human intimacy with God to others.

It will be shown how a coherent theology emerges out of Paul's own experience of the transformative power that gave rise to the early Christian movement. It is concerned therefore with how the different major themes of his theology interrelate. But a vital source for its original conclusions lies in its radical method for defining the foundational elements of Paul's theology, the individual words that he uses.

Words and meanings

The first significant benefit of studying New Testament Greek as an undergraduate came for me when looking at an important section of Paul's letter to the Romans, a passage that we will return to several times in this book:

> But now, irrespective of the law, the *righteousness* of God has been disclosed, and is attested by the law and the prophets, the *righteousness* of God through *faith* in Jesus Christ for all who *believe*. For there is no distinction, since all have sinned and fall short of the glory of God; they are now *justified* by his grace as a gift ... (Rom 3:21-24)

I can still remember the shock of discovering that 'righteousness' and 'justified' are translating words from the same Greek root, *dik-*: 'righteousness' is translating *dikaiosunē* and 'justified' is translating *dikaioō*. We will look at precisely what these Greek words mean in the first chapter but what I want to point out now is the cause of the shock that I first experienced. It seemed to me obvious that if Paul is using noun and verb from the same family then he is using them to resonate and connect in his reader's mind; that whatever 'the righteousness of God' is must have a direct connection with whatever Paul means by 'justified'. It was not possible to be immediately aware of this in conventional English translations. The same issue was even more evident in the translation of the noun, *pistis* ('faith'), and verb, *pisteuō* ('believe'), which are placed just six words apart in the Greek text of the passage above. In both these word groups, without a consistent English translation or some knowledge of the Greek, it is impossible for the reader in English to experience directly the connections Paul is making.

The cause of this situation is not mysterious. English does not have the verbs 'to righteous' and 'to faith' that would enable translations consistent with the nouns 'righteousness' and 'faith'. Making the nouns consistent with the way that the verbs are translated above is also not an adequate solution. The noun 'belief' which would match the verb, 'to believe', tends to be used in English in association with statements – believing in certain teachings – which does not carry the same sense as 'having faith'. If we fix on the verb 'to justify' and choose 'justification' to make the noun consistent with the verb we quickly find that 'justification' is too limited a translation; we will explore those limitations in the first chapter in a way that will help us get at precisely what Paul means.

Ten years later, given this earlier experience, I set about translating Paul's letter to the Galatians with the aim of putting all the Greek words into English in a consistent way. Most words were relatively easy to deal with but there were a few that gave greater difficulty. I had particular problems with the Greek word, *stoicheia* (Gal 4:3,9), sometimes translated into English as 'elements' or 'elemental spirits'. This problem became acute because, if it were possible, I wanted to translate nouns and verbs from the same Greek root with the same English root word or phrase. Galatians also contains *stoicheō* (Gal 5:25; 6:16), the verb related to *stoicheia*.

There are seven letters that can reliably be ascribed to Paul: Romans, 1 and 2 Corinthians, Galatians, Philippians, 1 Thessalonians and Philemon (the whole of the work that follows assumes this scholarly consensus; see Dunn, *Theology*, 13; Sanders, *PPJ*, 431f; Ziesler, *Pauline Christianity*, 6f.). In order to see if there was any way to resolve this difficulty I moved outside Galatians to see if there were other uses of these words in Paul. There turned out to be two: Romans 4:12 and Philippians 3:16. What I was finding was that although *stoicheia* and *stoicheō* did not appear to be weighty theological words in themselves, they were turning up in passages where Paul is dealing with several different substantial theological issues. And I found that I could not pursue my task of translating *stoicheia* and *stoicheō* in Galatians consistently without also translating a number of other words occurring in the same passages which I also wanted to translate consistently. So that quite quickly I found myself at work on some thirty different passages of Paul's letters (the words and phrases involved are listed in a separate index). Although no knowledge of Greek is necessary to follow the argument of this book, issues concerned with translation are central and some general points about the approach adopted to translation need making.

It was more than a year after beginning to work in this way (and by this time having translated all of Paul's letters) that I explored in some depth the questions about words and their meanings that had been raised for me. I looked again at an essay by Anthony Thiselton in which he argues for the importance of taking context seriously:

> [T]he meaning of a word depends not on what it is in itself, but on its relation to other words and to other sentences which form its context. (A. C. Thiselton, "Semantics and New Testament Interpretation" in *New Testament Interpretation*, ed. I. H. Marshall, Exeter: Paternoster, 1977, p. 78f.)

His concern in making this point was to counter an overemphasis on a particular kind of 'word study' in biblical scholarship. Much scholarly energy has gone into extracting key words in the Bible and analysing them in depth, particularly by looking at the meaning that they have in other writings of the time. This approach tends to imagine a more or less fixed meaning for the word which, if one could find it, would bring a sharper understanding. Thiselton is providing a necessary counter to that approach by making it clear how an approach which separates word from context is likely to distort the interpretation. Yet what I had found in my own work challenged the view that 'the meaning of a word depends not on what it is in itself'. That was clearly only part of the story; the meaning of a word is also carried by 'what it is in itself'. Indeed, having emphasized the importance of context, Thiselton then goes on to acknowledge that 'words do indeed possess a stable core of meaning'. This is crucial and one of the key texts on semantics that Thiselton refers to makes the same observation:

> There is no getting away from the fact that single words have more or less permanent meanings, that they actually do refer to certain referents, and not to others, and that this characteristic is the indispensable basis of all communication. It is on this basis that the speaker selects his words, and the hearer understands them... (G. Stern, *Meaning and Change of Meaning. With Special Reference to the English Language*, Goteborgs Hogskolas Arsskrift, 38, Gothenburg 1931, p. 85.)

Whilst I had indeed found that the meanings of individual words of Paul are shaped by the context in which they are used, it is also helpful and reasonable to assume that when Paul selects the same word to use in several different contexts that it carries a 'more or less permanent meaning' for him. Another scholar quoted by Thiselton describes this 'more or less permanent meaning' as 'a kind of hard core or "inner fortress" within the area of meaning' (S. Ullmann, *The Principles of Semantics*, Oxford: Blackwell, 1957, p. 64).

It is worth identifying a possible source of confusion here. In English there are words that carry two quite different meanings. 'Bank' can mean 'a place for keeping money' or 'a piece of sloping land'. This can happen in Greek too. But these are exceptional cases. Usually, when presented with a number of definitions in a dictionary it is possible to see that those definitions cover a range of meanings that can be represented by a core meaning. The second definition of 'bank' above could have a separate definition in the dictionary as 'a grassy slope' as this is a particularly common use for the word but this would only be a more specific use of the word which has become common enough to merit a dictionary definition of its own. Context will lead to the particular image of 'a piece of sloping land' that is evoked in the reader's mind, whether that is 'a grassy bank' or 'a bank of mud' or 'a bank of trees'. In all the cases in Greek that will be looked at, we will be seeking to find a consistent English word or phrase for representing the related range of meanings that a word carries. Single words which carry sharply different meanings do not feature in the argument.

The process of translation

In his work, *The Semantics of Biblical Language*, James Barr writes:

> Word meanings have to be investigated by asking what is specific about the word. (J. Barr, *The Semantics of Biblical Language*, London: SCM Press, 1961, p. 171.)

This simple observation provides the key for the type of investigation undertaken in the work that follows. Nothing reveals more clearly what is specific about a particular word than determining what is consistent about it in a number of different contexts. A superficial view of what this involves might suggest that the definition that emerges from such an enquiry will necessarily be a broader and more general one to fit the variety of contexts in which the word is used; however, it will be seen in Chapter 3 that this is not the case. There the translation of *stoicheō* and *stoicheia* provides a particularly good example of a word that can only fit the variety of contexts if its 'hard core of meaning' is more sharp and limited. It is worth spelling out the process followed with *stoicheō* and *stoicheia* in simple steps.

1. Investigation into the verb, *stoicheō*, started with an informed guess at its English definition in the particular passage being considered. That definition was chosen using the dictionary and other translations and by looking at the context in which the word was being used.
2. The proposed definition was then tried in a different passage where the word was used. When that first proposed definition did not make good sense in the new context another definition was tried. What was found was that the second definition worked in both passages, not because it had a more general sense, but, because it was actually sharper, shaped more specifically to fit into both contexts.

3. That sharpened definition was then tried in other different passages where the word is used by Paul. Because it made sense in those there was a high probability that this sharpened definition was the 'hard core of meaning' in the word as Paul uses it, particularly given that the different passages were concerned with a variety of different subject matter. 'What is distinctive about the word' was coming through very clearly. This became especially clear when the process moved to include finding a definition for the noun, *stoicheia*, that was consistent with the definition for the verb.

This process when it began had a major subjective component. There was, at first, no external check for the accuracy of the English word or phrase that I was choosing to replace *stoicheia* except my own perception of what Paul might be saying. What brings objectivity to this process is the complexity of interrelationships between different words. This becomes clear in the following further steps in the process.

4. In practice, as the process moved forward to examine new passages, each proposed change in the definition – and there were several along the way – then meant going back over the passages already considered to check that any revision would fit in all contexts.

5. If the proposed English word or phrase did not fit in one context then the definition needed to be 'sharpened' or 'reshaped' so that it would 'fit', i.e. work in that context. And that 'sharpening' or 'reshaping' could only be done in reference to all the earlier contexts which had already been considered to ensure that the word would continue to make sense in those texts too.

6. More or less simultaneously, this same process needed to be pursued with other different words in a number of sentences under consideration. This was because, as the suggested meaning in *stoicheō/eia* was becoming clearer, a particular difficulty in just one passage under consideration might not be indicating a problem with the definition of *stoicheō/eia*. The problem could be the inaccurate translations of other words in the passage. This was, of course, particularly the case where a sharp and clear meaning of *stoicheō/eia* was fitting in all contexts but one. In that case there was a strong indication that some other word or words in that one section needed to be reconsidered. And that reconsideration involved keeping the search for the definition of *stoicheō/eia* on hold whilst pursuing the same process outlined above for other words.

7. In time, it became apparent that only one sharp and clear definition for *stoicheō/eia* would work sensibly with sharp and clear definitions for a number of other key words in all the contexts in which *stoicheō/eia* was used. Those sharp and clear definitions are, I propose, the 'hard' or 'stable core of meaning' for these words and they are presented in the main text of the book.

An important quotation from Stern describes this process:

> With regard first to the *verbal context* ..., the words in a sentence provide determining elements for each other. The addition of attribute, verb, adverb, and so on, to the subject-noun, will greatly limit the number of referents that might possibly be denoted by the noun, cutting off, as it were, successively further portions of the referential range as not relevant; the noun likewise determines the precise meaning of the other words. Only meanings which suit all the words in a sentence can be intended by the speaker, since the sentence is to express a logically coherent thought. ... The mutual limitations exercised by the word meanings in a phrase may be sufficient to make the total meaning perfectly definite, and to reduce the number of possible phrase referents to one ... (Stern, *Meaning*, p.140f).

The last three stages outlined above are akin to the process of solving a problem like the following. To the left are five squares arranged in order. One of the squares has been left empty. To solve the problem, you have to find which one of the five squares on the right should take the place of the empty square. Alternatives need to be played out in the mind before all the elements fit together clearly and the only possible solution is seen:

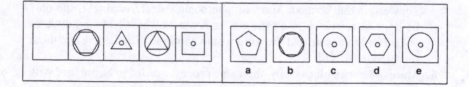

The above exercise is part of an intelligence test that is used for assessing children at the age of 10 or 11. It is not especially complex (the answer is 'd') . Some of the problems of assessing passages in Paul are considerably more complicated because of the numbers of words and sections of Paul's writing involved. However the process is fundamentally the same and leads to a similarly sharp and clear result. Or it would do if it were not for a factor that effectively limits and distorts this process.

Presuppositions: 'there is no neutral translator'

All the words considered in the work that follows either themselves carry the weight of traditional theological interpretation in the mind of the translator or they are embedded in passages which carry that similar weight. That is, at almost every stage in the process that has been described, choices are usually, to a greater or lesser extent, either prescribed or circumscribed by the weight of established theological interpretation. Certain lines of enquiry and solutions are either strongly expected or unthinkable. When the definition of even one element is limited and fixed in this way then this quickly introduces an extraordinary complexity into the process outlined, such that there appears to be no coherent solution to the question of how to put the various elements of Paul's thought together – whether of individual sentences or bigger elements of his theology. Paul then comes to be regarded as inconsistent or incoherent and this fact needs to be explained in some way. Scholars employ different approaches for dealing with this. E. P. Sanders, for example, seeks to present the view that Paul, while not being 'systematic', is still 'coherent', yet Sanders's definition of coherence severely limits its scope:

> ... I still see Paul as on the whole a "coherent," though not a "systematic" thinker.
> ... If each divergent statement comes from an identifiable "central conviction," I
> would call Paul a "coherent" thinker. If he does not relate his various conclusions
> to one another, he is "unsystematic". (*PLJP*, 147f)

That Sanders comes to this conclusion is particularly interesting because he is the scholar who, by overhauling one of the major scholarly foundations for the interpretation of Paul, had the most dramatic influence on Pauline studies in the latter part of the twentieth century. What he managed to establish was the recognition that for the greater part of the history of biblical scholarship the understanding of Paul has been shaped in relation to a distorted picture of the Judaism of his time. Paul – before coming to faith – was seen as guilt ridden, struggling under the weight of a law that made demands that could never be fulfilled. And hence the dramatic turnabout. Being now 'justified by faith' he feels liberated from the law, able now to be free of the sense of guilt and oppression. In *Paul and Palestinian Judaism* (*PPJ*), Sanders demolished this distorted picture of Judaism and in the process opened up the possibility of a reinterpretation of Paul.

The major part of *Paul and Palestinian Judaism*, some 428 pages, is not directly concerned with the thought of Paul. It consists of a detailed review of the Jewish literature from which we get our picture of Palestinian Judaism at the time of Paul (and Jesus). And together with this review, particularly in the first main chapter (some 200 pages in itself), is an engagement with New Testament scholars who have either created or accepted the distorted picture of Judaism, showing how the suspect conclusions of some have become the received truth of the many. Sanders's work is an extraordinary *tour de force* and could only be done by a scholar with very extensive linguistic tools and historical knowledge as well as an independence of thought to stand out against the many scholars for whom the prevailing distorted picture of Judaism was integral to their presentations of the thought and actions of Paul and Jesus.

As teacher of biblical studies, often working with students not especially interested in the Bible, I have used an image from my days in Yorkshire to give students a sense of what Sanders achieved. The Yorkshire dales are famous for their dry-stone walls. Strong walls are created without any cement by skilfully aligning the locally found stones with all their very different shapes with larger stones at the bottom, gradually reducing in size as the wall is built up. Imagining Pauline scholarship as an important part of a carefully worked on dry-stone wall, what Sanders did was analogous to using great strength to lever out the largest stone at the bottom of the wall and show that it had been completely misplaced and that there was a fundamental unsteadiness right at the base of the wall. However skilfully the stones above it had been placed (and they had been), the wall was vulnerable at the point Sanders pushed against. As a consequence of taking out this key stone, the rest of the stones (elements in Paul's theology) were together but somewhat scattered. All the care with which they had been put together was not lost but fresh work was needed to see how they could now be aligned together and the question about a stone to fill the gap left by the large stone needed to be answered. Was a new key stone needed (a new, previously unperceived centre to Paul's theology that would make sense of the rest)? Did the gap need to be filled at all? Would not a smaller wall made up of the remaining stones be what was required (maybe the scope and coherence of Paul's theology was not as impressive as had previously been thought)? Rebuilding the wall has been an engaging project for Pauline scholars of the past thirty years. Sanders's major work of demolition has been almost universally recognized as necessary; different scholars have tried different ways of reassembling the pile of stones that remains but with a continuing difficulty in getting the various major elements in Paul's thought to fit together in a way that makes coherent sense. So the work continues.

Expectations and experience

The expectations that we bring to the study of a text are important. They shape the kind of questions that we ask and, in a sense, determine what we are able to discover:

> A person who is trying to understand a text is always projecting. He (*sic*) projects a meaning for the text as a whole as soon as some initial meaning emerges in the text. Again, the initial meaning emerges only because he is reading the text with particular expectations in regard to a certain meaning. Working out this fore-projection, which is constantly revised in terms of what emerges as he penetrates into the meaning, is understanding what is there. (Hans-Georg Gadamer, *Truth and Method*, translated by J. Weinsheimer and D. G. Marshall, London: Sheed and Ward, 1975, p.267)

In December 1989 I went through a religious experience that changed the way I saw things. Staying at Buckfast Abbey in Devon, I attended a series of evening dialogues with American spiritual teacher, Andrew Cohen, author of *Embracing Heaven and Earth* (Lenox, Massachusetts: Moksha Press, 1999) and *Living Enlightenment* (Lenox, Massachusetts: Moksha Press, 2002). Cohen's teaching uses concepts from the Buddhist tradition but it was the sharpness and directness of his questions which triggered a change in me that I had not expected. My usual way of seeing things changed and a shift in perception occurred that became established for a number of weeks. As a result, my eyes were opened to possibilities about what happened in the beginnings of Christianity that I had not previously considered. Despite the non-Christian context of this change I still felt myself very much within the Christian tradition and embarked on a period of New Testament study at Oxford University. I came to that time of study prepared to pursue fresh lines of enquiry with a stubbornness which arose out of a conviction that, as far as I could tell, the scholarship that I knew had proceeded with only very limited openness to the extraordinary nature of the religious experiences that might underlie the beginnings of early Christianity and that this profoundly affected how the beginnings of the Christian movement were assessed.

Inevitably, as a scholar approaching the biblical text, one of the vital elements shaping the questions asked is the basic conviction about what is or is not possible. For example, in seeking to understand what happened around Jesus himself, the interpretation of any scholar will be shaped by his or her view on the possibility of miracles. The same is true in approaching the early Christian movement. Your interpretation of what went on – scholar or not – will be shaped by the nature of your own religious experience.

As I entered this period of study there is no doubt that my own recent experience was shaping the direction of my study. As a result of what had happened to me in Devon, my 'particular expectations', to use Gadamer's phrase, of what I might discover in the text had significantly changed. When it came to interpreting particular words and relating those meanings to the bigger theological concepts that they were part of, I was not only prepared to let go of traditional theological and scholarly interpretations but also had a new cluster of 'fore-projections' which shaped my enquiry. As I went back and forth, testing different translations of individual words in different settings and relating them to the bigger theological framework in Paul I quickly had a sense of a coherent picture emerging which made sense of Paul in a way that I had not previously discovered.

The experience of this process was akin to unravelling a tight cluster of complicated knots. Sometimes I had the sense of picking away at some tiny point of detail; at other times I was examining the knot, looking around it to find the next point to work on that would help unravel the whole. The focus of this work was all on the text of Paul's letters. Although all my earlier study of Paul and New Testament theology was clearly one of the influences shaping my approach, once I was embarked on this particular line of enquiry I only occasionally turned to the work of other scholars. All my attention was engaged with the interrelationships of different words and concepts in the text itself. It was only once I had finished unravelling a particular knot that I turned to look and see whether any scholar had come to the same or similar conclusions.

Relationship to other scholarship

The way my work proceeded has shaped the way that I have presented what I found. I have been concerned to keep the main text that follows as a clear presentation of the unravelling of the various 'knots' of translation and interpretation, showing how the unravelling of one knot leads on to picking away at another. Given that the effectiveness of the argument depends upon seeing the coherence that emerges, it is vital that no unnecessary complication enters the text itself.

The potential weakness of this mode of presentation is that, whilst the argument set out makes sense in itself, it is left spinning detached from the vast amount of scholarly work on Paul's letters and theology. To remedy this weakness, several important chapter sections are followed by a summary sentence of what has gone before leading to a discussion which relates the argument of the main text to the work of three respected Pauline scholars. These sections will be of particular interest to students of Paul but can be omitted by those who simply want to follow the main argument.

The engagement with scholarship has been limited to these three to better enable the reader to relate what is offered in the main argument to three other attempts to place details of Paul's understanding in a coherent relationship with the whole. Every section of this work presents a controversial view that could, in itself, be the subject of an academic thesis. To provide adequate conventionally argued scholarly support for each aspect of the argument presented here would lead to an impossibly long volume or even set of volumes. But it is a central point of this work that such an approach is not simply impossible to present because of the quantity of engagement that it would require; more importantly, it is not necessary. The strength of the argument is in its coherence and presenting the elements of that coherent view as simply as possible is all that is needed.

The approach taken can be likened to the way that the discovery of the arch in architecture made it possible for thin ribs of stone to carry the huge weight of a cathedral roof where previously only a heavy mass of stone would serve. There is a heavy mass of scholarship around every aspect of Paul's writing. Paul himself stated that what he had to say was difficult for the 'wise' because it does not have the 'cleverness' of Greek philosophical thought (1 Cor 1:21-25) – yet much Pauline scholarship is weighted down with heavy complexity. The parallel to the knowledge of the arch is the experience that opened up for me in the encounter in Devon. My claim would be that this gave me a much clearer sense of the experience that shapes Paul's theology. Without that knowledge, I would have assumed that the pillars that make up the construction of his theology have to be thick with scholarly justification; with that knowledge, I was able to proceed with the creation of a light structure, confident that the meeting point of the arch would provide the strength that the apparently spindly and inadequate ribs require. The separation of the main text from the engagement with other scholarship keeps the coherent lines of argument in the main text uninterrupted.

The three scholars, James D. G. Dunn, E. P. Sanders and John Ziesler, have been chosen because they have each worked both with important aspects of the detail of Paul's texts but also have attempted to integrate that detail into coherent presentations of Paul's theology as a whole. Full bibliographical details of the works used are at the front of the book. They represent the solid work that has continued since *Paul and Palestinian Judaism* in 1977. Despite demonstrating how the enterprise of scholarship can go seriously wrong, Sanders's work did not fundamentally change the way that biblical scholarship proceeds by building carefully on the precisely placed stones of those who have gone before. The present work offers a fundamentally different approach which can be illustrated by returning to the image of the dry-stone wall for Pauline scholarship.

Yorkshire has a number of impressive abbeys and monasteries that were destroyed during the reign of Henry VIII. What remains is now carefully preserved but for a long period they were a useful source of stone for buildings and walls in the surrounding areas. There is more than one section of Yorkshire dry-stone walling that contains stones that had previously served for arches in some Yorkshire abbey. The builder of dry-stone walls is not concerned to produce an arch; instead, these rather peculiar worked stone shapes are made to take their place among all the naturally shaped stones in the wall. In the image already introduced, the upheaval in Pauline scholarship caused by Sanders left a significant part of the wall dismantled with stones scattered about in piles but work has continued according to the old methods. Numerous bits of arch have remained scattered about or embedded in the remaining wall. Earlier, I likened my encounter in Devon to seeing how an arch functions. Returning to the work of scholarship, I could not forget what I had seen. I found myself drawn to the oddly shaped bits of arch that I could see embedded in the heavy earthbound dry-stone wall. Once I had turned to examine the stones in detail it became obvious how certain stones in the wall could be aligned together to produce something altogether more high and graceful than the functional dry stone wall. The three scholars chosen are all at work on restoring the dry-stone wall. Each of our three scholars illuminate points where stones of the arch are similar or related but the coherence and lightness of the whole arch remains absent from their work. This book carefully extracts the stones from the wall and erects the arch in its own right as coherent and strong. In this way, this book is a radical and original departure from all previous Pauline scholarship.

Work in progress

One final observation is required by way of introduction. As has been said, to get clear about the definition of particular words of Paul and particular elements of his theology, the attention in what follows is upon what is in the texts of his letters, specifically, upon the interrelationships of those elements. This particular focus means that virtually nothing will be drawn from what we might know of the historical context of Paul's letters. This is not because such an analysis is unimportant and might not be illuminating for our subject matter. My claim is that such work can be much better tackled once we have done this work on the texts first, rigorously excluding the inevitably more speculative issues of historical context.

It is as if Paul back in the first century had spoken a sentence that we in the twenty-first have not heard clearly. One way of seeking to get clear about what he said is to ask questions of the world around him. We are likely to discover that several of the words that he uses are similar to words that we find in other parts of the New

Testament. We may find similar words in the Jewish tradition or in Greek thought at the time. Another way of seeking to get clear is to compare what we think we have heard with the attempts of our own contemporaries who are also listening to what he said. We could turn especially to the world of Pauline scholarship and engage with the interpretations of others. Both of these ways of seeking clarity are vital parts of the process of understanding. But this work takes a third approach: to deliberately close our ears to the contemporary voices around Paul in his time and of interpreters today in ours in order to hear as clearly as possible the words that Paul is speaking in their relationship to each other. This approach brings a sharpness and clarity to Paul's words that can then bear much fruit as the vital tasks continue of hearing him in relation to his contemporary world and interpreting him in relation to ours. It is also especially important as an approach if, as is indicated in the presentation that follows, Paul is speaking in the light of an experience that was new in his own time and which may also be unfamiliar to us today.

One aspect of the consequences of this approach needs commenting on directly. Much of what we shall be giving attention to arises in passages where Paul is dealing with the relationship between, on the one side, the practice and belief of the emerging Christian communities and, on the other, the practice and belief of mainstream Jewish traditions. What emerges from this study throws a great deal of light on that relationship but adequately applying the findings of this present work to those issues will, in due course, need to be done alongside all the other evidence that we can glean of this relationship, especially through the other texts of the New Testament. That is a task for the future. Discovering the coherent theology in Paul and revealing how it emerges out of lived experience is a big enough task in itself and it is on that exciting and inspirational exploration that this book concentrates.

Book outline

The book is organized in four main sections. Part One, 'Liberation', explores how Paul contrasts law and faith as alternative ways of knowing God's will. The law of Moses, for Paul, is indeed God's will, but expressed for a limited time. Now, Paul says, God and God's will can be known directly. Given that God's living word is now being made known, the written form of God's will is no longer needed. Writing with this sense of direct knowledge of God's will, Paul not only speaks of a new way of being directly guided by God but also sees his old life in a different way and the need there was then for the law. It is only when this new freedom is revealed that it becomes clear why the law was needed and the nature of the liberation that makes the law redundant for Paul.

In Part Two, 'The Exposure of Sin', the focus is upon how Paul considers that everyone, whether Jew or Gentile, needs the liberation he speaks of. The subtle way Paul works with the image of childhood explored in Chapter 5, 'Childhood and Sin', has not previously been seen and provides the key to reveal Paul's understanding of exactly how all humankind has somehow become trapped and lacking both freedom and the way to discover it.

In Part Three, 'From Childhood to Adulthood', sense is made of the connection in Paul's thinking between the experience of liberation for himself and a few others with the absolute confidence that this is the beginning of liberation for the whole of humankind. Despite the popular view of Paul, far from being negative about our fleshly existence, Paul views the climax of creation as Spirit and flesh reconciled in the human body. Once that reconciliation comes, God is 'incarnate'; the body or 'flesh' of humanity is truly the image of God in creation. Paul's subtle use of the story of the fall of humankind from Eden explored in both Parts Two and Three enables him to make sense of the place of sin as essential in coming to the knowledge of good and evil necessary to be the true image of God in creation.

Part Four, 'The Source of Freedom', presents Paul's understanding of the action of God that has brought and is bringing about this universal transformation. The death of Jesus is presented as the beginning of absolute faith as humanity's way of relating to God. The transformation of Paul and others provides the key to understanding the nature of the transformation that humankind must undergo. The last section of the work explores how the only way people can truly 'see' God's revelation is by being transformed so that they become part of that revelation and instruments of transformation themselves.

PART ONE
Liberation

Chapter 1

A New Revelation

A key moment in the 16th century Reformation took place when Martin Luther was studying Paul's letter to the Galatians. He was seeking to understand what Paul meant when he used the Greek word, *dikaioō*, usually translated into English as 'to be justified'. Luther felt the same difficulty as many other interpreters down the years. Paul appears to be speaking of something momentous – a real change which in other contexts he can describe as a liberation. And yet this was not Martin Luther's own experience. Luther was acutely aware of the intense and continuing struggle in his own life – he did not feel this sense of 'liberation'. He continued to struggle with the reality of sin. To make sense of his own experience – and what he felt was the general experience of the Christian believer – he came to consider that Paul, when he used the word *dikaioō*, was indeed meaning a real change, but a change in the *status* of the individual in the eyes of God, not a felt change in the lived experience of the believer.

The interpretation of these sections of Paul continues to be problematical. There are questions about, what did Paul mean? And there are further questions about, how does what he says relate to the life of the Christian today? The difficult thing is that Paul seems to be speaking of a real change in the life of the believer in his time, which he describes as 'receiving the Spirit', a change so dramatic that there is no question for the person who has gone through it that they have experienced it; and yet this does not appear to be the widespread experience of Christians today or for most of Christian history.

So as we turn to interpret the thought of Paul today his meaning remains obscure when it comes to what is arguably the central experience of the Christian life as he understands it. As we seek to make sense of Paul this question is a central one: if Paul is speaking of a real change in the life of the believer, what was the nature of that change?

The source of action

A key word in interpreting Paul is *dikaiosunē*, traditionally translated as 'righteousness' but sometimes rendered as 'integrity' or 'justice'. By looking afresh at the way Paul uses the word in different contexts, seeking to discover a consistent translation, a meaning emerges which, while difficult to work with, is precise but subtle.

There turn out to be three elements crucial to the definition. In the first place, *dikaiosunē* is concerned with a fixed condition, most accurately described as 'a state or manner of existing'. In the second place this 'fixed' state is a way of acting: 'this established state subsists in a particular way of acting'. 'Subsists' is used here to indicate that the 'condition' and 'way of acting' are absolutely tied together. It is not, for example, that Paul is thinking of a fixed established state which from time to time issues in a certain kind of action; this separates the two elements and leads to inaccuracy. The established 'state' is a way of 'doing' or 'acting'. The third element in the meaning of the word can be easily added: the 'way of acting' is qualified by 'rightly'. It is describing a way of doing what is essentially 'right action'.

So, by *dikaiosunē*, usually translated into English as 'righteousness', Paul can be understood to mean *a state or manner of existing, which subsists in a way of doing what is right*. Although 'manner of existence' is the definition of 'state' that is being used here, and the two can be used interchangeably, it will be found helpful to keep in mind both renderings in all passages where Paul uses this word. The word 'state' in English tends to evoke something static for which 'manner of existence' provides a counter; 'manner of existence' does not comfortably express the unchanging condition intended by the word 'state'. Although this suggestion of a consistent meaning for *dikaiosunē* is clumsy when relayed into English, it does not mean that the concept itself is cumbersome. It is simply that there is not in English one word which can unambiguously evoke this sense in the English-thinking mind. The different contexts in which Paul uses this word will be examined as will the relationship between the noun, *dikaiosunē*, and the verb, *dikaioō*.

The definition proposed indicates that what Paul is speaking about is a universal human concern, not something peculiar to Jewish thought or peculiar to the world of the first century; he is dealing with the issue of how any person acts with integrity. The particular form that this right action takes is not usually Paul's primary concern when he uses this word; it is rather the original motivation in the individual out of which actions arise. Paul's concern is with an issue that every person has to consider: how am I to know and do what is right?

Paul uses the word in relation to both the life of faith and life under the law:

> What then are we to say? Gentiles, who did not strive for *dikaiosunē*/righteousness, have attained it, that is, *dikaiosunē*/righteousness through faith; but Israel, who did strive for the *dikaiosunē*/righteousness that is based on the law, did not succeed in fulfilling that law. (Rom 9:30f)

It is possible to replace the word 'righteousness' with 'a state/manner of existing which subsists in a way of doing what is right' on the three occasions when the word is used in this passage. It is no part of our purpose here to produce a smooth translation but rather to see clearly the meaning that this word carries for Paul:

> What then are we to say? Gentiles, who did not strive for a state/manner of existing which subsists in a way of doing what is right, have attained it, that is, the state/manner of existing which subsists in the way of doing what is right through faith; but Israel, who did strive for the state/manner of existing which

subsists in the way of doing what is right that is based on law, did not succeed in fulfilling that law. (Rom 9:30f, adapted NRSV)

Both law and faith are here being spoken of by Paul as ways of knowing and doing what is right consistently. It is clearly possible, as Paul says that Israel has done, to pursue the way of doing what is right based on law – to look to law as the way of consistently knowing and doing what is right. Using the clumsy but precise English phrase to follow Paul's argument here is vital. Paul is saying that it is possible to know and do what is right through faith in a way comparable to the following of law. He is saying further that the Jewish people have been consciously pursuing the way of knowing and doing what is right through law but have not succeeded in fulfilling it whereas Gentiles who have not been consciously pursuing a particular way of knowing and doing what is right have, through faith, attained it.

Paul makes a similar contrast in the letter to the Philippians:

> For [Christ's] sake I have suffered the loss of all things, and I regard them as rubbish, in order that I may gain Christ and be found in him, not having a righteousness of my own that comes from the law, but one that comes through faith in Christ, the righteousness from God based on faith. (Phil 3:8f)

Adapting the second half of this verse reads as follows:

> ... not having the state/manner of existing which subsists in the way of doing what is right of my own that comes from the law, but one that comes through faith in Christ, the state/manner of existing which subsists in the way of doing what is right from God based on faith. (Phil 3:8f, adapted NRSV)

Note that in this verse there is another important element not included in the Romans passage above: the state/manner of existing which subsists in the way of doing what is right through faith is stated, by Paul, to be 'from God'. Paul has to deal in other parts of his letters with the inference that can be drawn from this that 'the law' is not 'from God'. This he denies but, in doing so, clearly emphasizes the way of faith as the new and better way.

Part One of the book is concerned with exploring in depth this key issue of the relationship between living by law and living by faith. Our concern here is to see that they are both concerned with knowing and doing what is right and the passages above indicate that, while Paul considers that there is the state/manner of existing which subsists in the way of doing what is right that comes from the law, it is inferior to the state/manner of existing which subsists in the way of doing what is right that comes from faith. Specifically, it is possible to succeed in knowing and doing what is right by faith in a way that is not attainable in a life based on law.

A real change

> For there is no distinction; since all have sinned and fall short of the glory of God *they are justified* by his grace as a gift, through the redemption which is in Christ Jesus... (Rom 3:22-24, RSV)

This English translation, in common with most translations of this passage, does not indicate that the verb 'to be justified' (passive of *dikaioō*) comes from the same root as 'righteousness' (*dikaiosunē*). A connection can be made with the meaning of the noun already proposed: 'to be justified' can be understood to have the sense of *to be given a state/manner of existing which subsists in a way of doing what is right:*

> ...since all have sinned and fall short of the glory of God, they are *given a state/ manner of existing which subsists in the way of doing what is right* by his grace as a gift...

As with the noun, *dikaiosunē*, this proposal is cumbersome in order that the suggested meaning of the verb can be seen to show the three facets of the suggested definition of the noun. It is being used by Paul to describe a change that, while it is concerned with behaviour, is more precisely indicating a change in the state of the person, his or her manner of existing, from which what he or she does arises. Paul is not making a fundamental distinction between different aspects of behaviour but between different original motivations for action – whether a person's 'way of doing what is right' subsists in law or faith. What is the significance of this?

In order to answer this it is necessary to focus on the weakness of the proposed interpretation. While it indicates that Paul is concerned with a change in the root of behaviour, the interpretation places the emphasis on the new situation that comes about as a result of change – a person who 'has the state/manner of existing which subsists in the way of doing what is right by faith' – rather than the event of change itself (there is the same weakness in the translation 'to be made righteous'). This is the strength of the translation, 'to be justified'; it is clearly indicating an event: the event of 'justification'. But 'to be justified' and 'justification' as translations are unhelpful in other respects. In the first place the legal background of this word group – its connection with 'just' and 'justice' – makes for confusion when Paul is speaking of something that is explicitly 'apart from law'. But its main limitation is that it is not as accurate as it might be in relaying in English the nature of the change that Paul is describing. We are moving towards a new suggestion for translating this word into English but before this can be done an essential step must be taken in order to discern Paul's meaning.

A real change: summary sentence and discussion

Paul uses the passive of *dikaioō* to indicate a real change for the individual in which right action becomes possible.

Ziesler's view of 'justification' in Paul stops short of the radical change as defined above (88):

> Justification is strictly acceptance, restoration to fellowship, and not transformation of character (though that will follow).

Central to the argument of this chapter and this book as a whole is that when Paul uses the language of justification he is indeed speaking of a real 'transformation of character'. Later theological interpretation and the lived experience of later Christians have the power to distort the obvious meaning of Paul's words. 'Acceptance' and 'restoration to fellowship' are ways of presenting Paul which, on the one hand, allow the interpreter to give weight to the plain and obvious meaning of Paul's words, that he is speaking of a 'real change' in the believer, but, on the other, reduce that change to a change in the 'status' of the believer in the eyes of God. In this change of status, the believer does not feel for themselves a power that leads to a dramatically transformed life. This is the condition of most people who come to the life of faith and the interpretation of Paul is made to fit that fact.

Dunn speaks of the 'essentially relational character of Paul's understanding of justification'. He speaks of how God sustains the covenant partner in the covenant relationship 'despite the latter's continued failure' (344).

It is Sanders who clearly and consistently maintains that Paul is speaking of a real change enabling the person to do what is right. Commenting on Romans, he says (67/79):

> [Paul does not think] of righteousness as being fictitiously imputed to those who have faith, while they remain sinners in fact. In sharing Christ's death Christians have died to the old order. They no longer live in sin (6:2), but are "slaves" of righteousness, who have become obedient to God (6:15-18).

A new awareness of sin

The points already made are these:

(a) 'righteousness' (*dikaiosunē*), as Paul uses it, can be understood as 'a state/ manner of existing which subsists in a way of doing what is right';

(b) it is possible to pursue 'the state/manner of existing which subsists in the way of doing what is right' based on law or faith;

(c) the 'state/manner of existing which subsists in the way of doing what is right' based on faith is from God and there is a possibility of succeeding in doing what is right by faith that is not available through the law;

(d) 'to be justified' (*dikaioō*), as used by Paul, can be understood as 'to be given the state/manner of existing which subsists in the way of doing what is right by faith'.

Even a limited number of passages can be used to throw light on the change that Paul believed was taking place, the change indicated by his use of *dikaioō*. They indicate that, before people are given a way of doing what is right, their situation is associated with sin:

> For there is no distinction; since all have sinned and fall short of the glory of God, they are justified (are given the state/manner of existing which subsists in the way of doing what is right by faith) by his grace as a gift... (Rom 3:23f, adapted RSV)

> Do you not know that the unrighteous will not inherit the kingdom of God? ... And such were some of you. But you were washed, you were sanctified, you were justified (given the state/manner of existing which subsists in the way of doing what is right by faith) in the name of the Lord Jesus Christ and in the Spirit of our God. (1 Cor 6:11, adapted RSV)

Having said that 'all have sinned and fall short of the glory of God', Paul speaks of people being given a new manner of existing which he can also describe as being washed and sanctified. In order to show how Paul's description of a change from righteousness under the law to righteousness based on faith is also a move from a life associated with sin it is necessary to introduce a further text.

'All have sinned'

In Palestinian Judaism, a person was born into the covenant made by God with Israel which, for males, was ratified by circumcision. How a person becomes righteous was not therefore an issue. To be righteous was to be born within the people of Israel and to live within the covenant made by God with Israel by keeping the law. The law included remedies for transgressions, assuming that, even for those who were striving conscientiously to keep the law, these would be needed, and that such transgressions would not place the individual among the 'unrighteous'.

Yet the question about how someone becomes righteous is central in the writings of Paul. And it is not simply that Paul is concerned with a change in the situation of Gentiles who might now have the state/manner of existing which subsists in the way of doing what is right that has long been available to the people of Israel. The situation for Jews has changed too. In the letter to the Galatians where Paul is discussing the purpose of the law, he recalls an encounter with Peter at Antioch. While different translations disagree on whether Paul's direct quotation of what he said to Peter ends at v. 14 or at v. 21, the dispute with Peter clearly frames the whole section. He raises this question:

> But if, while we sought to be justified in Christ, we ourselves also were found sinners, is Christ a minister of sin? God forbid. (Gal 2:17, RV)

The importance of this can only be appreciated if it is noted that it is addressed from one Jew to another. Assuming that Paul is recalling his encounter with Peter, he is speaking to a fellow Jew who shares the same understanding of the difference between Jew and Gentile:

> We ourselves are Jews by birth and not Gentile sinners ... (Gal 2:15)

As Jews living within the covenant, Peter and Paul are 'righteous', set apart with a different status from the Gentile 'sinners'. Yet, 'we sought to be justified (given the state/manner of existing which subsists in the way of doing what is right by faith) in Christ'. Paul is reminding Peter that they both, even as 'righteous' Jews, came to see their need to be justified, their need to be made righteous. One way of interpreting Paul's question is that they had come to a sense of the inadequacy of the law. This is what Paul seems to say:

> We ourselves ... know that a person is justified not by the works of the law but through faith in Jesus Christ. ... [N]o one will be justified by the works of the law. (Gal 2:15f)

However, a further vital element needs to be seen.

The manner in which Paul expresses himself is illuminating; he speaks of himself and Peter *finding themselves* to be sinners. This points to a conclusion that needs placing alongside Paul's perception that the law was in some way inadequate. The inadequacy of the law is only revealed as Peter and Paul discover that they are sinners *in a way that previously they were unaware of*. It is not that, for the one living by the law, the law does not provide adequately for the sinner to be restored after transgressions. Paul shares with his fellow Jews the view of the Gentiles as 'sinners' and the Jews as 'righteous' even though they need forgiveness for their repeated transgressions. Paul's ironical question to Peter only makes clear sense when note is taken of the underlying assumption that both share a new awareness of what it is to be a sinner as a consequence of coming to faith. This paraphrase gives the sense:

> ... because in wanting to be justified in Christ we found even ourselves to be sinners, does that mean that Christ is the bringer of that sin. Of course not! It is rather that he has revealed something fresh to us about our condition.

We will see more clearly how the way that Paul consistently expresses himself indicates that he has a changed view of what it is to be righteous. No longer satisfied with being 'righteous' under the law, he seeks to be 'justified in Christ'. This is tied together with *a new perception of what it is to be a sinner* – Peter and Paul 'find themselves' to be sinners in a way that they had no awareness of before. Exploring this double sided revelation is the task of the whole book.

A new awareness of sin: summary sentence and discussion

An experience of their earlier state as sinful in a way not previously seen is integral to the transformation of individuals, like himself and Peter, that Paul is describing.

Ziesler states (24):

> [Paul] was a happy and zealous Jew, whose new belief that Jesus was the answer
> to human dilemmas made him find inadequacies in the Judaism that had hitherto
> satisfied him.

This statement, on its own, lacks an essential element for correctly understanding Paul and hence, as it stands, is misleading over this central issue. It is not simply that, for Paul, Jesus provides a better solution than Judaism to the continuing and universal 'human dilemmas' felt by Peter and Paul, but that the fundamental problem of the human condition from which all the human dilemmas arise is revealed clearly to them in their experience of transformation. Seeing for the first time their true condition – their 'plight' – is essentially bound up with coming to the new 'solution' that Peter and Paul discover in faith. This is what Ziesler later goes on to say (25):

> [P]aul seems not to have proceeded from a deeply felt problem to a solution in
> Christ, but the other way round: he first accepted Christ as centre and solution,
> and then saw with new eyes what the problem was.

It was only when he had been liberated that he understood his bondage.

Sanders has been instrumental in recognizing this movement from solution to plight (38/45):

> ... Paul did not come to Christianity with a pre-formed conception of humanity's
> sinful plight, but rather deduced the plight from the solution.

The important difference from Sanders in what is offered in the main text can be summed up in the contrast between 'deduction' and 'revelation'. For Sanders the 'revelation' to Paul is this (38/45):

> God intended to save the entire world by sending his Son.

At that point, deduction (and rather crude deduction in Sanders's view) takes over (38/45):

> Once [Paul] accepted it as revelation that God intended to save the entire world
> by sending his Son, he naturally had to think that the entire world needed saving,
> and thus that it was wholly bound over to Sin.

The main text proposes that the recognition of the 'plight' of humanity is indeed bound up with the experience of the 'solution' but both elements are aspects of the experience of 'revelation'. Essential to the liberation – the 'salvation' – that Paul is claiming has been effected in him by God, is the revealing of the slavery that he has been under which he has not previously perceived. Paul sees a universal significance in what he has been shown in his own experience: all are trapped in this 'plight' and all can be liberated from it by faith.

Dunn's view is that 'conversion for Paul meant becoming aware as never before of the power of sin in his own life' (*Romans 1-8*, 407). This does not quite capture the sense of a new insight into the very nature of sin as opposed to simply an intensification of a struggle that is already recognized. Dunn considers that this intensified struggle with sin is characteristic of the Christian life according to Paul, a view that will be returned to.

Absolution

It has been argued that by the passive voice of *dikaioō* Paul is meaning 'to be given the state/manner of existing which subsists in the way of doing what is right by faith'. It was noted that the subtle but significant weakness of this interpretation is that, while the Greek word is referring to a single event, the emphasis of this phrase is on the state that results from this event – 'the state/manner of existing which subsists in the way of doing what is right by faith'. The first stages have been made in showing how Paul associates life before this gift with sin. A more accurate single English word to express Paul's meaning when he uses the passive voice of *dikaioō* is 'to be absolved'. The Latin root behind the English words absolve and absolution is *absolvere* meaning 'to free'. The English dictionary definition of 'to absolve' includes 'to set free from the consequences of sin' (SOED). The difference between these two English translations is simple but important. 'To be justified' carries the sense of a change in status through something being added; either a good person or a bad one can be justified. 'To be absolved', however, has an integral connection with wrongdoing; a person who has done no wrong cannot be absolved. This is why Paul's question to Peter makes sense; it is only the sinner that can be absolved:

> But if, while we sought to be *absolved* in Christ, we ourselves also were found sinners, is Christ a minister of sin? God forbid. (Gal 2:17, adapted RV)

Paul's words to the Corinthians quoted earlier also make good sense with this translation:

> Do you not know that the unrighteous will not inherit the kingdom of God? ... And such were some of you. But you were washed, you were sanctified, *you were absolved* in the name of the Lord Jesus Christ and in the Spirit of our God. (1 Cor 6:11, adapted RSV)

More important still is the way this translation is appropriate in the Romans 3 passage looked at above. The proposal of 'to be absolved' fits vividly in the surrounding context:

> ... [S]ince all have sinned and fall short of the glory of God, *they are absolved* by his grace as a gift, through the redemption which is in Christ Jesus, whom God put forward as an expiation by his blood, to be received by faith. This was to show God's righteousness, because in his divine forbearance he had passed over former sins; it was to prove at the present time that he himself is righteous and that *he absolves* him who has faith in Jesus. (Rom 3:23-26, adapted RSV)

This proposal does not solve the problem of providing a consistent English translation which reproduces the consistency in the Greek. While 'to be absolved' may be a more appropriate English translation of Paul's meaning when he uses the passive voice of the verb *dikaioō* than 'to be justified', it is not possible to use the English noun 'absolution' for the Greek noun *dikaiosunē*. The problem is the same as with the word 'justification': 'absolution', like 'justification', has the sense of *a single event* and the Greek word *dikaiosunē* is describing a *consistent quality of action – a 'way' of acting*. What this proposal does is to facilitate a fresh look at the possible consistency in Paul's thought that underlies the consistency in his language. If 'to be justified' is better understood as 'to be absolved' there is the possibility of recognizing the crucial connection between noun and verb. It was proposed that by the noun *dikaiosunē* Paul means 'a state/manner of existing which subsists in a way of doing what is right'. Paul's understanding of 'sin' will receive further consideration in Part Two but, for the moment, can be interpreted as all that stands over against 'righteousness'/*dikaiosunē*. The interpretations of *dikaiosunē* and *dikaioō* that have been offered make it possible to understand Paul's meaning when he uses these words in a simple, consistent and literal sense: *the free gift of absolution from God is a real and effective liberation from sin that brings about a new state/manner of existing which subsists in the way of doing what is right by faith.*

Absolution: summary sentence and discussion

When Paul uses the passive voice of *dikaioō* he is referring to a lasting and effective liberation from sin.

Dunn, in interpreting Paul, emphasizes the traditional Lutheran view of justification, based on the subsequent lived experience of Christians – through history and today (386):

[T]he justified do not thereby become sinless. They continue to sin.

This, as Sanders states plainly in this important section, leads to a fundamental distortion of Paul's meaning (49/57f):

[Luther] was impressed by the fact that, though a Christian, he nevertheless felt himself to be a 'sinner': he suffered from guilt. Paul, however, did not have a guilty conscience. Before his conversion to being an apostle of Christ, he had been ... "blameless" with regard to "righteousness under the law" (Phil 3:6). As an apostle, he could not think of anything which would count against himself at the final judgement, though he left open the possibility that God might find some fault (1 Cor 4:4). Luther, plagued by guilt, read Paul's passages on "righteousness by faith" as meaning that God reckoned a Christian to be righteous even though he or she was a sinner. Luther understood "righteousness" to be judicial, a declaration of innocence, but also fictional, ascribed to Christians "by mere imputation", since God was merciful. Luther's phrase for the Christian condition was not Paul's "blameless" or "without blemish" (for example, 1 Thess 5:23), but rather *simul justus et peccator*, "at the same time righteous and a sinner": "righteous" in God's sight, but a "sinner" in everyday experience.

Put another way, Luther saw the Christian life as summed up in Romans 7: 21, "I find it to be a law that when I want to do right, evil lies close at hand", whereas Paul thought that this was the plight from which people were freed through Christ (Rom 7:24; 8:1-8). "You", he wrote, "are not in the Flesh, you are in the Spirit": and those in the Spirit, he thought, did not do the sinful deeds "of the Flesh" (Rom 8:9-17; Gal 5:16-24).

Luther's emphasis on fictional, imputed righteousness, though it has often been shown to be an incorrect interpretation of Paul, has been influential because it corresponds to the sense of sinfulness which many people feel ... Luther sought and found relief from guilt. But Luther's problems were not Paul's, and we misunderstand him if we see him through Luther's eyes.

Balancing this interpretation of Paul's radical claim for liberation from sin, Sanders notes later in his book (98/114): '[Paul's] view of Christian perfection did not correspond to empirical observation' and this raises questions to which we must return (Chapters 7, 8 and 11).

God's way of acting

In the Romans 3 passage considered above, Paul says that 'the righteousness of God' has now been 'disclosed' or 'shown' and it is clear that, by this 'showing', he considers that something about God and God's own way of doing what is right has been newly revealed:

> This was to show God's righteousness, because in his divine forbearance he had passed over former sins; it was to prove at the present time that he himself is righteous... (Rom 3:25f, RSV)

When Paul speaks about the righteousness based on faith he is speaking about *human* activity – the way people do what is right. What follows in this section is a proposal as to how human righteousness based on faith and God's righteousness are connected. The proposal will only be sketched at this stage but the various different aspects of the outline will receive further definition in later chapters.

It will be central to the argument that follows in this and subsequent chapters that, from Paul's new perspective, there is a sharp dividing line between that which is of God on one side and that which falls short of the glory of God on the other. To live according to the Spirit is to be on God's side of the line; to be a sinner places a person on the other side. In the Romans 3 passage, Paul says that 'all have sinned and fall short of the glory of God' (Rom 3:23); Paul has a conception of all humanity – Jew and Gentile – being, in a sense, over against God, or, at least, separate or on the other side of the line from God. Putting what was said in the last section in a different way, *dikaioō* ('to be justified' or 'to be absolved' in the passive voice) can be understood as meaning the transfer from one side of this dividing line to the other. The process of being absolved, that is, set free from sin and given the state/manner of existing which subsists in the way of doing what is right through faith, is a movement from being, in a sense, over against God to being on God's side.

To describe this transfer over the dividing line, Paul does not only use the word, *dikaioō*. He speaks of this change as a death, applying this understanding most dramatically to himself:

> I have been crucified with Christ; and it is no longer I who live, but it is Christ
> who lives in me. (Gal 2:20)

It has already been suggested that Paul understands the change that has been effected by God in himself and others as a change, not simply in the way of discerning what it is right to do, but in the fundamental 'state' or 'manner of existing' of the individual which issues forth in a particular way of doing what is right. Paul's description of the change he has gone through as a 'death' can be understood not simply as hyperbole but as something with a substantial meaning that fits into the whole framework of Paul's thought. In the passage where Paul refers to this change most fully as a 'death' he also connects it with the death of Christ and speaks of the way in which an individual goes through this death for him or herself as baptism:

> Do you not know that all of us who have been baptized into Christ Jesus were
> baptized into his death? Therefore we have been buried with him by baptism into
> death, so that, just as Christ was raised from the dead by the glory of the Father,
> so we too might walk in newness of life. For if we have been united with him in
> a death like his, we will certainly be united with him in a resurrection like his.
> We know that our old self was crucified with him so that the body of sin might be
> destroyed, and we might no longer be enslaved to sin. (Rom 6:3-6)

Clearly, Paul is speaking figuratively – those who have 'died' in the sense he is speaking of here are still alive – yet this should not obscure the fact that he is speaking of some kind of real death. It will be a central feature of the argument of this book that, by this death, Paul is speaking of the end of selfish assertion in the individual. In the passage above he speaks of the end of this selfish assertion as the death of 'our old self'. Attention will be given to exactly what is meant by this selfish assertion (Chapters 5 and 6), so that it becomes clear what it means to say that it is the sense of assertive individuality over against God and over against others that has to die.

This preliminary sketch of arguments that will follow in later chapters allows us, even at this stage, to indicate briefly how the ending of this sense of individual assertion over against God can be understood as a revelation or 'showing' of God's righteousness. There are two sides to the answer to be presented.

Firstly, it has been suggested how there is a sharp dividing line in Paul's thought with that which is of God on one side and that which falls short of the glory of God on the other. It has also been suggested that by 'sin' Paul is meaning the 'selfish assertion of the individual' and that this selfish assertion has to die for the individual to be transferred to 'God's side of the line'. If this presentation is accurate then, with the death of this assertion, all that is left in the individual is right action – the person consistently does what is right; the individual no longer acts against God but rather, on the side of God. Paul describes how individuals become 'slaves of God' as a consequence of this change (Rom 6:22); their actions are in conformity with the will of God and are therefore, in a real sense, God's actions. Paul is presenting the view that *after this 'transfer across the line', after the death of 'selfish assertiveness', after 'absolution', human actions themselves reveal or 'show' God's righteousness, God's manner of existing, God's way of doing what is right.*

Secondly, God's 'state/manner of existing which subsists in a way of doing what is right' is shown on a larger scale. A good deal will be made in the argument to come of Paul's use of the Genesis account of the fall (Chapters 5 and 6). He contrasts the figures of Adam and Christ:

> Therefore just as one man's trespass led to condemnation for all, so one man's act of righteousness leads to justification and life for all. For just as by the one man's disobedience the many were made sinners, so by the one man's obedience the many will be made righteous. (Rom 5:18f)

Behind this discussion of Adam and Christ is a simple but important issue: how could God have made a creature in God's own image, sharing God's glory and dominion over all creation, only for that creature to sin and fall short of the glory of God? Paul has a view of how that image is being restored by God. We will see how Paul connects this restoration with the death and resurrection of Christ – how this one event, which, for Paul, is the climax of the call of the people of Israel, has a significance and effect for the whole of humankind. This is part of the showing of God's righteousness. The 'condemnation' is brought to an end in this 'restoration'.

But we will see how the concept of restoration does not adequately express Paul's view. The idea of restoration still leaves something essential out of an adequate understanding of God's righteousness. It does not clearly indicate any purpose to the fall. It implies that something was simply lost which has now been restored. We will see how Paul's understanding is better expressed by the idea of fulfilment, that God has acted to restore humankind to bring to fulfilment or completion what was begun at creation. And we will grasp the nettle that is then presented. In order to adequately present God's righteousness, Paul also has to explain why the restoration of humankind is necessary; why did any dividing line between God and God's creation come about? Paul has to answer the question: *given God the creator's righteousness – given that God's state/manner of existing always subsists in doing what is right, why did sin occur at all? Why was it necessary that sin entered the world? How can it be that the existence of sin contributes to the 'showing' of God's righteousness?*

Conclusion

The first steps have been made in showing:

(a) how by *dikaiosunē* (righteousness) Paul means 'a state/manner of existing which subsists in a way of doing what is right';

(b) that this definition can apply to the different settings in which Paul uses this word: of both God and humankind and of human life based on both faith and the law;

(c) that by *dikaioō* ('to be justified' in the passive voice) Paul means 'to be given the state/manner of existing which subsists in the way of doing what is right by faith';

(d) that when he uses this word, Paul is indicating a real change in the individual which can be well expressed by the English word 'absolution' – a setting free from sin;

(e) that associated with this absolution is a new perception of what sin is.

A preliminary sketch has been made of how Paul could consider that God's righteousness was being newly revealed in setting people free from sin – understood as assertion against God – so that they, by their way of acting, themselves reveal God's righteousness. What has so far been sketchily drawn will be filled out in the chapters that follow.

Chapter 2

Faith's New Way of Listening

It has been argued that by 'righteousness' (*dikaiosunē*) Paul means 'a state/manner of existing which subsists in a way of doing what is right' and in the course of that argument reference was made to the fact that Paul contrasts 'the righteousness that comes from the law' and 'the righteousness that comes from faith' (Rom 10:5f). The way of doing what is right that is based on religious law is relatively easy to describe; it amounts to the determined and persevering observation of the commands contained within that law. But what of the way of doing what is right based on faith? This chapter will suggest how Paul considers that direction for behaviour can be given with just as much clarity through faith as through law.

Prophecy

When the coming of the Spirit on the feast of Pentecost is described in the Acts of the Apostles, the first thing that Peter is said to have proclaimed is a quotation:

> [T]his is what was spoken through the prophet Joel:
> "In the last days it will be, God declares,
> that I will pour out my Spirit upon all flesh,
> and your sons and your daughters shall prophesy,
> and your young men shall see visions,
> and your old men shall dream dreams.
> Even upon my slaves, both men and women,
> in those days I will pour out my Spirit;
> and they shall prophesy..." (Acts 2:17f; cf. Joel 2:28f)

In modern usage the verb 'to prophesy' usually means 'to foretell the future' but that is not its full sense; even in contemporary English it carries the richer sense of 'to speak by divine inspiration' (SOED). Although the Hebrew prophets were often concerned with the future, their essential task was to speak for God. When Jeremiah is called he protests because of his youth and God responds:

> 'Do not say, "I am only a boy"; for you shall go to all to whom I send you, and you shall speak whatever I command you...' Then the Lord put out his hand and touched my mouth; and the Lord said to me, 'Now I have put my words in your mouth...' (Jer 1:7, 9)

Ezekiel retells God's call in similar terms:

> Mortal, go to the house of Israel, and speak my very words to them. (Ezek 3:4)

With this richer understanding of prophecy, the sense of the words of Joel is not that in the last days all shall predict the future but rather that, in those days, God will speak in and through all God's sons and daughters.

The prophetic word of God

Paul's first letter to the Corinthians contains an extensive section on spiritual gifts (1 Cor 12-14). Paul's discussion includes an appraisal of the particular gift of speaking in tongues but a modern concern to understand this unusual phenomenon can obscure the no less extraordinary presupposition shared by Paul and his readers. The section opens with a contrast which begins to make the point. Paul describes the former life of the community when they 'were enticed and led astray to idols that could not speak' (12:2) and immediately follows this with a point about discerning when someone is 'speaking by the Spirit of God' (12:3). The main concern of the passage is about discernment but the object of that discernment is how the living word of God is heard and recognized in the community. *That God is speaking in the community through its members in contrast to the dumb idols of the past is the unquestioned assumption of the whole passage.*

It will be the argument of this chapter that Paul considers that clear direction for action comparable to the directions given by law comes through the prophetic word – God's word given directly – sounding in the community. As a preliminary support for the argument reference can be made to an example that Paul relates from his own experience. He describes how he pleads to the Lord for the removal of what he calls a 'thorn in the flesh' and records the response that he receives:

> [B]ut he said to me, 'My grace is sufficient for you, for power is made perfect in weakness.' (2 Cor 12:9)

Paul goes on to use this prophetic word as an explanation of why he glorifies in weakness and hardships. The important thing to note for the argument here is that the fact that he hears this teaching and accepts it in order to advance his understanding of the purposes of God passes without comment and he assumes that, just as he ascribes this word to the Lord, so will his readers. That the voice of the Lord is speaking in the community is a shared assumption which Paul does not need to establish.

In Paul's discussion of prophecy and speaking in tongues he discusses the relative value of these two spiritual gifts to the community:

> For those who speak in a tongue do not speak to other people but to God; for nobody understands them, since they are speaking mysteries in the Spirit. On the other hand, those who prophesy speak to other people for their upbuilding and encouragement and consolation. Those who speak in a tongue build up themselves, but those who prophesy build up the church. Now I would like all of you to speak in tongues, but even more to prophesy. One who prophesies is

greater than the one who speaks in tongues, unless someone interprets, so that the
church may be built up. (1 Cor 14:2-5)

Prophecy, Paul says, is of clear and practical benefit; it builds up the church, giving
encouragement and consolation.

Further very clear evidence of the presence of prophecy in the community comes
as Paul gives instruction about the way things are to be done when the community
are gathered:

> Let two or three prophets speak, and let the others weigh what is said. If a
> revelation is made to someone else sitting nearby, let the first person be silent.
> For you can all prophesy one by one, so that all may learn and all be encouraged.
> And the spirits of prophets are subject to the prophets... (1 Cor 14:29-32)

When the community gathers, listening to the prophetic word is central and Paul is
ensuring that this word is heard and that all may benefit. Paul is giving instructions
on how to hear it in an orderly way and also, briefly, on the right way to test that the
word that is heard is truly the word of God:

> Let two or three prophets speak, and let the others weigh what is said. ... [T]he
> spirits of prophets are subject to the prophets... (1 Cor 14:29, 32)

Again, the fact that there are prophets speaking the word of God and that this is a
central part of the life of the community are realities that Paul can assume in what
he says.

One final and very telling point can be drawn from the concluding section of this
extended passage; Paul claims of himself that what he has written on the subject of
prophecy itself has prophetic authority:

> Anyone who claims to be a prophet, or to have spiritual powers, must acknowledge
> that what I am writing to you is a command of the Lord. Anyone who does not
> recognize this is not to be recognized. (1 Cor 14:37f)

Because of his absolute confidence that what he has written is not his own instruction
but that of the Lord, Paul sets forward agreement with his own words as a mark of
the true prophet.

Paul and the prophetic word

Support for the argument of the chapter so far as to how direction and instruction
were received by the members of the early Christian communities comes from Paul's
own account of the source of the gospel that he preaches. From the very beginning of
the letter to the Galatians, Paul is concerned to establish that his calling came to him
directly from God and did not come through any other person:

> Paul an apostle – sent neither by human commission nor from human authorities,
> but through Jesus Christ and God the Father, who raised him from the dead...
> (Gal 1:1)

In the early part of the letter, Paul gives a further insight into his calling which leads
to an interesting connection:

> But when God, who had set me apart before I was born and called me through his
> grace, was pleased to reveal his Son to me [Gk 'in me'], so that I might proclaim
> him among the Gentiles, I did not confer with any human being... (Gal 1:15f)

Given the right background information, it becomes clear that Paul is making here
a very specific point. For the main part of that information it is necessary to see the
close parallels between the above text and the beginning of the book of the prophet
Jeremiah:

> Now the word of the Lord came to me saying, 'Before I formed you in the womb
> I knew you, and before you were born I consecrated you; I appointed you a
> prophet to the nations.' (Jer 1:5)

Jeremiah's words 'before I formed you in the womb' and 'before you were born'
parallel Paul's 'before I was born'; Paul regards himself as 'set apart' which is very
close in sense to the 'consecration by God' that Jeremiah speaks of; just as Jeremiah
was appointed 'a prophet to the nations', Paul says that God 'was pleased to reveal
his Son "in" me, in order that I might preach him among the Gentiles'.

Paul's last phrase in the section above emphasizes the direct, prophetic source
of his calling: 'I did not confer with flesh and blood'. Paul is arguing that his gospel
did not come to him through any natural means. His words clearly echo the passage
which records the call of Jeremiah and the essential foundation of that prophetic
call is not the reference to being called before birth or being sent to the Gentiles
(important as this latter aspect is) but rather *the coming to the prophet of the word
of God*. The call is not based on any vague general sense of the presence of God but
clearly indicates that Paul is attributing his gospel to that same prophetic word as
came to Jeremiah.

How the Spirit comes

As we have seen above, the prophet is understood as the mouthpiece of the Lord:

> Now I have put *my words* into *your mouth*. (Jer 1:9)

The words come out of the mouth of the prophet; yet, at the same time, the words that
he speaks are not his own – they are the Lord's. This same combination is evident
in the way Paul speaks about the Spirit; the Spirit is seen in the words and action
of an individual but it always remains the Lord that is acting. This is of importance

because, as in the calling of the prophets as well as in the passage from the prophet Joel quoted in Acts, the coming of the word of God is associated with the coming of the Spirit:

> ... I will pour out my Spirit upon all flesh, and your sons and your daughters shall prophesy ... (Acts 2:17; cf. Joel 2:28)

It is not difficult to find evidence in Paul's letters that he considered the coming of the Spirit to a community or to individuals as something arriving upon them, as it were, from outside. Right at the beginning of the first letter to the Thessalonians, Paul remembers what happened in his early preaching to them:

> For we know, brothers loved by God, that he has chosen you, because our gospel came to you not simply with words, but also with power, with the Holy Spirit and with deep conviction. (1 Thess 1:4f, NIV)

Paul is recalling a similar event among the Galatians when he asks them:

> Did you receive the Spirit by doing the works of the law, or by hearing with faith? (Gal 3:2, RSV)

Paul conceives of the Spirit as remaining objective even while assisting the believer:

> Likewise the Spirit helps us in our weakness; for we do not know how to pray as we ought, but that very Spirit intercedes with sighs too deep for words. (Rom 8:26)

Paul is able to remind the early faith communities of the coming of the Spirit as a definite event. This is particularly in evidence in the continuation of the passage from the letter to the Galatians quoted above:

> Having started with the Spirit are you now ending with the flesh? Did you experience so much for nothing? (Gal 3:3f)

Paul is calling them to remember how it was in the beginning; there was a particular event at a particular time in which many things were experienced.

Paul also describes the Spirit as entering into the believer:

> ...God has sent the Spirit of his Son into our hearts, crying, 'Abba! Father!' (Gal 4:6)

> Or do you not know that your body is a temple of the Holy Spirit within you, which you have from God, and that you are not your own? (1 Cor 6:19)

> If the Spirit of him who raised Jesus from the dead dwells in you, he who raised Christ from the dead will give life to your mortal bodies also through his Spirit that dwells in you. (Rom 8:11)

Paul, interpreting his own experience and that of the early communities with which he was involved, speaks of the Spirit coming to the early Christians in an objective way, that is, always identifiably 'other' or different from the individuals themselves and yet entering those individuals and dwelling within them.

This Spirit is described by Paul as providing both direction for behaviour and the power to see it through. It is in this that the combination of its subjective and objective quality is evident. Paul speaks of the Spirit both directing the community in moral behaviour and directing individuals into specific tasks of service. So Paul says to the Galatians:

> [L]ive by the Spirit, and you will not gratify the desires of the sinful nature ... [T]he fruit of the Spirit is love, joy, peace, patience, kindness, goodness, faithfulness, gentleness, self-control... (Gal 5:16, 22f, NIV)

To the Corinthians he says that

> ...there are varieties of gifts, but the same Spirit... To each is given the manifestation of the Spirit for the common good. (1 Cor 12:4, 7)

He then lists various forms of service to the community. Once again the thing to note is the objective character of the Spirit as understood by Paul and the specificity of the directions it gives, not only for the community but also for individuals.

Section conclusion

The Spirit as presented by Paul comes from outside the community and individuals but its work is done through them. While the Spirit remains other than them, that is, objective, its activity becomes the activity of the individuals and communities who have received it. This is the same curious combination as was described with regard to the words of the prophet; while remaining the words of the Lord, they are spoken by the mouth of the prophet.

How the Spirit comes: summary sentence and discussion

The coming of the prophetic word is bound together with the coming of the Spirit: both are described by Paul as coming to and operating in the individual and, at the same time, as being clearly from God, that is, distinct from the individual.

Ziesler comments on a series of texts where Paul gives his judgment on aspects of the life of the communities to whom he is writing. He notes the connection between the experience of the Spirit and confidently speaking the word of God (124):

> In all these passages, Paul is guided not by a rule but by the Spirit in the light of the concrete situation. ... These sentences demonstrate Paul's confidence that Christ's Spirit is working and speaking through him.

Dunn comments on the coming of the Spirit and how, when talking to the communities, Paul could confidently refer to it as a shared, if extraordinary, experience (429f):

> In Christian tradition it has become customary to think of the gift of the Spirit as a deduction to be drawn from a correct confession or properly administered sacrament. The new church member is in effect given the assurance: "You believed all the right things and/or received the sacrament of baptism and/or laying on of hands; therefore you have received the Spirit, whether you know it or not." With Paul it was rather different. He asks the Galatians, not "How did you receive baptism? What confession did you make?" but "How was it that you received the Spirit?" (Gal 3.2). Their reception of the Spirit was something he could refer them to directly, not merely as a deduction from some other primary factor.
>
> The same point follows from the "definition of a Christian" in Rom 8.9 and 14. Paul does not say: "If you are Christ's, you have the Spirit; since you are sons of God, you are led by the Spirit." In both cases, Paul puts it the other way round: "if you have the Spirit, you are Christ's; if you are being led by the Spirit, you are God's sons." The fact which was immediately discernible was not whether they were Christ's – attested by baptism or confession – a fact from which their possession of the Spirit could be deduced as a corollary. That which was ascertainable was their possession of the Spirit; that was the primary factor from which their relation to Christ could be deduced. Their Christian status was recognizable from the fact that Christ's agent was in evident control of their lives.

Note that, in these last two sentences, Dunn speaks of the Spirit with the same combination of 'subjective' and 'objective' referred to in the main text. The Spirit is described as something that Christian believers 'possess' and yet this 'possession' is 'in evident control of their lives'. Dunn also states clearly the link between the Spirit and the prophetic word (419f):

> In 1 Thessalonians, Paul reminds his readers how they received the word "with joy of the Holy Spirit" (1.6). He characterizes God as "the one who gives his Holy Spirit to you" (4.8). That this definitive statement ... appears in Paul's earliest letter signals a theme which remains consistent throughout Paul's letters. At the end of the letter he reminds them of the characteristically charismatic character of their worship (5.19-20); the soteriological Spirit [the Spirit which brings salvation] is also the Spirit of prophecy.

Faith's 'heard thing'

The main suggestion of the chapter so far has been that the guidance which Paul claims for enabling the early Christian community to know and do what is right comes by the prophetic word. A further point made was to indicate the curious combination of objectivity and subjectivity that is present in the idea of the prophet who speaks the words of the Lord. The same combination is present in Paul's understanding of the Spirit: the Spirit acts in and through the individuals in the community while remaining objective. These points will now be used to offer an explanation of a distinctive phrase Paul uses which combines 'faith' (*pistis*) with the noun from the Greek word for 'to hear' (*akoē*). There are three passages to consider.

Galatians 3:2,5

Paul writes to the Galatians:

> Let me ask you only this: Did you receive the Spirit by works of the law, or by
> hearing with faith? ... Does he who supplies the Spirit to you and works miracles
> among you do so by works of the law, or by hearing with faith? (Gal 3:2, 5,
> RSV)

From the way Paul puts this question it is clear that there can only be one answer, 'by hearing with faith', but what is meant by this phrase? In order to carry the weight of Paul's argument here, whatever is meant by 'hearing with faith' must be some shared experience easily identifiable to his readers. The RSV translation of this phrase above stays close to the AV which renders the phrase, 'by the hearing of faith'. Most modern translators, because of the obscurity of a literal translation of the Greek phrase, make a judgment about what Paul is describing here and then paraphrase Paul's Greek. The assumption is generally made that Paul is here contrasting doing 'works of the law' with the traditional Christian idea of 'believing the gospel message' and different translations render this understanding more or less explicitly:

> Did you receive the Spirit by doing works of the law or by believing what you
> heard? (NRSV)
> How was it that you received the Spirit – by the practice of the Law, or by
> believing in the message you heard? (NJB)
> (D)id you receive God's Spirit by doing what the Law requires or by hearing the
> gospel and believing it? (TEV)
> (D)id you receive the Spirit by keeping the law or by believing the gospel
> message? (REB)
> Did you receive the Spirit by observing the law, or by believing what you heard?
> (NIV)

A significantly different interpretation can be made of Paul's meaning.

There are three other passages where Paul uses the word, *akoē*. The strength of the definition to be proposed here is that it can be used in each of these passages. What makes it different from the translations set out above is that it takes into consideration the combination of objective and subjective in the activity of the Spirit and the prophetic word.

The various translations above all provide a meaning that is solely objective. *Akoē* is most straightforwardly understood as referring to something that is heard: a 'heard thing'. In English we do not have a noun that keeps the accuracy of this clumsy phrase. It is understandable then that the translations quoted assume that what is heard arises from outside the hearer. Having made that simple assumption, the issue then becomes the assessment of the nature of the external thing that was heard; the translations above all suggest that it was the gospel message that was preached. The material presented earlier in the chapter lends support for a different proposal: the simple sense of the Greek word used by Paul does not necessarily indicate something external to the hearer; it simply indicates something that is heard. There are many things that can be heard – a report, a message, a rumour – and normally these come from outside the hearer but the proposal to be made here is that *Paul is using this word in connection with faith to indicate the prophetic word that gives guidance to the individual and the community and which is associated with the coming of the Spirit. This word is heard, as it were, 'within' but remains objective – 'other' than the one who hears.* It will be argued that the word *akoē* (translated 'hearing' in the AV and RSV) is accurately interpreted as a 'thing that is heard' *within* the believer, that is, the *prophetic word or the word that is heard from God.*

> Did you receive the Spirit by works of law or by faith's 'heard thing (word of prophecy)'? (Gal 3:2)

The two other important passages in which this word is used will provide still clearer evidence for the proposed meaning.

Romans 10:15-17

In the passage from which these verses come, Paul is contrasting righteousness based on the law and righteousness based on faith. Support for the interpretation of *akoē* as 'the prophetic word that is heard within' comes earlier in the passage where Paul seems to be arguing that, in contrast to the law, the righteousness from faith is revealed within the individual:

> But the righteousness that comes from faith says, 'Do not say in your heart, "Who will ascend into heaven?"' (that is, to bring Christ down) 'or "Who will descend into the abyss?"' (that is, to bring Christ up from the dead). But what does it say? 'The word is near you, on your lips and in your heart' (that is, the word of faith which we proclaim) ... (Rom 10:6-8)

A little further on in the text, the word we are examining occurs three times:

> As it is written, 'How beautiful are the feet of those who bring good news!' But not all have obeyed the good news; for Isaiah says, 'Lord, who has believed our *akoē*?' So faith comes from the *akoē*, and the *akoē* comes through the word of Christ. (Rom 10:15-17, adapted NRSV)

As in the Galatians passage above, some translations clearly equate *akoē* with the gospel message:

> As it is written, 'How beautiful are the feet of those who bring good news!' But not all the Israelites accepted the good news. For Isaiah says, 'Lord, who has believed our message?' Consequently, faith comes from hearing the message, and the message is heard through the word of Christ. (Rom 10:15-17, NIV)

Inserting the proposed interpretation yields the following sense:

> As it is written, 'How beautiful are the feet of those who preach good news!'
> But not all have obeyed the good news, for Isaiah says, 'Lord, who has had faith
> in our "heard thing (word of prophecy)"?' So faith comes from the 'heard thing
> (word of prophecy)', and the 'heard thing (word of prophecy)' comes through the
> word of Christ. (Rom 10:15-17, adapted NRSV)

These quotations come in the midst of an extended section where Paul is seeking to
explain how the failure of the Jews to accept the gospel does not mean that God's
promises to them have been broken. It is a section where he is concerned to illustrate
his points from scripture. Both his references in the passage above come from the
same discourse of the prophet Isaiah. Using the proposed translation to interpret
the passage makes good sense of it. Paul is using the quotation to argue that, just as
the failure to accept the prophetic words of Isaiah in his time ('who has had faith in
the word of prophecy that we have heard?') did not mean that God's word (God's
'good news') was false, so the failure of the Jews to recognize the word of prophecy
spoken through Paul and his fellow apostles is, again, not a sign that God's word is
false or has failed. If this interpretation is correct then Paul is affirming that the word
of prophecy spoken in the preacher is the word of Christ:

> So faith comes from the word of prophecy, and the word of prophecy comes
> through the word of Christ. (Rom 10:17, adapted NRSV)

He seems further to be stating that faith arises from the word of prophecy. But to gain
more precision on this proposed relationship between the word of prophecy and faith
it is necessary to turn to the third passage; once this is done the consistent pattern of
thought underlying all three passages will emerge.

1 Thessalonians 2:13

For this next passage the most literal English translation of the Greek is that made
in the Revised Version:

> And for this cause we also thank God without ceasing, that, when ye received
> from us the word of the message, *even the word* of God, ye accepted *it* not *as* the
> word of men, but, as it is in truth, the word of God, which also worketh in you
> that believe. (1 Thess 2:13, RV [translator's italics])

Akoē is rendered above as 'the message'. A second point brings a further sharpening
of the translation. The translators of the Revised Version were particularly concerned
with remaining close to the Greek and whenever they added words not in the Greek
in order to make the sense in English clearer they put them in italics. In the phrase,
'the message, even the word of God', 'even the word' is in italics and is not in the
Greek; 'it' and 'as' in the following phrase can be omitted on the same basis. With
these changes and replacing 'message' with *akoē*, the passage now reads:

> [W]hen ye received from us the word of God's *akoē*, ye accepted not the word
> of men, but, as it is in truth, the word of God, which also worketh in you that
> believe. (1 Thess 2:13, adapted RV)

It can be seen that, of the three passages we are examining in this section, this verse
most dramatically favours the interpretation of *akoē* as the prophetic word:

> [W]hen ye received from us the word of God's 'heard thing (word of prophecy)',
> ye accepted not the word of men, but, as it is in truth, the word of God, which also
> worketh in you that believe. (1 Thess 2:13, adapted RV)

It evokes an image of Paul speaking the word of God, understood as words from
God, spoken as a prophet speaks, accepted as such by the community ('ye accepted
not the word of men, but ... the word of God'), and then, as a consequence, the
community becoming a medium of the same prophetic word ('which also worketh
in you that believe').

Noting how 'faith' is closely linked in Paul's understanding with the 'prophetic
word' opens up the possibility of a new clarity to the contrast between 'righteousness
by faith' and 'righteousness by law'. 'Faith' can provide direction for right action
just as the law can; it gives the hearer guidance from God on what to do.

The obedience of faith

Closely related to the Greek phrase *akoē pisteōs* is *hypakoē pisteōs*. As we have seen,
the phrase *akoē pisteōs* is usually translated 'the message of faith' or sometimes
'hearing of faith'; *hypakoē pisteōs* is usually translated 'the obedience of faith'.
The English translation 'obedience of faith' is well chosen as, in its Latin root, it
includes the element of hearing or listening. 'Obedience', in its Latin root, breaks
down into *ob + audire*. *Audire* is 'to listen' and in the word 'obedience' the prefix
'*ob*' characterizes the kind of listening as deep and responsive so that the word
'obedience' signifies the 'doing' of what is heard.

The closeness of these two ideas is suggested by the use of the verb *hypakouō* in
relation to *akoē pisteōs* in the Romans passage examined above:

> And how are they to proclaim him unless they are sent? As it is written, 'How
> beautiful are the feet of those who bring good news!' but not all have obeyed
> (*hypakouō*) the good news; for Isaiah says, 'Lord, who has believed our *akoē*?'
> (Rom 10:15f)

But the indication of the importance of the phrase, *hypakoē pisteōs*, and what it
means for Paul comes in Romans where he uses it at both the beginning and end
of the letter to sum up the task that he believes he has been given by God. Right in
his opening introduction Paul says that he has 'received grace and apostleship to
bring about *obedience of faith* ... among all the nations' (Romans 1:5). As we shall
see, 'apostleship' means 'one who is sent'; 'by God' is implied. The prophets are

all described as being sent by God (note how in the Isaiah passage above Paul is speaking of the 'beauty' of the one who is sent with good news). The interpretation of *hypakoē pisteōs*, if made in the light of the meaning of *akoē pisteōs* that has been offered, is that Paul is stating that he has been called and sent to bring about 'the hearing and acting upon the directly given word of God' among all nations.

There is further confirmation of the interpretation of this phrase in these prophetic terms at the end of Romans. It should be noted that the Pauline authorship of these final few verses is disputed among scholars:

> Now to him who is able to strengthen you according to my gospel and the preaching of Jesus Christ, according to the revelation of the mystery which was kept secret for long ages but is now disclosed and through the prophetic writings is made known to all nations, according to the command of the eternal God, to bring about the obedience of faith – to the only wise God be glory for evermore through Jesus Christ! Amen. (Rom 16:25-27, RSV)

Here again, right at the very end of the letter, we find the phrase 'obedience of faith' (*hypakoē pisteōs*) used to sum up the purpose of Paul's work. The phrase is related to the intriguing reference to the 'prophetic writings' which, the text says, is making known to all nations a mystery which has been kept secret for long ages. It seems very unlikely that what is being referred to here are the prophetic writings of the Hebrew scriptures. It is much more likely that 'prophetic writings' is a description of writings like the letter of Romans itself – Christian documents written under prophetic inspiration which are playing their part alongside the direct contact of Paul and others in spreading news of an experience of the Spirit which itself is 'the mystery which has been kept secret for long ages' and is now being revealed.

Faith's 'heard thing': summary sentence and discussion

> **For Paul the prophetic word of God is central to faith and gives just as clear guidance on right action as the law but is directly available to all.**

An extended section of comment is needed at this stage to show how each scholar affirms the centrality for Paul of living a new life, guided by the Spirit, but also, how each scholar, in different ways and in different degrees, is reticent to explore what that claim meant in the experience of Paul and others and to draw out the consequences of that claim for his theology. The main text has presented the idea that integral to that claim to being guided by the Spirit is the experience of hearing and responding to the prophetic word from God. This theme is supported and developed by the rest of the main text that follows; it is the whole argument of the book on which this thesis stands or falls. At this stage the task is simply to establish, as a preliminary but significant step, that the interpretation offered here is a legitimate one for further exploration.

Sanders on Paul's principles for behaviour

As we have seen, Sanders takes very seriously the idea of a real change for the Christian. A person who is 'righteoused' is transferred from being 'under the law to being under grace'

(48/57). Sanders argues from Romans 6 that Paul considers that Christians 'no longer live in sin (6: 2)', and 'that Christians, being "in the Spirit", are able to put to death evil deeds and to fulfil what the law requires' (67/80). At the same time, Sanders seems to undermine this view of 'real change' when he suggests that Paul, in speaking on particular aspects of behaviour, often simply seeks 'to impose Jewish behaviour on his Gentile converts' (116/135). Sanders does concede that Paul, when thinking more creatively, 'offers ... the beginnings of a code of behaviour that is founded on the Jewish principle of love of neighbour and his new principle of union with Christ' (116/136). Here are certain 'principles' from which right behaviour is worked out (109/127): 'the body of the Christian is part of the body of Christ' and 'a temple of the Holy Spirit' are both used as arguments for Paul's condemnation of the Christian going to a prostitute (1 Corinthians 6:13b-20). But Sanders is seriously reserved about the real foundation for Paul's new principles (109/1):

> [I]t is likely that the argument about union with Christ and being the temple of the Spirit is rationalization to support a point arrived at on another basis: he was Jewish and followed strict Diaspora practice.

This all seems a good way from the idea of the 'word of the Spirit' guiding believers but one of the most telling situations Paul has to deal with is the man who is cohabiting with his stepmother (1 Cor 5:1-5). Sanders presents the view that the man believes he is acting 'in the name of the Lord Jesus' and notes how most translators connect that phrase with Paul's response 'I have condemned the one *in the name of the Lord Jesus*' or the role of the community 'when you are gathered together *in the name of the Lord Jesus*'. Sanders says (107/124f):

> The simplest rendering ... provides the readiest explanation of the man's behaviour: he acted "in the name of the Lord Jesus". It is clear what had happened: Paul had said 'you are a new creation' and 'live in the Spirit'. The man took seriously his being a new person and concluded that old relationships had passed away. He then consulted the spirit within him and began cohabiting with his stepmother. He had thought through Paul's own principles in a way Paul had not considered ...

This interpretation of the situation provides support for the argument that there was a new basis for behaviour in the early Christian communities; they had a sense of their actions being done 'in the name of the Lord Jesus'. However, Sanders again reduces the motivation for this extraordinary action to the man 'thinking through Paul's principles'. The picture proposed in the main text would suggest that a more likely explanation is that the man had such a powerful sense of being directly guided by the Spirit that he was prepared to act in a way that Paul describes as immorality 'not found even among pagans' (1 Cor 5:1). Paul's response gives principles to deal with the big issue that arises: how to discern if such guidance is truly from the Spirit.

Dunn on faith and prophecy

Dunn affirms that 'the experience of the Spirit as gift was a common – should we not say, universal? – experience of the first believers (419)' and that the Spirit which brings salvation 'is also the Spirit of prophecy (420)'. In a section on prophecy Dunn also argues for the widespread nature of this experience in the Christian community (582):

> Prophetic authority was not limited to prophets. Only an apostle could exercise apostolic authority. But anyone might prophesy. Paul clearly expected that

members of the assembly other than the recognized prophets could be granted a prophetic charism that is, a word of prophecy (1 Cor 14.1, 5, 24, 31).

Dunn indicates how 'faith' and 'prophecy' are connected in Paul's thought (581):

> ...[P]rophets should speak "in proportion to faith" (Rom 12.6), that is, within the limits of their confidence that their words were God's words.

And Dunn refers to contemporary Jewish interpretation of the story of Abraham and Isaac to help explain Paul's use of the important words in Gen 15:6: 'Abraham believed God and it was reckoned to him as righteousness.' Dunn notes (375):

> ...Gen 22 [Abraham's faithfulness when tested in the offering of Isaac] showed what Abraham's believing involved. His *pistis* [faith] was his "faithfulness" under test, that is, his unquestioning obedience to God's command.

Dunn on *akoē pisteōs*

Although, as we have seen above, Dunn is very positive about the reality of prophecy for Paul and in the early Christian communities, when he comes to offer close commentary on the text of Romans 10:16-17, prophecy is not considered in his interpretation. The view presented in the main text was that in this section of Romans when Paul uses the phrase 'the word of God' or 'the word of faith' he is speaking of 'the prophetic word' rather than 'a message that is preached and heard'. Romans 9-11 deals with the relationship of the gospel to Israel. Dunn describes it as 'a carefully composed and rounded unit ... with 9:6a giving the text or thesis to be expounded ... – has God's word failed? (*Romans 9-16*, 518)'. In Dunn's interpretation, 'God's word' = God's 'promise to Israel' and 'the gospel of Christ' (*Romans 9-16*, 539). Both these definitions focus on the *content* of God's word, the 'message' whether that is 'God's word of call and promise to Abraham (*Romans 9-16*, 518)' or 'the good news of Jesus Christ (*Romans 1-8*, 10)'. The interpretation proposed in the main text suggests that when Paul speaks of 'the word of God' he is thinking first of the 'prophetic word' in itself which raises the question: how is the word of God that is spoken among us related to the word spoken to Abraham, especially as that word included a promise to the people of Israel? That question is acute for Paul because the experience that he and his fellow Jewish Christians have of God's directly given word makes them overwhelmingly confident that God's promise, God's word to Israel is now being fulfilled. And this leads to the obvious question: why, if this is the case, is there so little positive response among the Jewish people to 'the prophetic word of God spoken among them' and such a positive response from many Gentiles?

Dunn includes a paragraph on *akoē* to support his interpretation of Romans 10:16-17 (*Romans 9-16*, 623). The paragraph begins: '*akoē* can have the sense both of "(act) of hearing" and of "that which is heard" ... But whereas in v. 16 *akoē* is best taken in the latter sense, as almost all agree, in v. 17 the former sense seems to be required...' The argument in the main text has been that 'that which is heard' is the consistent meaning and can be sustained with clarity once the 'thing that is heard' is interpreted as 'the directly given word from God' rather than 'a message that is preached and heard'. Dunn's first point in support of his shift in translation has to be defensive: 'What seems unnatural to us because we have to use two different words ("report" and "hearing") would not seem so to the Greek hearer; the range of meaning of one and the same word is simply being exploited.' This is seriously questionable (see pp. xiii-xiv, 6, 11-12 108-11, 117-8 which deal with the same issue in other passages). It is true that the Greek word can carry a range of meaning but it is clearly preferable to look for an interpretation in which the meaning is consistent within the same argument (in this case within the space of seven Greek words), particularly because Paul's use of *akoē* is so central in this passage. It seems clear that the Isaiah quote in v. 16 is being used to support what he says in v. 17 precisely because it uses the word *akoē*. Dunn himself notes 'the verbal link effected by the use of *hypakouō* (v. 16), *akoē* (vv. 16-17), and *akouō* (v. 18), which is impossible to reproduce in English, but which the original audiences would no doubt have appreciated (*Romans 9-16*, 620).'

What the 'thing that is heard' is can be seriously confused by the translation of the Greek word, *hrēma*, which occurs in v. 17 and which Dunn looks at in his next point. Dunn has no difficulty in interpreting *hrēma* as 'the word we preach'. The RSV translation agrees. Its translation of v. 17 runs: 'what is heard comes by the preaching (*hrēma*) of Christ'. What the reader in English cannot know is that this same Greek word occurs several times earlier in the passage where the RSV gives it the more obvious and straightforward translation 'word':

> The word (*hrēma*) is near you, on your lips and in your heart (that is, the word [*hrēma*] of faith which we preach). (Rom 10:8, RSV)

Interpretation of 'word of faith' as a 'message preached about Jesus' in this verse seems to be supported by the phrase that follows:

> ...because if you confess with your lips that Jesus is Lord... (Rom 10:9, RSV)

This translation indicates that, by this 'word', Paul is meaning some kind of 'statement of faith', an acceptance of the 'message preached about Jesus', but the word translated 'confess' is *homologeō* which Dunn notes is only used on this occasion by Paul. It is a combination of *homo*, 'the same' and *logos*, word, and has the core sense of 'to speak the same word as'. The translation of this phrase with the sense, 'if with your lips you speak the same word as the Lord Jesus' would support and be supported by the broad interpretation being offered of this whole passage (see pp. 178-84 on 'the faith of Jesus'). Right through the passage, the idea that Paul is speaking of 'the word of prophecy' rather than 'the word that is preached' leads to more straightforward translations of individual words. Arguably, the difficulty with this interpretation is that 'the word that is preached' is something known and understood by translators today whilst 'the word of prophecy' is not something widely experienced.

Dunn's final point refers to the parallel use of *akoē pisteōs* in Gal 3:2,5 where he suggests that 'hearing' is the most 'natural sense'. Interestingly in support of this translation in the Galatians passage he says, 'it is precisely faith as the responsive hearing/acceptance of the gospel/Spirit which Paul clearly has in mind (*Romans 9-16*, 623)'. 'Hearing of the Spirit' as opposed to 'hearing/acceptance of the gospel' is a vivid phrase to describe the experience that, it has been argued, Paul is referring to in these passages. Dunn does not refer to Paul's only other use of *akoē* in 1 Thessalonians 2:13 which, as was suggested above, offers the clearest support for the translation proposed in the main text.

Dunn on *hypakoē pisteōs*

In Dunn's interpretation of *hypakoē pisteōs* just about all that he says can be applied to the interpretation of *hypakoē* as 'hearing and responding to the directly given word of God'. In a section on 'faith and "the law of faith"' (634-642) Dunn seeks first to establish that faith is not just about the point of conversion, 'the means through which individual and church receive the saving grace of God'. He goes on (634):

... [F]aith is just as important in Paul as an ethical concept, as that out of which believers live. It could hardly be otherwise, since for Paul faith is the human response to all divine grace, the junction box, as it were, through which the transforming power of God flows into and through the life of individual and church.

Direct guidance could easily be what Dunn is speaking of here as in the next paragraph where he presents the relationship between *hypakoē*, *akoē* and *akouō* (634f):

It is a striking and insufficiently noted fact that Paul's first and last references to faith in Romans carry precisely the connotation of a means to responsible living. Paul introduces himself in Rom 1.5 by describing the purpose of his apostleship as "for the obedience of faith." The term "obedience" (*hypakoē*) was a little-known word at Paul's time. But its establishment in Christian terminology may be yet another case of a term which Paul in particular brought into active service through his theology. Its derivation from the verb "hear" (*akouō*) means that it retains the richer meaning of the Hebrew *shama'*, "hear (responsively)" – "obedience" as responsive hearing. ... By implication, that response is given not only in the immediate act of commitment, but in the obedience which follows.

Dunn elaborates on Paul's presentation of the figure of Abraham as the example of faith (641):

... [F]aith for Paul meant complete trust in God, like Abraham's, total reliance on God's enabling. *That* was the root of obedience for Paul. ... The "obedience of faith" is that obedience which lives out of the sort of trust and reliance on God which Abraham demonstrated.

Dunn understands Paul to hold that there is a continuing place for the law as 'a measure of righteousness' but only when 'understood aright', when it is lived 'in faith and out of faith' (641). In Chapter 4 it will be argued that Paul, in fact, allows no continuing place for the law, and that the reason he presents Abraham as the example of faith is that his faith comes before there is any external law. As Dunn himself says in a sentence quoted above (375):

[Abraham's] *pistis* [faith] was his "faithfulness" under test, that is, *his unquestioning obedience to God's command* [italics added].

For Abraham that command was directly given to him by God; it was what we have called 'the prophetic word from God' or 'faith's prophetic word'.

Ziesler on the prophetic word

Ziesler's assessment of the prophetic word in Paul is inconsistent. On occasion he indicates that it has a central significance in understanding Paul but on others it disappears from his thinking. It receives particular attention in two sections. In the first he is seeking to explain why Paul shows so little interest in the traditions about Jesus (22f):

In the end we are reduced to two alternative explanations. First, that Paul did not know the Jesus-tradition in any detail. ...
  The alternative explanation is that Paul had little interest in the Jesus-tradition. He concentrated on Jesus crucified, risen, and exalted, the present

reigning and saving Lord now active through the Spirit. This, and not stories about Jesus and his teaching, was what mattered. In teaching, he relied more on the present direction of the Spirit in the church than on words of Jesus from the past. The church's authority was not the teacher of Galilee but the risen Lord speaking through the Spirit. He does not attribute quotations because it is not important to do so. What matters is what God is saying now. In many ways this is theologically attractive, but few have been entirely happy with it, if only because on a very few occasions he can quote Jesus-sayings without qualms.

The problem is unsolved ...

Note how Ziesler formulates the second explanation for Paul's lack of interest in 'the Jesus-tradition'. He speaks of 'the present direction of the Spirit' and 'the risen Lord speaking through the Spirit' and 'what God is saying now'. Ziesler's conclusion is interesting, indicating that, although Ziesler can see that the 'alternative explanation' is 'theologically attractive' he is not prepared to commit himself to it. The argument that this is because 'on a very few occasions [Paul] can quote Jesus-sayings without qualms' is weak; there is no reason why words of the historical Jesus might not be recalled and used for inspiration and guidance even if, as argued in this book, the prophetic word is the main source of guidance.

Confirmation that the idea that what matters to Paul is 'what God is saying now' really is theologically attractive to Ziesler comes when he returns to this theme later in his book. Ziesler asks a key question for this discussion (116):

> The Law gave Israel divine guidance for the whole of life. If for Christians it is no longer the key authority, then where do they look for guidance? ...

And the answer Ziesler gives is confident of the place for Paul of 'the present direction of the Spirit' (116):

> He who is justified by faith dies to the old self, and lives under the authority and power of Christ and the Spirit.

Having made this affirmation, Ziesler then seems to vacillate over how 'living under the authority and power of Christ and Spirit' might give guidance that can replace the law, so a little later he says (121):

> [Paul] seems to assume (e.g. in Rom 6) that his readers will know what righteousness means in practice, and that whether from their knowledge of high pagan morality or from their reading of the Old Testament, they will have commonly accepted standards which can fill in the outlines of general moral exhortation.

In this statement all reference to the Spirit as source of guidance has disappeared.

Shortly after this, Ziesler has a section headed 'Love in the community' and he talks there about the 'centrality of love' and looks at its 'practical outworking' in three questions for the community. He then gives this description of the source of guidance for the community (124):

> Consideration for others, and their existing or potential adherence to Christ, is the guiding rule; in other words, love.

Whilst no-one would dispute the centrality of love for Paul, what disappears in this analysis is the clarity of guidance for the community through 'what God is saying now'. What is interesting is that it does reappear in the concluding paragraph of this section but *only applied to Paul's decision making* in relation to the issues being considered (124, italics added):

> In all these passages, *Paul is guided not by a rule but by the Spirit* in the light of the concrete situation. *There is a conviction that in Christ immediate illumination is given on questions of behaviour.* This is underlined by the occasional practice of uttering what have been called 'sentences of holy law' in the form 'If someone does *x*, then he will be *y* (by God)' or '*God* will *x* him'. An example is in 1 Cor 3:17: 'If anyone destroys God's temple, God will destroy him.' 'God's temple' here is the church. The confident uttering of judgment or anathema betrays a tacit claim to complete and divine authority (see also 1 Cor 5:3-5; 14:38; 16:22; Gal 1: 9). God's final judgment is anticipated in his apostle's utterance. These sentences demonstrate Paul's confidence that *Christ's Spirit is* working and *speaking through him.*

This last section is a strong affirmation of the reality of the prophetic word functioning in the early Christian community but with a substantial difference from what has been proposed. It is only to Paul that Ziesler can confidently ascribe this gift. This will be returned to in Chapters 8 and 11.

To sum up, we have seen that although Ziesler affirms confidently that Christians now 'live under the authority and power of Christ and the Spirit' what that means in practice for him lacks real substance. Do the early Christians (a) respond obediently to the words from God of Paul the prophet or (b) work out what to do out of 'love' understood as 'consideration for others' or (c) have 'commonly accepted standards ('whether from their knowledge of high pagan morality or from their reading of the Old Testament') which can fill in the outlines of general moral exhortation'? The widespread – if not universal – access to the life of the Spirit, understood as the Spirit of prophecy, which Dunn presents and which is a major theme of the current work is missing from Ziesler.

Conclusion

When Paul uses the phrase *akoē pisteōs,* usually translated as 'a message that is heard' like 'the gospel message' or 'the message of faith', it is possible to maintain a consistent translation of the single Greek word *akoē* if Paul is understood to be speaking of something heard within the believer. It has been proposed that this is indeed what Paul means and that what is heard in association with faith and the coming of the Spirit is the prophetic word from God guiding the actions of those who receive it. It is with this word of prophecy that Paul claims to speak. In what Paul writes to the Thessalonians he indicates that by their recognition of the prophetic word spoken by him they themselves become recipients of the same prophetic word. Paul's question to the Galatians examined earlier can be understood with this sense in the following paraphrase:

> Was it through works of the law or when you heard the word that comes by faith, the word of God spoken through me, that you received the Spirit of prophecy that empowers and guides, the same Spirit by which I spoke?

The Spirit and word of prophecy can be understood as being directly from God, objective and yet appreciated within the individual, that is, subjectively. This points to the possibility that in speaking of 'righteousness by faith', that is, the way of doing what is right by faith, Paul is referring to a life guided by the word of prophecy. Paul can directly contrast righteousness by faith with righteousness by the law *because they are both ways of knowing what to do*. The difference is in the directness or immediacy of guidance by the prophetic word from God. The mediation of law is no longer required in those who have the way of doing what is right through faith. Paul can summarize his task as being to bring about the 'obedience of faith' (*hypakoē pisteōs*) among all the nations: 'the hearing and acting upon the directly given word of God.'

Chapter 3

The Freedom of Obedience

The subject of this chapter is Paul's understanding of the contrast between faith and law as ways of knowing what it is right to do, in other words, of knowing God's will. The conclusion of the last chapter was that 'the mediation of law is no longer required in those who have come to faith'. This chapter makes clear the sharpness of the dividing line in Paul's thinking between the life of faith guided by the Spirit, and life under the law. The tool for discovering this clarity again lies in pursuing consistent translation along with a willingness to see the consequences for our understanding of Paul's theology.

In the introduction, the image of picking away at a cluster of knots was used for some of the translation work involved in pursuing the argument of this work. Much of this chapter is akin to picking away at a particularly tightly pulled knot. Patience is required to keep the focus on a small area of string. Analogous to the loosening of the knot is the opening up of new clarity on Paul's view of the law, crucial to appreciate Paul's understanding of freedom.

The whole of the chapter is concerned with the examination of the plural noun, *stoicheia* and the verb, *stoicheō*. These are words that, in themselves, are peripheral in the framework of Paul's thought but the examination of this noun and verb from a single Greek root reveals the subtlety with which Paul describes what it means to live by faith. It reveals how Paul seeks to maintain that, while the life of faith is a way of freedom and does not involve the obligation which is present in the obedience to the law, it still involves a direction for living.

Direction for Living

Peripheral to the thought of Paul, this verb and plural noun from the single Greek root do not represent a concept that Paul is trying to *explain*, but rather one of the many concepts Paul is using as *a means of explaining* the new and extraordinary nature of his gospel. In English translations of the bible, the meaning that will be offered for this verb and noun do not appear. In the case of the verb this is because the consistent core of meaning in this word is not considered to be significant and its meaning is taken to vary according to the context in which it is used. In the case of the noun, it will be seen that a dramatic distortion has taken place, entirely separating its meaning from that of the verb.

The root meaning of the noun *stoicheia* to which the verb *stoicheō* is related is a 'row' or 'series'. It will be argued here that the verb *stoicheō* is best translated, 'to keep aligned' and that Paul is using it in connection with behaviour. Although it is stretching English usage to use the word 'alignment' in this way – we would not generally say 'keep aligned by your faith' – there are several English idioms that do contain this same connection. We might well talk of faith 'giving a direction to our lives' or 'keeping us on the right path' or 'keeping us in line'. The importance of using the image of 'alignment' lies in its precision. The RSV translates the word as 'to walk' (Gal 5:25, 6:16) and 'to follow' (Rom 4:12). The NRSV also uses 'to follow' (Gal 6:16; Rom 4:12) and 'to be guided' (Gal 5:25). Both these do relay something of the quality of 'alignment' but without the precision that can help us get really close to Paul's meaning. It will be proposed that Paul is using this word to communicate the clarity and firmness of guidance that is present in living by faith without equating that guidance with the obligation that is present in living by the law.

Before turning to an examination of these passages, it is worth making a further preliminary point: the fact that this word, *stoicheō*, is used in passages important for understanding central elements of Paul's theology is what leads to it being considered by translators as a word whose meaning can change within a broad spectrum depending upon the context. The central elements of Paul's theology inevitably receive particular attention from scholars and translators. In order to do their job, translators must have a clear idea of the meaning of these central elements. What can happen is that the hardening of a theological or scholarly position on one of these concepts, a hardening that is inevitably involved in the process of definition, can mean that the central abstract concepts are then shaping the interpretation of the images rather than vice versa as was clearly Paul's intention. So because this word is peripheral, it can be mistakenly assumed that its meaning is not only relatively insignificant but that the word carries no consistent hard core or skeleton of meaning. The argument in this chapter will assume the simple point that because a word is peripheral does not mean that it has no unvarying and significant core of meaning. The simple spatial image of 'alignment' with which this word is concerned is employed by Paul just because it is precise and thus useful for bringing definition to more abstract ideas.

'Straight-line thinking': translating *stoicheō*

Keep aligned by the Spirit

In the letter to the Galatians, Paul first uses the word *stoicheō* in the context of living by the Spirit (using the RSV in this section allows the key point about translation to be seen most clearly). The translation of *stoicheō* as 'walk' occurs right at the end of the passage and is italicized:

> But I say, walk by the Spirit, and do not [Gk – 'you definitely will not'] gratify
> the desires of the flesh. For the desires of the flesh are against the Spirit, and the
> desires of the Spirit are against the flesh; for these are opposed to each other, to

prevent you from doing what you would. But if you are led by the Spirit you are not under the law. ... [T]he fruit of the Spirit is love, joy, peace, patience, kindness, faithfulness, gentleness, self-control; against such there is no law. And those who belong to Christ Jesus have crucified the flesh with its passions and desires. If we live by the Spirit, let us also *walk* by the Spirit. (Gal 5:16-18, 22-25, RSV)

Paul is discussing the motivation for behaviour and making an absolute contrast between walking by the Spirit and walking by the flesh. The verses that have been omitted above simply list the consequences in behaviour of living by the flesh. By leaving out these verses it is possible to get a clearer view of the significant issue of translation to be examined here.

In sharp contrast to the RSV and most other translations, the sense of the Greek in the opening sentence is emphatically different: '[W]alk (*peripateite*) by the Spirit, and you will *definitely not* gratify the desires of the flesh.' Paul uses 'a double and thus strengthened negative, "assuredly not"' (Dunn, *Galatians*, 297). Paul says further that 'if you are led by the Spirit, you are not under the law'. The point is very simple and is stated clearly in the next sentence quoted above: against the fruit of the Spirit 'there is no law'; in other words, such is the kind of life that you will live if you are led by the Spirit that no law will be necessary, you are no longer 'under the law'. Paul then states how this has come about. The flesh, which is the source of those aspects of human behaviour which the law opposes, has been crucified in those who belong to Christ Jesus; the passions and desires of the flesh which necessitate law are no longer operative. This is the straightforward sense of the Greek.

We come now to the interpretation of *stoicheō*. It needs a little careful attention to see the effect of the RSV translation in significantly distorting Paul's meaning. That distortion occurs because of the way the sentences at the beginning and end of the above passage are translated. To see this it is helpful to quote them together:

> But I say, walk (*peripateite*) by the Spirit, and do not gratify the desires of the flesh. ... If we live by the Spirit, let us also *walk* by the Spirit. (Gal 5:16, 25, RSV)

To put the issue simply, by imprecise translation of these two sentences which frame this passage on the Spirit, Paul's meaning has been changed from a *description* of life in the Spirit to a general *exhortation* to live by the Spirit. Compare this alternative, which as well as significantly changing the meaning of the first sentence also introduces the image of 'alignment' for *stoicheō*:

> But I say, walk by the Spirit, and you will definitely not gratify the desires of the flesh. ... Those who belong to Christ Jesus have crucified the flesh with its passions and desires. If we live by the Spirit, let us also keep aligned by the Spirit. (Gal 5:16, 24f, author's translation)

This second translation aims to capture the sharp dividing lines that are there in the meaning of Paul's Greek. There is no vagueness. Those who walk by the Spirit will *definitely not* gratify the desires of the flesh; this is why they have no need of law. This has come about because the flesh, which the law exists to check, has now been crucified. Once this clear meaning in the passage is seen, the sense in the last sentence also clearly emerges.

The first half of the sentence ('if we live by the Spirit') is concerned with the initiation into a new way of living; it connects directly with the previous sentence. The flesh was crucified and the new life came by the Spirit. There is an exhortation here but it is very precise. Paul is not saying: because you now live by the Spirit carry on as someone who lives by the Spirit ought to live ('walk by the Spirit'). Rather he says this: you came to life by the Spirit, now stay aligned, keep being guided, by that Spirit. We have already seen how Paul can remind them of the coming of the Spirit (Gal 3:2f). He is stating that that dramatic beginning in which the Spirit was first evident in the community brought a transformation which still provides the way of living – the way of determining what to do. To put this another way, his exhortation is not about conduct; it is rather about remaining in a fundamentally changed way of living that *inevitably* brings a transformation of behaviour. If the interpretation proposed here is accurate then this indicates that, in Paul's conception, the fruits of the Spirit and the lack of the passions and desires of the flesh both issue without any doubt from living by the Spirit.

Keep aligned by faith

This section is concerned with the first of two passages which, whilst interesting in themselves, are presented here primarily to confirm that the core meaning in this word is accurately to be connected with the image of alignment. A brief examination of these passages precedes an enquiry into the interpretation of the noun *stoicheia*, the interpretation of which can significantly clarify or distort the sharp lines in Paul's understanding. In the example just examined, it has been argued that Paul is exhorting the Galatians to keep aligned or directed by the Spirit; in the first of these second two examples, Paul speaks of *stoicheō* in relation to faith; in the second, of *stoicheō* in relation to the cross.

In the following passage, Paul is speaking of Abraham. The English translation for *stoicheō* is italicized:

> The purpose was to make him the ancestor of all who believe without being circumcised and who thus have righteousness reckoned to them, and likewise the ancestor of the circumcised who are not only circumcised but who also *follow the example* of the faith that our ancestor Abraham had before he was circumcised. (Rom 4:11f)

'Follow the example' is a paraphrase of the Greek. The NIV takes us nearer to a literal translation:

> And he is also the father of the circumcised who not only are circumcised but who also *walk* in the footsteps of the faith that our father Abraham had before he was circumcised. (Rom 4:12, NIV)

The phrase 'in the footsteps' which disappears in the NRSV translation is there in the Greek. The meaning of *stoicheō* is being understandably treated in a malleable way in order to relay the Greek words idiomatically into English. 'Walking in the footsteps' in the NIV is a good image to accurately convey what Paul is saying. What is of real importance for our purpose here is that, while 'to walk' is used in conjunction with 'in the footsteps' to create a comfortable English idiom, using our proposed precise sense for the word *stoicheō*, 'to keep aligned', leads to exactly the same image in this passage. 'Keeping aligned in the footsteps of', whilst not an idiomatic English phrase like 'walking in the footsteps of' has exactly the same sense; it is the vivid and meaningful image of walking, as it were, in single file along precisely the same path as Abraham. The significance of this is the support it gives for the assertion that this word has a simple precise meaning which varies very little, if at all, in the variety of contexts in which it is used. Translating *stoicheō* as 'to keep aligned' in this passage has not led to any change in sense from other English translations. This is not true of the passage to be examined next in which the connection of *stoicheō* with alignment brings a sharp vividness to the passage which is not present in other translations.

Keep aligned by the cross

Like the first example, this use of the verb *stoicheō* is from the letter to the Galatians, this time in a different context. The whole of the letter can be understood as an argument by Paul against the idea that Gentiles need to be circumcised in order to fully receive the benefits of faith. Paul is finishing the letter by saying that those who are insisting on circumcision are doing so, 'only in order that they may not be persecuted for the cross of Christ'. He continues:

> May I never boast of anything except the cross of our Lord Jesus Christ, by which the world has been crucified to me, and I to the world. For neither circumcision nor uncircumcision is anything; but a new creation is everything! As for those who will *follow* this rule – peace be upon them, and mercy, and upon the Israel of God. (Gal 6:14-16)

The RSV uses 'walk' instead of 'follow' to translate *stoicheō*:

> Peace and mercy be upon all who *walk* by this rule, upon the Israel of God. (Gal 6:14-16, RSV)

Using either 'follow' or 'walk' for *stoicheō* in this passage means that the vivid force of the image Paul is presenting is completely lost. For that image to emerge depends on the interpretation of two other words in addition to *stoicheō*: 'cross' and 'rule'.

To begin with the word translated 'cross' (*stauros*). Although now the word is understandably almost totally identified with the Roman instrument of execution, the Greek word simply means a 'pale' as in 'a spiked post for a fence' or 'stake'. While 'pale' is rarely used in modern English, it does allow an insight into the vivid way in which Paul is speaking of himself:

> May I never boast of anything except the pale (*stauros*) of our Lord Jesus Christ,
> by which the world has been impaled (*estaurōtai*) to me, and I to the world. (Gal
> 6:14, adapted NRSV)

The sharp wooden stake in the ground on which Jesus died has become the means by which the world has died to Paul, and Paul to the world.

The word translated 'rule' (*kanōn*) has a closely related meaning. The reason that the word comes to be used for 'rule' is that its root meaning is that of a straight stick. However, a straight stick, as well as being useful as a ruler, can also be used as a boundary marker and the Greek word can also carry the sense of a demarcated territory. Paul himself uses the word with this latter sense in the second letter to the Corinthians when he speaks of the particular area in which he has preached the gospel. In the RSV, *kanōn* is translated 'field':

> We do not boast beyond limit, in other men's labours; but our hope is that as your
> faith increases, our *field* among you may be greatly enlarged, so that we may
> preach the gospel in lands beyond you, without boasting of work already done in
> another's *field*. (2 Cor 10:15f, RSV)

In this passage Paul is clearly distinguishing the areas designated to him for preaching the gospel from areas designated for others – the NRSV replaces 'field' with 'sphere of action'. Although the RSV translates the word *kanōn* as 'field', the sense the word contains can still be detected in our ancient words for pointed sticks, 'stake' and 'pale'. We still speak of someone being 'beyond the pale' meaning 'outside of the accepted limit', and of 'staking out a claim' meaning 'marking out our area'. Although the English word 'stake' may now carry unhelpful resonances, it still enables sense to be made of the passage:

> ...our hope is that as your faith increases, our stake among you may be greatly
> enlarged... (2 Cor 10:15, adapted NRSV)

The very clear and powerful image that is operating in Paul's thought opens to us once the literal meaning of these words is seen. It comes through connecting the pale on which Jesus died with 'a boundary marking stake' rather than 'rule', combined with the proposal of 'to keep aligned' rather than 'to walk':

> May I never boast of anything except the *pale* of our Lord Jesus Christ, by which
> the world has been *impaled* to me, and I to the world. For neither circumcision
> nor uncircumcision is anything; but a new creation is everything! As for those

who will *keep aligned by* this *stake* – peace be upon them, and mercy, and upon the Israel of God. (Gal 6:14-16, adapted NRSV)

The 'pale' referred to is the cross; Paul says that this is the 'stake' or 'boundary marker' by which to keep aligned; nothing else, whether circumcision or uncircumcision, can be trusted.

Confirmation for the accuracy of this vivid image follows in the next verse, in which Paul again refers to the cross as a sharp pointed stake:

From now on, let no one make trouble for me; for I carry the marks of Jesus branded on my body. (Gal 6:17)

The Greek word translated here 'marks' (*stigma*) is the source of our English word, 'stigmata' and means 'marks made by a something pointed'.

Section conclusion

It has been shown how *stoicheō* always carries the sense of 'alignment' in Paul's writing and that Paul uses the image of 'alignment' to indicate direction for behaviour. He speaks of keeping aligned or directed by the Spirit, by faith or by the cross. The sections where *stoicheō* is considered in relation to faith and the cross, whilst interesting in themselves, have been examined primarily to establish the clarity and sharpness of the image of 'alignment'. The way that Paul uses this word in relation to living by the Spirit is of greater value in the overall interpretation of Paul's thought in that it provides confirmation for the view that the Spirit without law on the one side and the flesh under the check of the law on the other provide alternative sources of motivation and guidance from which different kinds of behaviour inevitably arise. This examination of the verb has been a preparation for enquiring into the meaning of the plural noun *stoicheia* which provides such strong evidence for the sharpness of the dividing lines in Paul's way of thinking on faith and the law that some very difficult but creative questions are inevitably raised about key elements in Paul's theology.

Translating *stoicheō*: summary sentence and discussion

The verb *stoicheō* carries the simple and unchanging sense of 'to keep aligned' and is used by Paul in connection with faith, the cross and the Spirit to indicate the direction from which right action comes: those who 'keep aligned' by the Spirit naturally bring forth the 'fruits of the Spirit' and no longer need the law.

In commenting on *stoicheō*, Dunn notes that it 'is not simply a synonym for "walk" (as RSV/ NRSV)' but retains 'something of its basic sense of "stand in line" (*Galatians*, 317f)'. He then follows conventional interpretation in which the sharp, clarity of the alignment image recedes to be replaced by more malleable concepts: '"to keep in step with" (NIV), "hold to, agree with, follow" (BAGD, *stoicheō*), "be in harmony with" (TDNT, vii. 668-9)'. This matters because the sharpness of Paul's clear rejection of the law as a source of direction for right action is lost in Dunn's interpretation. It needs a couple of steps to see this. Dunn translates Galatians 6:14-16 as follows (*Galatians*, 334 [italics and Greek added]):

> But as for me, God forbid that I should boast except in the *cross (stauros)* of our Lord Jesus Christ, *through whom (di' hou)* the world has been *crucified (estaurōtai)* to me and I to the world. For neither circumcision counts for anything, nor uncircumcision, but a new creation. And as many as will *follow (stoichēsousin)* this *rule (kanōni)*, peace be on them and mercy ...

The issues involved here are subtle but central for interpreting Paul. Dunn acknowledges that his translation '*through whom* (our Lord Jesus Christ) the world has been crucified' is unconventional; '*through which* (the cross) the world has been crucified' is followed by 'almost all commentators' (*Galatians*, 334, n.2). This is not the main issue but Dunn's translation here is part of the way in which the centrality of the image of the cross is lost in Dunn's interpretation. Our central concern is with the phrase 'as many as will follow this rule'.

By treating *stoicheō* as if it were a malleable concept and could in this case be translated as 'follow' and by translating *kanōn* as 'rule', in which the image of the cross as a wooden stake is lost, Dunn misses the clear image of alignment involved in Paul's juxtaposition of *stoicheō*, *stauros* and *kanōn*. Instead of 'the pale', the cross, being the stake by which to keep aligned, Dunn considers that by 'rule' Paul is indicating that there is a literal 'norm' or 'standard' to follow. And the rule to follow is given in verse 15: 'neither circumcision counts for anything, nor uncircumcision'. This is Dunn's interpretation (*Galatians*, 343):

> As a summary of his own teaching, verse 15 provides the norm and standard by which [Paul] hopes the Galatians will judge and act in response to the pressure from the other missionaries. His hope is that, like him, they will sit loose to issues of ethnic identity and ritual distinction, and that such issues will be seen to be of irrelevant significance beside the gospel of the cross.

Here is an expression of Dunn's view that it is only those aspects of the law which mark 'ethnic identity and ritual distinction' that Paul rejects. This is a central element of Dunn's interpretation of Paul and the law and it will be returned to in the final comment section in this chapter and in the next chapter. What is important to observe now is that it leads him to affirm a positive continuing role for law in the life of the Spirit. According to Dunn, the gift of the Spirit makes possible 'a more effective keeping of the law' which had long been hoped for within the Jewish tradition (*Theology*, 644):

> For it is important to recall that the hope which Paul saw as thus fulfilled in the Spirit was not hope for another law or a different Torah. The fulfilment of that earlier hope had not been perceived as dispensing individuals or communities from keeping the law. On the contrary, the hope was for a means to a more effective keeping of the law. Only a circumcision of the heart would enable an adequate keeping of the law (Deut 30.8-10). Contrary to popular opinion, the promise of a new covenant in Jeremiah is not of a new or different law. The promise is plain: "I will put my law within them, and I will write it on their hearts" (Jer 31.33). Likewise the new heart and spirit promised in Ezekiel has in view a more effective keeping of the law: " I will put my spirit within you, and make you follow my statutes and be careful to observe my ordinances" (Ezek 36.27). It is this hope, precisely this hope, which Paul claims to have been fulfilled in the gift of the Spirit to those who put their faith in Messiah Jesus. The coming of Christ

and of faith in Christ had brought emancipation from the law in its temporary, constrictive function (Gal 3.19-4.7). That was still the case. But nothing that Paul says indicates that for him Christ had brought emancipation from the law as God's rule of right and wrong, as God's guidelines for conduct.

As we will see, this interpretation leads to confusion.

In a section headed, 'The Law is irrelevant to salvation', Ziesler concludes (115): 'Undoubtedly the Law has been moved from the centre.' Whilst Paul 'nowhere says that Jewish Christians must not keep the Law', and allows that there are some Jewish Christians who 'continue to keep the Law', it is clear for Ziesler that Paul sees no continuing need for 'the Law' (115):

> It is not ... the way to salvation. It is also not ... the way to lead a righteous life.

Sanders's interpretation of Paul and the law flows from his view that Paul believed a 'real change' had come about in Christians, 'that people who were in Christ were "a new creation" and that they lived in the Spirit' (71f/84):

> Paul seems not to have spent his time in each city teaching ethics. We find him having to give elementary ethical admonition by letter, and he seldom appeals to the readers to remember what he had told them when present. The apparent explanation of this strange fact is that he thought that correct behaviour was the consequence of baptism and that deeds related to people as fruit to trees.
>
> The Corinthian correspondence shows how realistically some or all of Paul's converts understood the change which he proclaimed; they really were new people (cf. 1 Cor 4: 8). When we add this realism to the fact that in his correspondence Paul often gives very basic ethical instruction on major issues, with no indication that he had given it before, we must conclude that he and his converts thought that their membership in the body of Christ really changed them, so that they would live accordingly. He thought that his converts were dead to sin, alive to God, that conduct flowed naturally from people, and that it varied according to who they really were. Those who were under sin naturally committed sins: 'those who are in the Flesh cannot please God' (Rom 8:8); those who were in Christ produced 'the fruit of the Spirit' (Gal 5:22).

So we could sum up Dunn and Sanders by saying that whereas Dunn strongly affirms a continuing role for the law, Sanders affirms the centrality of a real transformation of individuals as a consequence of which the law is no longer required. If this were all, we could state plainly that Sanders is supportive of the view that 'those who "keep aligned" by the Spirit naturally bring forth the "fruits of the Spirit" and no longer need the law' and Dunn would reject it. But neither position is so straightforward. For when Sanders looks at the law and correct behaviour he notes that 'for the most part [Paul] agrees with the behaviour which the law requires' (85/99). And whereas Sanders affirms that for Paul 'Christians are free, and in particular free from observing the law' (85/101) he also offers extended comment on Paul's statement that the single commandment 'Love your neighbour as yourself' 'fulfils "the whole law" (Gal 5: 14, quoting Lev 19: 18) (85/99)' and interprets this as Paul's 'embrace of "the whole law"' (86/101). In the last section of comment it will become clear that this confusing denial and affirmation of the place of the law is a misinterpretation of Paul.

Dunn's position is also confusing for when he says more about what he means by law 'fulfilled in the gift of the Spirit' Dunn talks of 'the law understood as guidelines for Spirit-directed conduct' which 'is the law thus rightly perceived and experienced (647)'. And yet Dunn then asks (647):

And what does this mean in practice for Paul? Paul presumably had in mind a conduct informed and enabled out of a direct and immediate apprehension of the divine will. This is already implied in his earliest letter: "you yourselves are being taught by God to love one another" (1 Thes 4.9).

These confusing interpretations are an attempt to make sense of the mix of positive and negative statements on the law that we find in Paul. In the rest of the chapter, Paul's view on the law will emerge more clearly in a way that makes the solutions of Sanders and Dunn untenable.

'Keeping to the straight and narrow': translating *stoicheia*

The passage in which the plural noun *stoicheia* occurs is of great significance and, as the argument of this book is followed through, it will be seen how incorrect translation of this word seriously impairs an understanding of Paul's meaning. Paul's two uses of the plural noun occur close together in a single passage and, in the RSV, are translated 'elemental spirits':

> I mean that the heir, as long as he is a child, is no better than a slave, though he is owner of all the estate; but he is under guardians and trustees until the date set by the father. So with us; when we were children, we were slaves to the *elemental spirits* of the universe. But when the time had fully come, God sent forth his Son, born of woman, born under the law, to redeem those who were under the law, so that we might receive adoption as sons. ... Formerly, when you did not know God, you were in bondage to beings that by nature are no gods; but now that you have come to know God, or rather to be known by God, how can you turn back again to the weak and beggarly *elemental spirits*, whose slaves you want to be once more? You observe days, and months, and seasons, and years! I am afraid I have laboured over you in vain. (Gal 4:1-5, 8-11, RSV)

The comment of E. P. Sanders on this section of Galatians is that '[Paul's] statements would make a systematist shudder' (*Paul, the Law and the Jewish People*, 68). What it is important to see at this stage is the issue that makes Paul's thought seem unsystematic in this passage.

Paul is contrasting the past 'when we were children' with the present now that the time has 'fully come'. He is speaking of himself and his readers when he says that 'we were slaves to the elemental spirits of the universe'. There is no doubt that he is speaking of both Jews and Gentiles when he speaks of that former situation. To put Jew and Gentile on the same footing as slaves to the 'elemental spirits of the universe' is extraordinary. While he affirms in other places that both Jew and Gentile need to come to the faith that Jesus has made possible, Paul always affirms the importance of the Jewish commitment to the one true God in contrast to the pagan worship of 'unrighteous' Gentiles. But, as his argument is followed through in this translation, the next use of the word seems to confirm that this is his view. He says to the Galatians, 'you were in bondage to beings that by nature are no gods' and then chides them for seeking to turn back again 'to the weak and beggarly elemental spirits'. Given that the larger issue which Paul is dealing with is that of whether the Gentile Galatians need to be circumcised, what Paul is saying is that it is precisely by being circumcised, that is, by accepting a prescription of the law of Moses, that the Galatians will be turning back to be 'in bondage to beings that by nature are no gods'. The implication in Paul's words is that to follow the law of Moses is equivalent to the worship of elemental spirits – 'beings that by nature are no gods' – an identification that Paul makes nowhere else. The purpose of the following argument will be to make clear that it is in the inaccuracy of the translation 'elemental spirits' that Paul's meaning becomes distorted and apparently unsystematic. Several points will need to be presented in sequence in order to support a fresh interpretation of this passage.

It will be suggested that the word *stoicheia* which is translated above 'elemental spirits', being the plural noun related to *stoicheō*, has a core meaning in English of 'things which keep aligned' or 'things that give direction'. There is no single English word to replicate this phrase and in order to follow the argument we will use the Greek word with the clumsy phrases 'things that keep aligned' and 'things that give direction for behaviour' in brackets.

Step 1

With this change, the two phrases where the word occurs now read as follows:

> ... we were slaves to the *stoicheia* (*things that 'keep aligned'/'give direction for behaviour'*) of the universe. (Gal 4:3, adapted RSV)

> ... how can you turn back again to the weak and beggarly *stoicheia* (*things that 'keep aligned'/'give direction for behaviour'*)? (Gal 4:9, adapted RSV)

Step 2

In the first of these phrases, 'enslaved to the *stoicheia* (things that 'keep aligned'/ 'give direction for behaviour')', the preposition 'to' [Gk *hypo*] is more simply translated 'under' as in the AV and NIV:

> ... we were slaves *under* the *stoicheia* (things that 'keep aligned'/'give direction for behaviour') of the universe. (Gal 4:3, adapted RSV)

Step 3

No detailed attempt will made here to investigate the meaning of the word translated 'universe' (*kosmos*). In the NRSV it is translated 'world'. What is important for the present discussion is that Paul uses the word to contrast created things – the things of 'the world' – with the things 'of God'. One example will suffice to demonstrate the point:

> Now we have received not the spirit of the world (*kosmos*), but the Spirit that is
> from God ... (1 Cor 2:12)

To clarify the proposed translation it is helpful to assume that the same contrast is
there in Paul's mind when he is speaking of the *stoicheia*. In modern English, the
translation 'worldly' points to the way Paul is using the word of something that is
created and inferior to something of the divine order:

> ... we were enslaved under the *worldly stoicheia* (things that 'keep aligned'/'give
> direction for behaviour'). (Gal 4:3, adapted RSV)

Step 4

'To be enslaved', a translation which carries strongly negative associations, can be
just as accurately rendered 'to be in servitude' or 'to serve'. As was stated above,
Paul's first use is referring to both Jew and Gentile:

> So with us; when we were children, we were *in servitude* under the worldly
> *stoicheia* (things that 'keep aligned'/'give direction for behaviour'). (Gal 4:3,
> adapted RSV)

The 'us' and 'we' indicate that Paul is quite able to refer to the law of Moses as one
of the 'worldly *stoicheia*'. In the second use of the word, Paul is definitely referring
to his Gentile audience who, unlike the Jews, 'were in bondage to beings that by
nature are no gods':

> Formerly, when you did not know God, you were in bondage to beings that by
> nature are no gods ... (Gal 4:8, RSV)

The passage continues:

> ... but now that you have come to know God, or rather be known by God, how can
> you turn back again to the weak and beggarly *stoicheia* (things that 'keep aligned'/
> 'give direction for behaviour') ...? You observe days, and months, and seasons, and
> years! I am afraid I have laboured over you in vain. (Gal 4:9f, RSV)

Having omitted one phrase in the above, a clear meaning of *stoicheia* can be seen
which carries the same sense whether Paul is talking about something that the Jews
were 'in servitude under' or something 'weak and beggarly' that the Gentiles were
in danger of turning back to. Neither of these two uses are necessarily referring to
something that is served in itself. Two points on either side of the use of *stoicheia* in
the passage above help make the meaning clear. Paul finishes by lamenting that 'you
observe days, and months, and seasons, and years!' Paul is using an exclamatory
phrase to refer here in shorthand to the central fact that unites the previous practice of
both Jew and Gentile. The observance of a religious calendar is a central part of any
religious law. And he is contrasting this former state of religious observance for both
Jew and Gentile with the direct experience of God's will. The distinction in Paul's

mind is between a mediated way of knowing God's will and coming 'to know God, or ... be known by God'. You have come to that better knowledge; do not go back. If this interpretation is correct, *stoicheia* is the word Paul is using for 'religious laws or observances' – things which give 'direction for behaviour' or 'keep the religious adherent aligned on their path' whether those directions come from the law of Moses or the religious traditions of the Gentiles.

Step 5

What makes this simple identification of *stoicheia* with religious laws apparently impossible is a phrase that follows the second use of the word:

> Formerly, when you did not know God, you were in bondage to beings that by nature are no gods; but now that you have come to know God, or rather to be known by God, how can you turn back again to the weak and beggarly *stoicheia*, *whose slaves you want to be once more?* (Gal 4:8-10, adapted RSV)

In the phrases which speak of being 'in bondage' to 'beings that by nature are no gods' and being 'slaves' to 'the weak and beggarly *stoicheia*', 'to be in bondage' and 'to be slaves' are both translating the same Greek word. Paul is saying that the Galatians, who were formerly in bondage to beings that by nature are no gods are now wanting to be in bondage once again. The ordering of the sentence in the RSV translation above can only lead to one conclusion: the *stoicheia* must be describing those 'beings that by nature are no gods' to which the Galatians once again wish to be in bondage. If this is the case then it means that the attempt to link the meaning of *stoicheia* and *stoicheō* in the way pursued above breaks down. However, close attention to Paul's Greek yields an alternative sense for the second section of the passage.

The alternative translation, which significantly alters the meaning of the passage, hinges on the interpretation of one pronoun, 'whose', of the phrase, 'whose slaves you want to be once more' which has been put in italics above. *There is no grammatical reason why this pronoun and with it this whole phrase which is connected in English translations with 'elemental spirits' cannot instead refer to the 'beings that by nature are no gods'.* It is difficult to translate this smoothly into English but Paul's sense then becomes this: by turning back to the *stoicheia*, in this case, the practice of the law of Moses, the Galatians want to leave being 'kept aligned' by the living Spirit of God and to turn back to a weak and beggarly form of religious direction. Paul is making a polemical point in saying that, for Gentile Galatians, turning back to the old world of religious rules implies that they are wanting to turn back to what they had served in the past: 'beings that are no gods'.

Paul's sentence seems to be overloaded and what follows is a paraphrase but one which seeks to stay as close as possible to the phrases of the RSV translation we have been following:

> Formerly, when you did not know God, you were in bondage to beings that by
> nature are no gods, *whose slaves you want to be once more*, for now that you
> have come to know God, or rather be known by God, how can you turn back to
> the weak and beggarly *stoicheia* (things that 'keep aligned'/'give direction for
> behaviour')? You observe days, and months, and seasons, and years! I am afraid
> I have laboured over you in vain. (Gal 4:8-10, adapted RSV)

In this translation, 'beings that by nature are no gods' are not themselves *stoicheia*
but Paul is referring to the fact that the service of them must involve the following
of religious rules including the observance of a religious calendar and in this respect
there is common ground with the law of Moses. *So Paul is saying that the Jews were
in servitude under the law of Moses and the Gentile Galatians served 'beings that by
nature are no gods' but not that the law of Moses has an equivalent status to 'beings
that by nature are no gods'. The equivalence in the situation of Jew and Gentile was
in the servitude under religious 'directions for behaviour'.*

Comment – Colossians

There is disagreement among scholars over whether the letter to the Colossians can
be definitely ascribed to Paul and because of this uncertainty it has not been used
in this work as a source for Paul's thinking. However, given how few occasions the
word *stoicheia* is used by Paul, there is value in considering the verses in Colossians
where the word is used, 2:8 and 2:20:

> See to it that no one takes you captive through philosophy and empty deceit,
> according to human tradition, according to the *elemental spirits of the universe*,
> and not according to Christ. (Col 2:8)

Replacing 'elemental spirits of the universe' with the understanding presented above
of 'worldly *stoicheia* ('things that keep aligned'/'directions for behaviour')' makes
good sense:

> See to it that no one takes you captive through philosophy and empty deceit,
> according to human tradition, according to the *worldly stoicheia* (things that
> 'keep aligned'/'give direction for behaviour'), and not according to Christ. (Col
> 2:8, adapted NRSV)

The 'worldly *stoicheia*' are being linked with 'human tradition' and contrasted with
the way of Christ.

The second use that comes a few verses later offers striking support for the
proposed interpretation:

> If with Christ you died to the *elemental spirits of the universe*, why do you live
> as if you still belonged to the world? Why do you submit to regulations, 'Do not
> handle, Do not taste, Do not touch'? All these regulations refer to things that
> perish with use; they are simply human commands and teachings. (Col 2:20)

The thrust of the question as it is in Greek is more literally expressed in the adaptation below:

> If with Christ you died to the elemental spirits of the universe, why do you submit to regulations, living as if you still belonged to the world?

In the light of the work on *stoicheia* above, this passage now makes very clear sense:

> If with Christ you died to the *worldly stoicheia* (things that 'keep aligned'/'give direction for behaviour'), why do you submit to regulations, living as if you still belonged to the world? 'Do not handle, Do not taste, Do not touch'? All these regulations refer to things that perish with use; they are simply human commands and teachings. (Col 2:20, adapted NRSV)

The same contrast occurs here as was noted in the previous section but even more clearly. Coming to Christ involved dying to religious regulations – a worldly form of direction for behaviour. It is clear that Paul can refer to the Jewish law in this way. 'Do not handle, Do not taste, Do not touch'; Paul's point is that these regulations are all concerned with 'earthbound, worldly things', literally, as stated in this passage, 'things that perish with use'. Having come to faith, to pick up such regulations again is turning away from the freedom of the living God and turning back to earthbound traditions.

Comment – from rudiments to spirits

A speculative account can be given as to why, in the centuries after Paul had written, a word which he used with the sense of 'the things which keep aligned' came to mean 'elemental spirits' can be briefly outlined. There is no intention here of presenting a full argument from the linguistic evidence available, only to demonstrate briefly that such a case is possible and plausible. This suggestion draws on material in Kittel's *Theological Dictionary of the New Testament*.

As was stated at the beginning, 'row' or 'series' is the root meaning of *stoicheō* and *stoicheia*. It is understandable, therefore, that the word came to be used for letters of the alphabet, the ABC, and that, as in English we speak of the ABC of a subject, so, in Greek, the word was used for the 'rudiments' or 'principles' or 'elementary stages' of something. Along with, or arising from, the identification of *stoicheia* with 'rudiments' or 'principles' or 'an elementary stage' was its use for 'the material elements of the universe': earth, air, fire and water. In particular, it came to be used for the stars which were thought to be composed of fire. Given that the heavens were considered to be an abode for spirits and gods and that *stoicheia* was used for heavenly bodies, it is a plausible development in the meaning of the word for it to be associated with spirits and gods. It can be seen how there is the potential in this development for *stoicheia* to be identified with 'beings that by nature are no gods'.

The ambiguity in Paul's Greek then opens up the possibility of confusion. As was noted above, the pronoun 'whose' in Galatians 4:9 can equally well refer to either 'beings that by nature are no gods' or *stoicheia*. If Paul was using the word in an unusual way to capture the sense we have identified of 'direction for behaviour' without the obligation associated with rules and regulations, then it is indeed possible that his subtle meaning could be lost and replaced by a meaning that could be identified with 'the beings that by nature are no gods'. It is helpful to remember how much influence the Authorized Version of the bible has had on shaping the English language. The Greek text of the bible was equally influential once it was widely read and seems here to have led to the redefinition of a word. It is beyond the scope of this section to identify the precise steps in this process but enough has been presented to suggest a possible development. The combination of ambiguity in Paul's Greek and a separate evolution of the meaning of the Greek word towards a sense that could be identified with 'beings that by nature are no gods' may well be the process by which the latter came to be identified as the *stoicheia*. It is then possible that it was precisely this mistaken identification in Paul's Greek that shaped later Greek where the word came to mean 'a spiritual being'. This evolution is confirmed in modern Greek where the word means 'a ghost'!

Translating *stoicheia*: summary sentence and discussion

The interpretation of the plural noun, *stoicheia*, as 'elemental spirits' is incorrect and destroys the logic in Paul's argument; it is used by Paul for 'things which keep a person aligned', which, in more idiomatic terms, give 'direction for behaviour' or 'keep a religious adherent on the right path'.

Both Dunn and Sanders find limited value in pursuing the debate over the precise meaning of *stoicheia*. In his major section on Gal 3:19-4:10 in *Paul, the Law and the Jewish People*, Sanders only refers to the definition of *stoicheia* in a footnote; he accepts the identification of *stoicheia* with pagan deities that Paul seems to make in Gal 4:8f (*PLJP*, 88, n.21):

> It is not necessary to enter the discussion of what these *stoicheia* were. I take Gal. 4:8f. to show that Paul had pagan deities in mind.

Dunn thinks Paul is working with a broad definition of *stoicheia* (*Galatians*, 212):

> The long-running dispute over the precise meaning of the phrase (*ta stoicheia tou kosmou*) here (iv. 3, 8) and in Col ii. 8, 20, is another example of either-or exegesis ... Does it denote 'the elemental substances' of which the cosmos is composed, earth, water, air and fire ...; or ' the elementary forms' of religion ..., now superseded by the coming of faith in Christ; or 'the heavenly bodies, the stars' understood as divine powers which influence or determine human destiny ... ? The answer is probably 'All three!' Or more precisely, that Paul did not have such distinctions in mind. Rather we would do better to suppose that this phrase was his way of referring to the common understanding of the time that human beings lived their lives under the influence or sway of primal and cosmic forces, however they were conceptualized.

Note Dunn's definition of *stoicheia* as 'primal and cosmic forces under the influence of which, in the common understanding of Paul's time, human beings live their lives'. Dunn considers that Paul does not conceptualize or make mental distinctions between these different primal and cosmic forces. We have begun to see how Dunn presents Paul as having a continuing place for the law in the life of the Spirit, once the boundary marking elements of the law – 'the issues of ethnic identity and ritual distinction' – are removed. In Dunn's view, Paul identifies the Jewish law as a whole, which the Gentiles in Galatia are being tempted to accept, as a primal and cosmic force which functions in the same way as false gods to which they had previously been enslaved (*Galatians*, 226):

> The situation and status to which they were in danger of reverting were those of enslavement 'under the elemental forces of the world' (iv.3). Here the inference continues to be clear that Paul counted the law as one of these 'elemental forces'. That is to say, the law regarded in the way it typically was within contemporary Judaism, the law being treated as it was by the other missionaries and the judaizing Gentile converts, was functioning in effect as one of those cosmic forces which were then popularly thought to control and dominate life ... Life under such a power was a life dominated by fear of infringing its taboos and boundaries .... Since they had already experienced freedom from precisely such slavery Paul found it hard to credit the reports that they wished to exchange their slavery to things which were in reality no gods for a slavery to the law misrepresented to function just like another false god.

Dunn finds logic in Paul's position on the law because he believes that Paul makes a sharp distinction between the law lived in the power of the Spirit with 'taboos and boundaries' removed and the law 'regarded as it typically was within contemporary Judaism' as in this Galatians passage: the first is entirely positive; the second can be categorized with pagan deities.

For Sanders, who does not make this sharp distinction which is so crucial for Dunn, Paul's logic in the *stoicheia* passage in Galatians completely collapses. He talks of an 'extraordinary series of statements' (*PLJP*, 69). And, as we have already noted in the main text, says that Paul's 'statements would make a systematist shudder' (*PLJP*, 68). Sanders does not try to defend Paul's logic. For him it breaks down. And the reason he gives for this affirms one of his central positions on Paul: that Paul is so overwhelmingly concerned with the 'solution' – 'everyone needs to be liberated from bondage by Christ' (*PLJP*, 69) – that he is not concerned to offer a coherent position on the human plight that Christ liberates people from. It is specifically, Sanders says, when Paul comes to describe 'the plight' that 'his statements would make a systematist shudder'; 'all need faith in Christ' and this is 'the ground on which the plight of Jews and Gentiles is equated' (*PLJP*, 68). This view, based upon Sanders's generally accepted observation that Paul's thought runs 'from solution to plight' supports one of Sanders's major conclusions on Paul, that Paul is a theologian – 'he was deeply worried about theological problems' – but not a 'systematic' one (*Paul*, 128/149). Particularly on the law his statements 'when set alongside one another, do not form a logical whole (*PLJP*, 4)'.

The interpretations of *stoicheia* and this passage in Galatians offered by Dunn and Sanders are both to be rejected. In both cases, the mistaken identification of *stoicheia* with pagan deities or cosmic forces and the difficulties this raises for finding the logic in Paul's argument leads them both to argue that it is necessary to reject the explicit sense in his words in order to discover the 'concepts' in Paul's mind. For Dunn, Paul is able to do this because he has a broad conception of *stoicheia* as primal forces and two conceptions that can be evoked when he uses the word 'law', one strongly positive, one negative. It is the negative conception of the law as a power that dominates 'by fear of infringing its taboos and boundaries' that Paul identifies as a primal force like a pagan deity. For Sanders, the lack of logic in the explicit sense of Paul's words means that this passage provides a very good example of how Paul's conviction of liberating power of faith in Christ for all overwhelms any interest he has in conceptualizing coherently the different kinds of 'plight' that Jew and Gentile need liberating from.

Paul's logic in this Galatians passage ceases to be a problem once the correct definition of *stoicheia* is seen and consequently there is no need to make a split between his 'explicit sense' and his 'mental conceptions' (*PLJP*, 69). For Paul, it is in their common ability to offer 'direction for behaviour' that the law and pagan religion can be placed in the same category.

Ziesler does not analyse Paul's use of the the word *stoicheia* but in the section below – which includes the image of the law 'keeping Israel in line' – there is precise support for the view that will be explored in more depth in subsequent chapters (80f):

> Unlike sin, Law is not malignant ... In Galatians one answer is that it was a divinely appointed guardian whose day is now over, so that to remain in its guardianship now that the freedom of Christ and of his Spirit has arrived is anachronistic bondage. Its function was to keep Israel in line, preparing her for the coming freedom (Gal 3:21-6). To remain in its tutelage now is to reject the freedom of the sons of God (Gal 4:5).

No place for religious law

It has been proposed that the accurate core of meaning in Paul's use of the Greek word *stoicheō* is 'to keep aligned'. Further, it has been argued that Paul's two uses of the plural noun *stoicheia* in his letter to the Galatians are directly connected with the definition of the verb and carry the core meaning of 'the things which keep aligned' in the sense of 'things that give direction for behaviour'.

Despite the fact that this word is not central to Paul's thinking, this proposed interpretation does have one vital consequence for understanding Paul's theology. Before this can be indicated, the interpretation itself merits further comment now that both verb and noun have been examined.

The English definition of the verb *stoicheō* that has been used, 'to keep aligned', is clumsy and will hardly serve as a translation. In the case of the noun, we were not able to use an English alternative and fell back on using the Greek word, *stoicheia* with 'things that "keep aligned"/"give direction for behaviour"' in brackets. We have been concerned to show that the consistent meaning in both words is concerned with the simple spatial image of 'alignment'. Taken together, the way that the verb and the noun are used give very powerful evidence that Paul was using this word with its simple sense of alignment in connection with behaviour. In all the uses of the verb, Paul is speaking of the motivating source of action; we have seen that he speaks of keeping aligned by faith or the Spirit or the cross. Dramatic confirmation of the connection of this image of alignment with behaviour comes in his use of the noun. On both occasions when Paul is speaking of the things which keep aligned it is clear that he is speaking of law, religious law in particular, including the law of Moses. This is a very simple yet important point. Law is one of those things that keeps a person 'aligned', that is, on a certain path, or practising a certain kind of behaviour. This word, while not theologically significant in itself, occurs in important passages where there is a vital point at issue: the question of the right motivating source of behaviour in the new life of freedom, whether it is, on the one side, faith, the Spirit or the cross, or on the other, religious law.

Paul is saying that all written codes of religious laws are worldly *stoicheia* which are inferior to the Spirit or faith as a way of determining what it is right to do. Paul qualifies the *stoicheia* to which the Galatians contemplate returning as 'weak and beggarly'. This proposed interpretation makes Paul's question to the Galatians simple and straightforward; a paraphrase will demonstrate the precise content and force of his appeal to the experience of his listeners:

> Now that you have come by faith to know God, or rather to be known by God, in that God's will is revealed to you directly, how can you go back to the old second rate, inferior way of discovering God's will, by following a written code of law, even the law of Moses? (Gal 4:9, author's paraphrase)

Living by the Spirit is entry into a new intimacy with God, characterized by a knowledge of or being known by God. Guidance from the Spirit arises from this new openness to God in which God's will is revealed directly; any law, even the law of Moses, is, by comparison, an inferior way of knowing God's will.

While there is a simplicity and coherence about the interpretation presented here it raises significant questions about central themes in Paul's theology. The reason is that, if the sharp definition of this verb and noun is correct, it must lead to a reinterpretation of major aspects of Paul's theology. Just as when discussing the verb the attempt was made to demonstrate that the defence of a consistent skeleton of meaning in this peripheral word would have consequences for appreciating Paul's understanding of the Spirit, so, if the interpretation made above is correct, there can be no question of Paul retaining any place for religious law in his understanding of life in the Spirit. The sharpness and precision of his thought rules this out. Paul directly contrasts living by faith, by the Spirit, by the cross with living by any religious law, Jewish or Gentile.

One further point needs to be made about this contrast. We have seen how Paul can characterize life in the Spirit as knowing or being known by God. More commonly he describes life in the Spirit as a life of freedom:

> For freedom Christ has set us free. Stand firm, therefore, and do not submit again to a yoke of slavery. (Gal 5:1)

Paul is encouraging the Galatians to remain firm in the life of faith. For him to return to that weak and beggarly *stoicheion* (direction for behaviour) which is the law is, in Paul's eyes, to choose slavery in contrast to the freedom of living by the Spirit. The rest of the book will contain further detailed examination of what precisely Paul is meaning here by slavery and freedom but one point is relevant now. As has been shown, Paul talks of 'keeping aligned' by faith, by the Spirit, by the cross. We have also seen how 'the Spirit' and 'faith' are directly connected with the prophetic word. What is important to note now is that Spirit and faith both provide direction for behaviour but in a way which can be characterized by Paul as 'freedom'. There is a pointer here to the real transformation that has already been spoken of (pp. 6-7) but needs investigating in more detail. The implication is that the guidance from the Spirit or faith is not experienced as coming from an external directing force that constrains freedom. Faith's prophetic word provides guidance which arises within the individual and the community (pp. 20-25).

'Keeping aligned' is a concept that captures well the sense that this prophetic word does provide guidance but without any coercive force. Actions flow naturally from it. As we have seen, Paul does not say, if you live by the Spirit these are the things that you ought to do, these are the ways that you ought to behave, but rather, live by the Spirit and these are the ways that you definitely will behave. Life in the Spirit leads to such behaviour as naturally as trees bear fruit. For Paul, being guided – 'keeping aligned' – by faith, by the Spirit, by the cross is to experience a life of freedom, without needing to follow any external direction. Living by the law is, in contrast, a form of enslavement.

There is a consistency in this with what was noted about the sharpness of his contrast between living by the Spirit and living by the flesh (pp. 38-40). These two different sources of life both issue inevitably in a certain kind of behaviour. There is no blurring between them. Because living by the Spirit produces the fruits of the Spirit, no law is necessary for one living in this way. It is to deal with the desires of the flesh that the law exists and the force with which Paul argues against going back to any law is that such a step also means abandoning living by the Spirit. This is a controversial understanding of Paul's meaning but it is the consistent and precise sense that emerges through the interpretation of *stoicheō* and *stoicheia* offered above. So in order to defend this proposal for a precise and consistent definition of a word that is peripheral and, in itself, inessential to Paul's theology, further central elements of Paul's theology need to be looked at afresh.

No place for religious law: summary sentence and discussion

> **Understanding *stoicheō* and *stoicheia* as carrying the sharp and simple image of alignment establishes the view that Paul sees all religious law, including the Torah, the law of Moses, as 'weak and beggarly' and that there is no need and therefore no essential place for law once an individual has come to the freedom of knowing God's will through the Spirit.**

Ziesler is clear that coming to Christ brings about a break with the law (112):

> No one can serve two masters; for Paul, serving Christ means freedom from the rule of the Law.

However, Ziesler misses the nature of the contrast between 'serving Christ' and 'the rule of the Law'. In Ziesler's view, Paul is not contrasting his new and better way of doing what God requires – a way which is experienced as freedom – with the law, now experienced as 'weak and beggarly' and a form of slavery, but is primarily concerned with what it takes to be accepted by God (90):

If acceptance with God comes about only through Jesus Christ and faith in him, then it does not come about by circumcision and consequent Torah-observance. Since Paul believes that faith in Christ is not only the necessary but also the sufficient condition for acceptance, even something as holy as the Law cannot be imposed as a further condition, hence 5:4: 'You are severed from Christ, you who would be justifed by the law; you have fallen away from grace.' Those who want Gentiles to accept circumcision and the Law in addition to having faith in Christ are really dethroning him, and proposing not an addition to faith but a substitute for it. This is why Gentiles not only need not but must not be circumcised.

While Ziesler uses clear and strong language to indicate the existence of the line between 'faith in Christ' and 'circumcision and the Law', the precise contrast between 'faith' or 'Spirit' and 'law' as alternative ways of knowing what to do is not there. This passage evokes a more traditional Christian understanding of coming to faith in Christ as coming under the lordship of Jesus Christ which is primarily conceived of as 'the sufficient condition for acceptance [by God]'. The confidence of Ziesler's view that this sharply separates faith and law lies in this belief in the sufficiency of faith in Christ such that any additional requirement amounts to 'really dethroning him'.

However, even though the source of Ziesler's clarity on the sharp dividing line between law and faith differs significantly from what has been proposed in this chapter, because of that clarity, his interpretation of Paul's more positive statements on the law is thoroughly consistent with the view presented in the main text (112):

The nearest [Paul] comes to being positive about the Law's role for Christians is when he speaks of love of neighbour as the fulfilling of the Law (Gal 5:14; Rom 13:8-10) and when he says that those who walk by the Spirit fulfil the Law's requirement (Rom 8: 4). In all these instances, however, the controlling factor is not the Law but the new life in Christ and his Spirit, and he is talking about the divine intention behind the Law, not the Law itself. He cannot mean, for instance, that loving one's neighbour literally fulfils, in the sense of carrying out, the command to be circumcised.

Despite Paul's statements that 'if you are led by the Spirit, you are not subject to the law' (Gal 5:18) and 'Now we are discharged from the law, dead to that which held us captive, so that we are slaves not under the old written code but in the new life of the Spirit' (Rom 7:6) both Sanders and Dunn argue that Paul supports a continuing role for the law in the life of faith. In presenting this view both of them put the weight of their argument on a particular interpretation of the two passages Ziesler mentions where Paul speaks of the faith 'fulfilling' the law (Gal 5:14; Rom 13:8-10).

Sanders interprets these more positive statements on the law differently to Ziesler. As we have seen, he is concerned to make clear that Paul links faith with real change (74/87):

He thought that God could actually change the most intractable part of the creation – humanity.

Not only that, Sanders states clearly that 'acceptance by God' which he caricatures in what follows as God altering his opinion about people, is a far from adequate interpretation of Paul's view (72f/86):

... Paul thought that God did something other than keep track of people and alter his opinion about them. God 'righteoused' the person of faith as well as 'reckoned' the person to be righteous. ... This means not just that the person's name was moved from one side of God's ledger to another, as 'reckon' might imply, but that the person was transferred to another sphere, called variously 'the body of Christ', the Spirit, and the like. In this transfer a real change was effected ... As a result of the change the new person found that good deeds flowed out naturally and that everything which the law had required was 'fulfilled' in his or her life (Rom 8: 4).

This all supports the view presented in the main text of the chapter but a surprising shift occurs in Sanders's section on 'The law and correct behaviour' (85-91/99-107). Sanders begins (85f/99) by referring to the same Galatians and Romans texts which speak of 'fulfilling the law' commented on by Ziesler:

> [Christians] should love one another, as the law said – 'Love your neighbour as yourself.' This fulfils 'the whole law' (Gal 5:14, quoting Lev 19:18). In Romans 13 Paul states that 'the one who loves the neighbour has fulfilled the law', and he then lists four of the ten commandments: the prohibitions of adultery, murder, theft and covetousness (Rom 13:8-10). In Romans 8 he claims that in Christians the requirement of the law is 'fulfilled' (Rom 8:4).

As we saw, Ziesler does not find in these passages any support for the view that Paul is arguing for a following of the law, however modified. His view is that in these passages Paul is talking positively 'about the divine intention behind the Law, not the Law itself' and that the source of motivation, or what he calls 'the controlling factor', is not obeying 'the Law' but 'the new life in Christ and his Spirit'. 'Fulfilling the Law' is fulfilling 'the divine intention behind the Law' so that Paul can say 'Love your neighbour as yourself' 'fulfils "the whole Law"'.

Sanders, in interpreting these same texts, completely sets to one side his statements that Paul regards Christians as changed people who can now naturally do good deeds. Instead, he embarks on an investigation into which bits of the law Paul is meaning when he makes these positive statements on the law. He asks the question (86/101):

> How can we understand his embrace of 'the whole law' if he did not accept parts of it?

Two important points need to be made about the way Sanders frames this question. Firstly, Sanders is interpreting Paul's very limited positive statements on the law as meaning that he 'accepted' parts of the law. This implies that in Sanders view, for those 'parts of the law' that are 'accepted', Paul approves a conventional relationship with the law: looking to the law for direction and then making an effort to live by what the law requires. Sanders's question then becomes how could Paul claim that this limited acceptance of the law is an 'embrace' of 'the whole law'. Secondly, note how Sanders has moved from using Paul's word 'fulfil' to speaking of his 'embrace' of the whole law. Sanders's language is revealing here because he uses three words which are not used by Paul but which strongly evoke a conventional understanding of how people relate to the law. We have already seen how he speaks of Christians '*accepting*' the law (86/101). He also interprets Paul as saying 'that Christians should *keep* the "whole law" (91/106)' and that 'his followers should *observe* "the whole law" (91/106)'. This is a significant shift which needs examining in more detail.

Sanders's placing of 'the whole law' in inverted commas in these phrases means that he is clearly referring to the quotations in Romans and Galatians with which he started the section. It is important to consider what Paul actually says:

> Owe no one anything, except to love one another; for the one who loves another has fulfilled (*plēroō*) the law. The commandments, 'You shall not commit adultery; You shall not murder; You shall not steal; You shall not covet'; and any other commandment, are summed up (*anakephalaioō*) in this word, 'Love your neighbour as yourself.' Love does no wrong to a neighbour; therefore, love is the fulfilling (*plēroō*) of the law. (Rom 13:8-10)

Although in the NRSV, the translation of *plēroō* in this verse of Galatians is inconsistent with the Romans passage, the sense is clearly identical:

> For the whole law is summed up (*plēroō*) in a single commandment. 'You shall love your neighbour as yourself.' (Gal 5:14)

In the main text we examined the passage that follows on from this Galatians text (5:16-25) because it contains *stoicheō*. In that passage Paul's list of 'the fruits of the Spirit' is headed by love. The list also includes 'joy, peace, patience, kindness, generosity, faithfulness, gentleness, and self-control' and finishes with the statement: 'There is no law against such things.' This conclusion is directly related to the conclusion in the Romans 13 passage. There Paul lists statements in the law that prohibit wrong actions towards a neighbour: adultery, murder, stealing, coveting. He then states as a definition that actions of love do no wrong to a neighbour and says, therefore, that 'love is the fulfilling of the law'. In the Galatians passage, Paul says that if you live – 'keep aligned' – by the Spirit this will naturally issue in actions of love. There is no law against such 'actions of love'. In other words, the law is unnecessary for one acting from the love that the Spirit enables. The law is fulfilled in the sense that it has become unnecessary for the one who acts in love. In each passage, Paul is affirming that there is an alternative and more effective 'source of motivation' than the law. To say that his purpose in these passages is to affirm that the law should be 'accepted' or 'observed' or 'kept' is seriously missing the point.

For Sanders the 'controlling factor' of behaviour has changed for Paul and, in the light of that change, some aspects of the law are still to be 'kept'; some to be dropped. The new controlling factor for Paul is his sense of mission to the Gentile world (91/106f):

> [Paul] rejected ... the aspects of the law which were against his own mission, those which separated Jew from Gentile in the people of God. Once he excluded circumcision, food, and days from 'the commandments of God' ..., he could say, without contradicting himself, that his followers should observe 'the whole law': they should accept it after he redefined it.

Dunn's analysis of Galatians 5:13f and Romans 13:8-10 leads him to agree with Sanders that when Paul speaks of '"fulfilling" the law' he is intending that phrase to mean that there is a continuing function for the law (655):

> ... Paul did not teach that the law was to be wholly discarded or abandoned. His critique of the law was more specific and in effect peeled away from the law the functions that it no longer should serve to leave its continuing function all the clearer. In both Gal 5:13-14 and Rom 13:8-10 Paul talks about "fulfilling" the

law as something which evidently meets the requirements of the law (Rom 8:4)
and is still desirable and necessary for believers. In so doing he indicates clearly
that he had in mind the whole law. Not just the moral commands within the ten
commandments, but "any other command" too (Rom. 13.9).

Dunn goes on to clarify what he considers to be the 'continuing function' of the law. It is 'the
whole law' redefined in the light of the command to love (656f):

> [W]here requirements of the law were being interpreted in a way which ran counter
> to the basic principle of the love command, Paul thought that the requirements
> could and should be dispensed with. On the other hand, it was still possible in his
> view for the *whole* law, and *all* its commandments, to be fulfilled in a way which
> did not run counter to the love command.

Having examined each scholar's position it is possible to compare them in summary
form:

(a) Ziesler argues that Paul rejects law on the basis of a new principle: all people
    are now judged and accepted by God on a new basis, their relationship to
    Jesus Christ;
(b) Sanders argues that Paul reinterprets the law on the basis of a new principle
    which arises from his confidence in the God-given nature of his mission to
    the Gentiles: all elements of the law that separate Jew and Gentile in the new
    people of God are excluded;
(c) Dunn argues that Paul reinterprets law on the basis of a new inward principle:
    the command to love which leads Paul to reject the elements of 'ethnic
    identity and ritual distinction' in the law which create 'a life dominated by
    fear of infringing its taboos and boundaries'.

Each scholar argues that law is abrogated (Ziesler) or reinterpreted (Sanders and Dunn)
according to a new principle. The argument of these opening chapters is that what is central
for Paul is not a 'new principle' from which right action can be 'worked out' but a new
experience which involves a new and better way of determining what God requires: guidance
from the immediate, living, prophetic word. What that word requires may be identical to what
the law requires but the law is no longer what gives direction. Paul speaks of this new way
of determining what to do using the image of alignment (*stoicheō* and *stoicheia*) with 'faith,
Spirit, the cross'. These images all evoke this new sense of direction and suggest that that new
sense of direction is combined with an inward change. Having done enough to establish the
possibility of this interpretation, the nature of that change will be explored in later chapters in
a way that will also strengthen the argument already presented.

Dunn's position needs a little further comment. In that the principle Dunn considers central
to Paul is 'the command to love', it is a principle that is 'inward' and has an affective quality that
makes it more than a new 'rule' or 'command' which simply needs to be intellectually applied.
This does allow important points of connection with the radical inward transformation that is
the subject of the main argument. As we have seen, Dunn acknowledges the importance of the
living, prophetic word at work in the community. He also states that it is only the new 'Spirit-
prompted and enabled lifestyle' that can empower a life lived in the way that the law requires
(435). The crucial difference lies in Dunn's affirmation of a continuing essential place for law
alongside an inward transformation. Central for Dunn is 'the balance Paul evidently sought to
maintain between what we might call internal motivation and external norm' (668):

The external norm can be variously defined. It can be defined in terms of traditional wisdom, vices and virtues commonly recognized as such, notions of what is right and wrong accepted by all those of good will, ideas of communal interdependence and good order at the heart of society. ... Again, given the through and through Jewish background of Pauline Christianity, the external norm, not surprisingly, may also be defined as the law.

It is important to note that, as we have seen, Dunn can only sustain this affirmation of the law in Paul's thought by positing two sharply opposed views on the law operating in Paul's mind. The law as he now sees it lived in the power of the Spirit is good; the law as it was traditionally perceived to function as a boundary marker to sustain the special privileged identity for Israel is bad.

The interpretation of *stoicheia* and *stoicheō* offered in the main text reveals the simple and consistent sharpness in Paul's thought: the law is an inferior – 'weak and beggarly' – way of knowing God's will. His clarity on this issue makes it necessary for Paul to answer the question – given that you say God gave the Torah, which now you say is a 'weak and beggarly' way of knowing God's will, why then the law? What was its purpose? Paul addresses this precise question in both Galatians and Romans and it is the subject of the next chapter.

Conclusion

It will be argued that the existence of a sharp dividing line in Paul's thinking that is indicated by the above analysis makes good sense of difficult elements of his understanding. The crucial links that have been made so far are these:

(a) coming to live by the Spirit involves a real liberation from sin which necessarily issues in transformed behaviour;
(b) Paul uses the idea of 'faith' in close connection with the coming of the prophetic word, understood as direct guidance from God for the individual and the community;
(c) for those who live by the Spirit, guided by the prophetic word, this liberation from sin is also liberation from the need for law.

It will be argued in the second part of the book that the image that Paul uses to describe this change is that of the movement from childhood to maturity. In the whole of the Galatians 4 passage in which the two uses of *stoicheia* occur, Paul is working with this image. To illustrate the situation of both Jew and Greek prior to the coming of faith, he pictures an heir, who, whilst still a child, is 'no better than a slave', being 'under guardians and trustees'. And having introduced the image he says, 'when we were children, we were slaves under the earthbound *stoicheia* ('directions for behaviour'). This image reveals an understanding of a real change within the individual, as a consequence of which, all things, whilst having some continuity with the past, are different. In particular this applies to the law which Paul says is necessary for childhood but not for maturity. Without this understanding of a real change it can seem that Paul is simply contrasting two ways in which it is possible to choose to live: law and faith. Without the acknowledgement that Paul considered that a real change was involved in coming to faith, this is an incomplete and misleading way of describing Paul's position. By looking carefully at other aspects of what Paul says, it is possible to get a more full and vivid sense of the nature of the real change which is illuminating in itself and reveals far more clearly the coherence in Paul's understanding. We will discover that, for Paul, coming to faith, like coming to adulthood, involves a real change through which the direction for behaviour ceases to come from outside but becomes part of the responsible individual who can now act in freedom without the external obligation of the law.

Chapter 4

Childhood under Law

The interpretation of *stoicheō* and *stoicheia* presented in the last chapter suggested that Paul considered there to be an equivalence in the situation of Jew and Gentile: without faith, both are 'in servitude' under religious law. This chapter contains two sections which will support and build on that interpretation. The first will consolidate the view that Paul considered all people, prior to the acceptance of faith, to be under law. It confirms the interpretation of *stoicheia* presented in the last chapter which implies that, from the perspective of the direct guidance provided by the prophetic word, Paul could place Gentile and Jew in the same category with the same need to be liberated from the 'weak and beggarly' guidance of the law. The second argument will begin to show how Paul could hold such a view without thereby undermining the consistency, the faithfulness, the integrity of God. For this is the serious problem which emerges from this view. If there is one God, as Paul and his fellow Jews believed, and if, therefore, the law of Moses which brought into being and sustained the Jewish people was given by the same God who is now revealing that law to be inadequate, how can that be so without undermining God's faithfulness, without calling into doubt a consistency and coherence in what God does which can be absolutely relied upon?

'The law' does not equal 'the Torah'

A principle of translation and interpretation

An important preliminary point needs to be made about translation and interpretation. The point will be made first with a word other than 'law' in order to make the appreciation of how Paul speaks of 'law' more clear. In the second letter to the Corinthians, Paul is advising the community about how to treat someone who has done serious wrong. Remember that the purpose of presenting this passage is simply to make a theoretical point rather than to spend time on its particular meaning:

> [S]o you should rather turn to forgive and *comfort* him, or he may be overwhelmed by excessive sorrow. So I *beg* you to reaffirm your love for him. (2 Cor 2:7f, RSV)

The words in italics are both translating the same Greek word, *parakaleō*. It is a word that Paul uses often and is variously translated into English in the RSV, 'to exhort, to comfort, to console, to encourage, to beg or beseech, to admonish'. Because it is variously translated in English, we could easily say that it is a Greek word with a number of meanings but this would be inaccurate. It is true that a word can have two or more distinct meanings and for someone who is familiar with a language there is usually no problem about understanding which distinct meaning is accurate from the context, but here the situation is different. The issue can be clearly seen because of the proximity of the two uses in the above passage. There simply is not one English word that can serve for both uses and in English two different words have to be used but – and this is the point – this does not mean that Paul himself did not have one concept operating when he used this same word in consecutive sentences. *Paul's two uses of this one word in close proximity indicates that he had one concept in mind when he used this one word, but a concept which contains a number of aspects that can only be variously translated in English.*

The Greek word being translated here breaks down into two basic components, one is the verb 'to call', the other is a prefix which has the sense of 'alongside'. Insight into this issue can be gained by recalling an old English word, 'to midwife'. 'To midwife' is a very particular task, but one that contains several components. It is helpful to evoke the image of the midwife alongside the mother in labour, at one time encouraging, at another begging, at another comforting, at another admonishing. It is not being proposed here that Paul had this precise image for this word. It is enough to acknowledge the possibility that, for him, the one word he used carried these various meanings without ceasing to be one precise concept. For English speakers who do not have a word that can replace the one Paul is using, it is important to see that, just because we do not have the word, it does not mean that a unifying concept does not exist. But that is what we do presume when we say that this particular Greek word has several different meanings. In truth, it has one meaning with a number of different aspects which can only be expressed in English with a variety of different words, chosen according to context.

'The Law'

Something very similar happens in the interpretation of Paul and the law, only here the consequences are very damaging because an oversimplification of how to interpret Paul's Greek in English leads directly to a misinterpretation of the place 'law' has in Paul's thought which in turn makes it impossible to get a clear sense of the nature of the experience that Paul is claiming is now possible. A number of passages will illustrate this point about translation:

> Then what becomes of our boasting? It is excluded. On what *principle*? On the *principle* of works? No, but on the *principle* of faith. For we hold that a man is justified by faith apart from works of *law*. (Rom 3:27f, RSV)

In this passage the words 'principle' and 'law' are translating the one Greek word, *nomos*. The way the majority of scholars interpret this passage, as reflected in the RSV translation, is to accept that Paul in this brief section is using this one Greek word in two different ways. 'Works of law' at the end of the passage is uncontroversially interpreted as an almost technical designation, 'works of Torah', the Jewish law. It is then argued that it is impossible that Paul is speaking in the first part of the passage of the 'Torah of faith' and consequently the conclusion is reached that, while Paul is clearly speaking about works of Torah in the last sentence, in the first part of the passage the meaning of *nomos* is 'principle' or 'rule' or 'regime' to indicate the more general sense of a fundamental basis for action.

The passages where the Torah, the law of Moses, is the meaning in *nomos* most to the fore are those where, not surprisingly, Paul is explicitly discussing the situation of the Jew in relation to the new experience of faith:

> But if you call yourself a Jew and rely on the law and boast of your relation to
> God and know his will and determine what is best because you are instructed in
> the law ... (Rom 2:17f)

What else can 'the law' mean here but only and precisely 'the Torah'? However, both the immediate context and the consistency of Paul's thought in the whole of the letter must shape the interpretation. It is of the greatest importance that the above passage, specifically addressed to Jews, follows a section where Paul has been deliberately stretching the concept of 'the law' as Jews would understood it:

> For it is not the hearers of the law who are righteous in God's sight, but the doers
> of the law who will be justified. When Gentiles, who do not possess the law, do
> instinctively what the law requires, these, though not having the law, are a law to
> themselves. (Rom 2:13-15)

This is a significant element in seeing that Paul, in the whole of the first section of the letter to the Romans, is working with the idea that, before faith, all, both Jew and Gentile, are under law.

Paul begins the letter to the Romans with a greeting, a thanksgiving and a brief summary of the theme of the letter; his first statement then is to explain how the knowledge of God's will has been available to all humankind:

> For the wrath of God is revealed from heaven against all ungodliness and
> wickedness of those [all people] who by their wickedness suppress the truth.
> For what can be known about God is plain to them, because God has shown it to
> them. Ever since the creation of the world his eternal power and divine nature,
> invisible though they are, have been understood and seen through the things he
> has made. So they are without excuse; for though they knew God, they did not
> honour him as God or give thanks to him, but they became futile in their thinking,
> and their senseless minds were darkened. (Rom 1:18-21)

In this opening section, Paul asserts that all people can know God through seeing God's 'eternal power and divine nature' through 'the things he has made'. As his argument continues, as we have seen, he also states that Gentiles can do the law, knowing 'instinctively what the law requires'. He is seeking to indicate clearly how Gentiles can be under the law even though they do not have the Torah:

> They ['Gentiles, who do not possess the law'] show that what the law requires is written on their hearts, to which their own conscience also bears witness ... (Rom 2:15)

In a further important passage it can be clearly seen how there is an explicit separation in Paul's mind between a 'spiritual' understanding of the law and a 'literal' one. 'Law' as Paul is referring to it here transcends 'the written code and circumcision', in other words, the Torah of the Jews. This separation enables him to affirm clearly that the physically uncircumcised can 'keep the law':

> So, if those who are uncircumcised keep the requirements of the law, will not their uncircumcision be regarded as circumcision? Then *those who are physically uncircumcised but keep the law will condemn you that have the written code and circumcision but break the law*. For a person is not a Jew who is one outwardly, nor is true circumcision something external and physical. Rather, a person is a Jew who is one inwardly, and real circumcision is a matter of the heart – it is spiritual and not literal. (Rom 2:26-29)

Two further meanings of *nomos* can be added to 'Torah' and 'principle': God's will for all revealed through (a) the things that are made and (b) in the heart.

Subtle consistency

What follows is an extremely important passage and will be returned to later in the book (pp. 66, 99, 108-24, 176); the only aim at present is to examine Paul's use of *nomos* which in every instance in this passage is translated 'law':

> There is therefore now no condemnation for those who are in Christ Jesus. For the *law* of the Spirit of life in Christ Jesus has set me free from the *law* of sin and death. For God has done what the *law*, weakened by the flesh, could not do: sending his own Son in the likeness of sinful flesh and for sin, he condemned sin in the flesh, in order that the just requirement of the *law* might be fulfilled in us, who walk not according to the flesh, but according to the Spirit. (Rom 8:1-4, RSV)

In this case the translation does not reveal the problem but the issue quickly emerges when any interpretation is attempted. Without doubt, the obvious interpretation of the latter two uses of the word 'law' is that Paul is specifically referring to the Jewish law, the 'Torah': 'For God has done what the Torah (the law of Moses), weakened by the flesh, could not do ... in order that the just requirement of the Torah (law of Moses) might be fulfilled in us...'. It can be argued that the sense of the second use is: 'the Torah of sin and death', although this is a particularly severe description, given Paul's positive view of the Torah at other points. Given the very clear contrast we have already identified in Paul between the life of 'faith' and life under the 'law', it does not make sense to interpret the first use as 'the Torah of the Spirit of life in Christ Jesus'. The precise meaning of 'The Torah' – 'the law of Moses' – cannot be linked in a sensible way with the phrase 'of the Spirit of life in Christ Jesus' and therefore a more general sense of *nomos* as a framework of how to live means that the interpretation 'principle' or 'regime' is required. The important question of interpretation is then: is it accurate to say that the meaning of the word changes in these two sentences?

This is where it is valuable to return to the example of 'to midwife'. The aim of introducing the verb 'to midwife' was to demonstrate that one clear concept can contain within it several different meanings. Though this one concept may need translating into English with a variety of words, it does not cease to be a single clear concept in the mind of Paul and those of his hearers who are familiar with the Greek language he is using.

A similar proposal can now be set forward on Paul's use of the word *nomos*. This is in one way an easier example than 'to midwife' in that the English word 'law' can be used with the variety of meanings that are there in the Greek word *nomos*; there is not here the same problem at the level of translation. As in the Romans 8 passage above, the one Greek word can consistently be translated 'law' right through every letter of Paul (NRSV translates *nomos* as 'law' in every use in the passages above). The solution is needed at the level of interpretation and can be observed in the way that our minds respond to a word which has a richness of meaning. We have examined several passages where Paul uses the word 'law' (*nomos*) and found that the word is used with four meanings: Torah, principle, God's will revealed through the created world and in the heart. The simple but vital observation needed in order to reach an accurate interpretation is this: *the fact that, in any one use of the word, one of these meanings is predominant or in the 'foreground' does not mean that, on that occasion, the other three meanings disappear altogether.*

This simple observation can have profound effects on interpretation. The fact that in Romans 3:21 in the phrase 'the law and the prophets' the word *nomos* can be clearly interpreted as 'Torah' does not mean that, even in this straightforward phrase, other meanings contained within the one concept 'law' are totally absent in the mind of Paul or his hearers. In the second passage above (Rom 8:1-4) the meaning 'Torah' *within* Paul's use of the word 'law' moves to the fore in the second half of the passage but is in the background in the previous sentence. To discover the consistency in Paul's use of this word it is necessary to acknowledge the subtle way that language works. In the case of a complex word with a range of different meanings like other theologically rich words such as (S)pirit, life, light, truth, it is simply a mistake to identify one aspect of the meaning contained in the word as the sole, exclusive meaning in any particular use of the word; other meanings that the word carries are always subtly present. The aim of gaining a clear understanding of Paul by defining precisely what he means can lead to a hard definition of a word that oversimplifies the way words carry meaning and therefore seriously distorts his sense. Paul's use of *nomos* reveals that the word does not keep shifting in his mind from one 'hard' and exclusive meaning to another but that it carries its meaning in a subtle and flexible way. In the consistent way in which Paul uses *nomos* there are always several meanings operating even though one of the meanings can be very much to the fore in a particular context. This is crucial in getting clear that when Paul speaks of people being 'under the law' he is referring to Gentiles as well as Jews, the 'whole world' (Rom 3:19).

'The law' does not equal 'the Torah': summary sentence and discussion

The fact that Paul can use the word *nomos* when his primary sense changes within a single short section between (a) the Torah – 'the written code and circumcision', (b) a consistent principle and (c) the perception that Gentiles have of (i) 'God's eternal power and deity' through 'the things that have been made' and (ii) the requirements of God 'written on their hearts' indicates that these meanings are all operating when he uses the word and when one meaning is to the fore the other meanings are not altogether excluded and enables him to argue in a subtle way his essential point that, before the coming of faith, all – both Jew and Gentile – are 'under the law'.

This extended discussion section is necessary to show how the simple fact of interpreting Paul's use of *nomos* too crudely is a major factor in obscuring the coherence in his view on the law.

Issues involved in the interpretation of *nomos* are most acute in Romans 3:27-31. Scholars' interpretations of this difficult but important passage are necessarily shaped by their view on these issues determined by other things Paul says; the circular process of interpretation where the meaning of a particular passage or word is both shaping and being shaped by scholars' views on the overall picture is very clearly operating in the assessment scholars make of this text. In giving attention to this passage we are thus plunged directly into all the difficulties raised by the interpretation of this one word and Paul's understanding of the law. In the NRSV, all uses of *nomos* in the passage are translated 'law':

> Then what becomes of boasting? It is excluded. By what law? By that of works? No, but by the law of faith. For we hold that a person is justified by faith apart from works prescribed by the law. Or is God the God of Jews only? Is he not the God of Gentiles also? Yes, of Gentiles also, since God is one; and he will justify the circumcised on the ground of faith and the uncircumcised through that same faith. Do we then overthrow the law by this faith? By no means! On the contrary, we uphold the law.

The interpretation and translation of *nomos* in this passage is related to scholars' views on three connected questions:

(a) what is meant by 'boasting':

    i. 'boasting in the law because it marks the "national privilege" of Israel as God's chosen people' or

    ii. 'the fundamentally flawed spiritual attitude of acquiring merit by one's own power'?

(b) what is the relationship between 'Torah' and 'faith'?

(c) how are Paul's positive statements on the law ('So the law is holy, and the commandment is holy and just and good' [Rom 7:12]) and negative statements on the law ('While we were living in the flesh, our sinful passions, aroused by the law, were at work in our members to bear fruit for death' [Rom 7:5]) explained?

Ziesler: *nomos* usually means Torah

Ziesler supports the view that *nomos*, while it usually means the Torah, should here be rendered 'something like the RSV principle' (Ziesler, *Romans*, 117f). He suggests that 'perhaps "regime" or even "system" would be better'. He rejects Torah as a translation. He says that 'in that case we have a Torah of works set in opposition to a Torah of faith'. This would make the difference of attitude with which a person approaches the Torah the central thing for Paul (*Romans*, 118):

> ... there were some people (Jews) who approached the Torah thinking that by observing it they earned God's favour, whereas Christians approached it knowing that they could never so earn that favour ...

Ziesler rules this view out because 'this whole contrast' – that the Jewish approach to the law reflected a fundamentally flawed spiritual attitude (a.ii above) sharply contrasted with the right approach of Christians – 'is under serious doubt' (*Romans*, 118). Rather, Ziesler is clear that 'boasting' should be understood in the sense of (a.i), 'boasting in the law because it marks the "national privilege" of Israel as God's chosen people' (*Romans*, 117):

> The boasting is of those who think they have a special status because they are Jews.

Ziesler acknowledges the difficulty in making coherent sense of Paul's positive and negative statements on the law (question c) and this affects his conclusions on Paul's view of the relationship between Torah and faith (question b). After examining the key elements of Paul's view on the law one by one, Ziesler states (*Pauline Christianity*, 115):

> A coherent account of his view of the Law is not easy to give ... because he never writes about it systematically, but also because he himself was perhaps somewhat ambivalent about it. He may have been torn between an inherited and instinctive reverence for the Law as divine revelation, and a Christian conviction that it was now a barrier against yielding centrality to Christ.

Ziesler here briefly refers to two explanations for the difficulty of finding coherence in Paul's apparently conflicting statements on the law (answering question c above). Firstly, the fact that Paul 'never writes about [the Law] systematically' and, secondly, that there is in Paul an inner 'ambivalence' between his Jewish past and his new Christian conviction.

Both these reservations about Paul's coherence will find support in Sanders's views but Ziesler presents two conclusions on the relationship between Torah and faith which indicate that, while it is difficult, it is possible to find coherence. The first picks up on the points made above on the centrality of Christ as opposed to Law (*Pauline Christianity*, 115):

> Undoubtedly the Law has been moved from the centre. ... If some [Jewish Christians] continue to keep the Law, it must not be allowed to become a central issue unless they start to demand that others join them, as in Galatia. Once this happens, Christ is dethroned and Paul's theological hackles rise.

The idea that Christ has replaced the Law at the centre of Paul's theology allows Ziesler to affirm both the positive and negative statements. While the Law is peripheral it can retain some positive place in Paul's scheme. But when Paul is arguing against those Jews who are making attempts to establish a central place for the Law among Christians is when he makes his strongest negative statements.

Ziesler's second description of Paul's view on the law occurs on the same page (115):

> ... we have no exception to the Pauline position about the Law's irrelevance to new life in Christ.

The idea that Paul's thought is framed by the different but related convictions that 'the Law has been moved from the centre' and 'the Law is irrelevant to new life in Christ' gives a subtle answer to the question of the relationship between Torah and faith (question b) and to how Paul's positive and negative statements on the law can be explained (question c). Fundamentally for Paul, in Ziesler's assessment, 'the Law is irrelevant to new life in Christ' but when he is dealing with fellow Jews who still practise the Law as Christians he allows that it can have a continuing, but peripheral, place. Paul's most antagonistic statements occur when he is challenging Jews who are arguing and seeking to persuade Gentiles that it has a central, essential place in the Christian life. This position is consistent with the emerging position in the main text.

Dunn: *nomos* consistently means Torah, Torah of works or Torah of faith

While Dunn recognizes that Paul's meaning when he uses the word *nomos* cannot always be contained by the concept of Torah, he argues that when he uses *nomos* Paul means Torah throughout Romans 3:27-31 and consistently in his other writings (Dunn, *Romans*, 133):

> [W]e may have to retain awareness that Paul wanted to make universal claims at various points, even when speaking of the Torah, the law of Moses as such. But as a rule we can assume that when Paul spoke of *nomos* ... he was thinking of the Torah.

For Dunn, the 'boasting' that Paul is rejecting is (a.i) above: 'boasting in the law because it marks the "national privilege" of Israel as God's chosen people'. When Paul says 'boasting is excluded' by 'the law of faith' and asks 'is God of the Jews only?' he is meaning that there is no boasting for the people of Israel on the basis of their special relationship with God; God is not God of the Jews alone but of Gentiles too and justification for both is available on the basis of faith. That basis of faith is revealed in the right approach to the law. Dunn clearly disagrees with Ziesler. He believes firmly that Paul is setting the Torah of works in opposition to the Torah of faith (*Romans*, 186f):

> It is two ways of looking at the law as a whole which he here sets in opposition: when the law is understood in terms of works it is seen as distinctively Jewish and particular features come into prominence (particularly circumcision); but when the law is understood in terms of faith its distinctive Jewish character ceases to hold center stage, and the distinctively Jewish works become subsidiary and secondary matters which cannot be required of all and which can be disregarded by Gentiles in particular without damaging ... its faith character.

Faith, for Dunn, does not bring the law to an end but enables a 'Spirit-led' following of the law once it is stripped of those elements which separate Jew from Gentile.

Dunn: the nature of the Torah of faith

It is important to note the difference and similarity between Dunn's proposal and the view Ziesler rejects. Dunn does not share the previously widely accepted interpretation of Paul that 'there were some people (Jews) who approached the Torah thinking that by observing it they earned God's favour, whereas Christians approached it knowing that they could never so earn that favour' (Ziesler, *Romans*, 118). Yet for Dunn it is still the attitude with which the law is approached that makes all the difference. If it is approached from a 'too narrowly Jewish perspective', 'misunderstood by a misplaced emphasis on boundary-marking ritual, ... sidetracked into a focus for nationalistic zeal' (Dunn, *Romans*, lxxii) then it is a negative force. If it is 'understood in terms of faith' (*Theology*, 639), approached with an attitude of faith, it is established in its true function. And what is that attitude of faith for Dunn? Dunn notes that, shortly after Romans 3:27-31, Paul presents Abraham as the example of faith (4:18-21) (*Theology*, 641f):

> [F]aith for Paul meant complete trust in God, like Abraham's, total reliance on God's enabling. ... This creaturely trust in and reliance on God could be expressed as "the law of faith" in that it is only living out this trust which produces the quality of living before God and for others which the law was originally intended to promote.

And Dunn, while he argues that for Paul 'the law of faith' refers to the function of the law as a whole, reveals much about his understanding of faith in relationship to law when he states how, in practice, faith modifies the content of the law (641):

> The law of faith, then, is the law in its function of calling for and facilitating the same sort of trust in God as that out of which Abraham lived. This is not a reference only to sections or parts of the law but describes the function of the law as a whole. Thus we can recognize the criterion by which Paul judged the relevance of the law as a whole and in any of its particulars. Whatever commandment directed or channeled that reliance on God or helped bring that reliance to expression in daily living was the law still expressive of God's will. Conversely, whatever law required more than faith, whatever commandment could not be lived out as an expression of such trust in God alone, whatever ruling hindered or prevented such faith, that was the law now left behind by the coming of Christ. With the gospel now making it possible for *all* to express such faith in God through believing in Christ, the law which was understood to demand more than that faith was in fact the enemy of that faith and should be regarded as redundant.

The sections above show clearly Dunn's answers to the questions (b) and (c) with which we started this section. Faith and law are not in opposition. The purpose of the law was always to bring about the reliance on God which is faith. Since the coming of Christ, that faith is now possible. Approached through faith the law is positive. The law is negative for Paul in two primary ways: the law as a whole when it is misunderstood as a mark of Israel's privileged status before God; the law when, in practice, it is at odds with faith, when particular commandments demand more than faith or cannot be lived out as an expression of total trust in God or hinder or prevent such faith.

In Chapter 10 there will be support for Dunn's view of faith as complete reliance or trust in God. What is at odds with Dunn in the main argument is the centrality of the prophetic word – direct guidance from God – in the experience of faith as spoken of by Paul. It has already been argued that it is in this respect that faith and law are in opposition: faith as openness to guidance by the prophetic word provides a better way of discovering what God requires (pp. 54-61). We have already seen that Dunn considers that the prophetic word was a significant part of early Christian experience (581f, quoted on p. 30) but in the continuing place that he believes Paul retains for the law, it is clear that Dunn does not see it replacing the law as a new and better way of seeking God's guidance.

Sanders: *nomos* almost always equals Torah

There are important points of connection between Sanders and Dunn even though their overall positions are remarkably different. Sanders is clear that when Paul asks 'what becomes of boasting?' it is 'the "national privilege" of the people of Israel' he is referring to (*PLJP*, 33):

> Paul proceeds to argue that God is the God of Gentiles as well as of Jews (3:29) and that he righteouses the uncircumcised and the circumcised on the same basis, faith (3:30). The argument, in other words, is in favor of equal status and against privilege – especially against boasting in privileged status.

He also, like Dunn, sees a continuing role for the law in the life of faith (*PLJP*, 104):

> Paul held ... that Christians should fulfill "the law" or keep "the commandments."

He considers that *nomos* for Paul almost always equals the Torah (*PLJP*, 3):

> In the study of " Paul and the law" we have before us a lot of unquestionably authentic statements by Paul on the subject; and, further, we know what law Paul was talking about. With a few exceptions, he meant ... the Jewish Torah.

The fact that Sanders speaks of 'a few exceptions' is crucial; these include Rom 3:27-31 and Rom 8:2 (also referred to in the main text). In the phrases that occur in these passages – 'the *nomos* of faith' and 'the *nomos* of the Spirit of life' – Sanders believes Paul is using 'wordplay' (*PLJP*, 62). At these points, Paul's meaning switches from 'Torah' to 'principle' (*PLJP*, 15):

> It is much better in both cases to take *nomos* to refer to the saving *principle* of faith or of the Spirit. It should be added that until very recently scholars generally (and correctly) understood *nomos* in Rom 3:27 ... to mean "rule" or "norm" ...

Sanders: the Torah does not bring salvation

Dropping the definition of *nomos* as Torah at this point enables Sanders to take up a very significantly different position from Dunn. While, as we have seen, Dunn's understanding of the climax of Paul's argument in this passage is that Paul is upholding the Torah of faith, that is, the Torah approached with the right inner attitude of trust in and reliance on God, Sanders rejects the view that a change in the interior attitude makes sense of Paul's statements (*PLJP*, 146):

I find no instance in Paul of a distinction with regard to the interior attitude with which one obeys the law. When Paul objects to "works of law," he never objects to the intention to achieve merit by them, and when he recommends obedience to the law he never mentions attitude one way or the other.

Note that Dunn, while he does not consider that Paul is objecting to the intention to achieve merit by 'works of law', does affirm that the 'interior attitude' of faith is central. For Sanders, the difference that faith brings is not in the attitude with which the law is approached but in its effectiveness in bringing about the transition to a new kind of life, something that the law cannot do (*PLJP*, 152):

> Thus we come to the following train of experience and thought: God revealed his son to Paul and called him to be apostle to the Gentiles. Christ is not only the Jewish messiah, he is savior and Lord of the universe. If salvation is by Christ and is intended for Gentile as well as Jew, it is not by the Jewish law *in any case*, no matter how well it is done, and without regard to one's interior attitude. Salvation is by faith in Christ, and the law does not rest on faith.

For Sanders, this sharp contrast in the effectiveness of faith and law to bring about change is central. Faith brings a change that enables the law to be 'fulfilled' and for Sanders, as we saw in the last chapter, that means effectively followed (p. 45). The distinction between the law as totally ineffective as the means of transition to the new life of faith but of value as a way of living once the transition is made gives Sanders the explanation of the mixture of positive and negative comments on the law made by Paul (question c above). In responding to different questions, some about transition – how to be 'righteoused' – and some about the continuing life of faith, Paul makes comments on the law that are not reconcilable with each other (*PLJP*, 145):

> The unsystematic character of Paul's thought about the law also comes distinctly to the fore when he discusses correct behavior. He makes no distinction between the law which does not righteous and to which Christians have died and the law which those in the Spirit fulfill. ... [E]ach statement (righteousness is not by the law; Christians fulfill the law) springs from one of Paul's central convictions. One has to do with how people enter the body of those who will be saved, one with how they behave once in. He did not abstract his statements about the law from the context in which they were made, nor did he consider them in their relationship to one another apart from the questions which they were intended to answer.

Dunn: the coherence of Paul on the law

Dunn strongly opposes Sanders's conclusion that Paul's various statements on the law are contradictory. His commentary on Romans 3:31 comes to this forceful conclusion (*Romans*, 191):

> In view of continuing blanket assertions that Paul "broke" with the law, or abandoned the law, or regarded it as superseded and abolished (as in Sanders, *PLJP*, 3 ...), it cannot be stressed too much that Paul had no intention of destroying the law. He sought only to undermine the law in its function as marking out Jewish privilege and prerogative (so characterized by "works of the law ...") – what was in fact its most fundamental and distinctive function in Jewish eyes.

> Once that point is grasped the continuing positive value he attributes to the law
> can be appreciated, and 3:31 ['we uphold the law'] ... ceases to be a contradiction
> ... We should do Paul the courtesy of taking his various assertions about the law
> seriously and of assuming that they made sufficiently coherent sense within his
> own theology. The conclusion that Paul's various statements on the law cannot
> be saved from outright contradiction should be a last resort and is more likely
> to indicate that the exegete has failed to enter sufficiently into the concerns and
> contexts of Paul's writing on the subject.

As we have seen, Sanders would agree with Dunn that Paul attributed 'continuing positive
value' to the law but his conclusion that Paul's positive and negative statements on the law are
responding to different questions means that he can also give full weight to Paul's negative
comments and talk of Paul's 'self-conscious' 'break with [the law]' (*PLJP*, 3). What Dunn
reacts against so strongly is that Sanders can only hold this position by arguing that Paul's
different statements on the law are not reconcilable. Dunn is not prepared to accept that Paul
lacks coherence on this central theme and believes that the consistency in Paul's statements is
established in a fundamentally positive view of the law, once it is seen to mean 'the Torah of
faith'. In commenting on the climax of Romans 3:27-31, 'we uphold' or 'establish the law' he
quotes favourably the NJB translation, 'we are placing the law on its true footing', and goes
on to say (*Romans*, 190f):

> Paul's object is not to make the law as though it had never been, but by
> universalizing it to confirm it in its proper function. When seen as directed to
> faith rather than to works, to bring all humankind under the Creator's rule rather
> than to divide off Israel from the nations, the law's role in the eschatological
> age (the "now" time) is established ... [O]nly when the *universal* function of the
> law is recognized can it fulfill its proper role, as the word of the Creator to his
> creatures by which he calls them to their proper creaturely response and by which
> he will in the end judge them all – Jew and Gentile. The law understood thus ...
> is "the law of faith" ...

For Dunn, any negative statements on the law are directed at those who continue to identify
its function with the privileged separation of the people of Israel.

Dunn and Sanders: a reduced 'whole law'

In order to support the view that the law has a continuing positive value for Paul, both Dunn
and Sanders rely heavily on interpreting Paul's statements that Christians 'fulfil the whole
law' as Christians 'obey' or 'keep' or 'follow' the Torah. In the last chapter this view was
rejected (pp. 56-61). It was argued that Paul deliberately uses 'fulfil' rather than 'obey', 'keep'
or 'follow' because his meaning is that it is the whole purpose of the law, what it was given to
effect, that is now 'fulfilled'. Those who come to faith live a life of freedom from law in which
what the law requires issues naturally from their transformed state as fruit from the plant
and consequently do not need to look to the law to determine what they have to do. There is
further support for the view that Dunn and Sanders are misinterpreting this brief but important
statement. In order for them to affirm that Christians 'keep' the whole law, both Dunn and
Sanders have to acknowledge that what Paul means by 'the whole law' has a significantly
reduced content. Sanders notes Paul's rejection of the law on circumcision, Sabbath and food
laws and comments that these were the laws that 'created a social distinction between Jews
and other races in the Greco-Roman world' and that 'they were the aspects of Judaism which

drew criticism and ridicule from pagan authors' (*PLJP*, 102). While it is clear which parts of the law Paul rejects, Sanders does not find in Paul a clear rationale for this reduction of the law and has to speculate on his motivation for this move (*PLJP*, 102f):

> I do not wish to propose that Paul consciously deleted from the law which Christians are to keep the elements which were most offensive to pagan society on purely practical grounds, so that pagans would find it relatively easy to convert. We should recall, rather, two of his principal convictions: all are to be saved on the same basis; he was called to be the apostle to the Gentiles. Putting these convictions into practice understandably resulted in deleting circumcision, Sabbath, and food laws from "the whole law" or "the commandments of God." Yet we must also bear in mind that Paul himself offered no theoretical basis for the de facto reduction of the law. We can say that he meant in fact a *reduced* law when he said that the law is fulfilled in the requirement to love the neighbor only because we can observe the ways in which he reduced it, not because he himself admits that he reduced it. He still calls it "the whole law."

This explanation fits Sanders's overall thesis that Paul does not consciously reconcile different elements of his theology. His view is that Paul can both claim that Christians obey the whole law but have only a limited awareness of how he was cutting parts out of the law (*PLJP*, 103):

> We cannot determine to what degree he was conscious of his own reduction of the law.

This suggestion that Paul does not see the consequences of his principal convictions is completely unsatisfactory to Dunn. He finds Paul coherent provided that it is seen that Paul is consistently contrasting two different ways of understanding the Torah, 'through works', by which Paul means the Torah misunderstood as primarily concerned with Jewish identity, and 'through faith', meaning the Torah observed with total reliance on God. But, as with Sanders, his view also necessitates the interpretation of 'fulfilling the whole law' as 'obeying' or 'keeping' the whole law. We must look again at his interpretation of Romans 3:27 this time focusing on his affirmation that, for Paul's argument to work, the phrase, 'the law of faith', must be referring to the Torah as a whole (*Romans*, 186):

> Granted that *nomos* here too refers to the Torah ..., Paul's meaning should not be short-changed. He does not mean simply the law as bearing witness to faith or even summoning people to faith ... Nor does he have in view the law reduced to some core and shorn of its peculiarly Jewish ritual requirements ... In both phrases, "law of works" and "law of faith," Paul has the law as such, the whole law, in view; otherwise his response here would be deficient from the start, and his concluding assertion (v. 31 ['we uphold the law']) critically undermined. "The law of faith" then must mean the law understood in terms of faith ...

He goes on to make the clear statement (*Romans*, 186)

> ... It is two ways of looking at the law *as a whole* which he here sets in opposition ... [italics added]

This puts the emphasis strongly upon the internal attitude with which the law is approached rather than any external difference between 'the law of faith' and 'the law of works' – a view rejected by Sanders. But even in the commentary that follows directly upon that statement, a section which we have already briefly considered, Dunn is acknowledging that 'the whole law' is significantly reduced by this changed way of looking at it (*Romans*, 186f):

> ... when the law is understood in terms of works it is seen as distinctively Jewish and particular features come into prominence (particularly circumcision); but when the law is understood in terms of faith its distinctive Jewish character ceases to hold center stage, and *the distinctively Jewish works become subsidiary and secondary matters which cannot be required of all and which can be disregarded by Gentiles in particular without damaging (indeed thereby enhancing – v. 31) its faith character* [italics added].

Dunn cannot evade the many occasions in which Paul indicates that faith releases people from keeping particular aspects of the law. So, in order to present a view that affirms the consistency in Paul's thought based on a continuing role for the Torah, he has to affirm that Paul says both (a) that the Torah of faith upholds the whole law which specifically is not 'the law reduced to some core and shorn of its peculiarly Jewish ritual requirements' and (b) that 'the subsidiary and secondary matters' contained in the law arising from its 'distinctive Jewish character ... cannot be required of all and can be disregarded'. At this central stage of his argument for the consistency of Paul's thought based on the interpretation of 'the law of faith' as the Torah 'understood in terms of faith' Dunn's interpretation becomes at least confusing if not downright contradictory.

This need for Sanders and Dunn to affirm that Paul both expects Christians to 'obey the whole law' and at the same time reduces – consciously or unconsciously – the content of 'the whole law' arises from their conviction that Paul gives a 'continuing positive value' to the whole law, in the context of which, his clear rejection of aspects of the law needs to be explained. The main text argues that Paul's consistent view is that, while the law has had its positive God-given place in preparing the way for faith, it is no longer necessary for those living by faith – they 'fulfil the law' in the sense that the life that the law was given to lead people to, they are now living. Living by faith in practice leads to similar moral actions as living under the law but the motivation is fundamentally different. Struggling to do what the law requires is no longer the experience of those who live by faith. Further, as Dunn and Sanders both acknowledge, significantly different actions follow in relation to those elements of the law which are primarily concerned with marking out the Jews as a people. For Paul, these elements have come to an end in the new life of faith.

All have knowledge of the law

Central to this new sense of motivation is the transition from seeking God's will through the following of law to seeking God's guidance through faith. Paul regards this transition from law to faith as one that all – both Jew and Gentile – must go through. In Chapters 5-7 we will explore in detail why this experience of the law is so central for Paul and the precise way in which it is bound up with sin but the exploration cannot take place without acknowledging the vital place in Paul's theology of the idea that all – both Jew and Gentile – have knowledge of the law. This is the purpose of the Romans 2 passage referred to in the main text (pp. 65f) The climax of this section is not that before faith all are under sin but that before faith all are under law (Rom 3:19), the Jews through having the Torah and Gentiles through seeing God's will in creation and through conscience. In assessing Rom 2:12-15 where Paul argues that Gentiles have knowledge of God's will through conscience, Dunn clearly sees this as part of the sustained argument of Romans 2 and 3 leading to the climax that all have knowledge of God's law (*Theology*, 136f):

> Above all 2.12-15 is largely directed to demonstrating that Gentiles who are "without the law" (2.12), and "who have not the law," nevertheless can be said to be "the law for themselves" (2.14). The grounds Paul gives for this assertion are that they "by nature do what the law requires ... [and] demonstrate the business of the law written in their hearts" (2.14-15). Their active consciences (usually understood as denoting a painful or disturbing awareness of personal wrongdoing) also bear the same testimony of a more universal moral sensibility (2.15). What precisely Paul had in mind in these verses has been a subject of much debate. But the point for us is clear enough. Gentiles could be said to have some knowledge of what God expected of humanity; and since the law was (for Jews generally) the highest and clearest expression of God's will, it could also be said that Gentiles were aware of the law. The law could thus be said to stand as the measure of God's requirement and judgment for the world of humankind as a whole (2.16; 3.6). And Paul could wind up his indictment appropriately: the law stops every mouth and makes all the world liable to God's judgment (3.19) – Jew first, and also Gentile.

This is not Sanders's view and in Romans 2 he finds Paul at his most unsystematic. The difficulty that Sanders has with the passage arises from his assessment that Paul, in order to demonstrate the universal nature of the human plight before the coming of Christ, is not seeking to show that Gentiles are under the law, but, instead, is seeking to establish that Jews are sinners as Gentiles are. For this to be the case, Paul has to argue that, even without Christ, it is possible to follow the law effectively, and the fact that they do not do this means that Jews can be regarded as sinners. In other words, in the argument of Romans 2, salvation was possible through the law (*PLJP*, 128f):

> The offer of salvation on the basis of fulfillment of the law is held out repeatedly, and not in terms which make one think that the offer is hypothetical or that the goal is impossible to achieve ...

This is a view that is explicitly rejected everywhere else in Paul; he consistently maintains that, in the light of faith, it can be clearly seen that no one is 'righteous' through the law. This leads Sanders to treat this section as exceptional and as not reflecting Paul's theology.

At the heart of Sanders's assessment of this passage is a blurring together of two related ideas in Paul: 'all have knowledge of the law' and 'all are sinners'. Sanders's summary of the consistent way Paul's thought moves from solution to plight has been influential and his view of Romans 1:18-2:29 is part of his argument (*PLJP*, 82):

> ... Paul's thought about sin and redemption is not based on a systematic, empirical account of the human condition. One often reads that Paul "demonstrates" that all are under sin. He does not, however, "demonstrate" it – not even in Rom 1:18-2:29, as we shall see – he asserts it. Since God sent Christ to save humanity, and to do so on a common basis, all are in the same situation, under sin (e.g., Rom 3:9). God had given the law before the coming of Christ. It does not save; therefore it is connected with sin, the common condition of everyone, and thus everyone, before Christ, was under the law.

While Sanders's observation that Paul's account of the human condition is not based on systematic, empirical observation is obviously true, clarity is obscured by Sanders's lack of precision over Paul's thought on the relationship between sin and law. As we have already seen (p. 10), he suggests that there is a naivete in Paul's thought that verges on caricature: 'God sent Christ to save humanity' therefore 'all are in the same situation', all are in need of saving, all are 'under sin'; the law was given before the coming of Christ; clearly 'it does not save' and 'therefore it is connected with sin'. Note the insubstantial nature of this link between 'law' and 'sin': because 'the law does not save ... it is connected with sin'. According to Sanders, this vague 'connection' in Paul's mind between law and sin has to bear the weight of Paul's argument that 'everyone, before Christ, was under the law'. Given that, according to Sanders, Paul simply asserts this view, this inevitably leads to the difficulties Paul has in arguing how it can be that all, including Gentiles who do not have the Torah, could be under the law.

That there is a close connection between law and sin is not in doubt. What is very questionable here is the way Sanders presents Paul's own thinking about this connection. Sanders's view that Paul's thought moves from solution to plight has been extraordinarily helpful; his hypothesis on the various mental steps Paul makes on that way from solution to plight assumes, at best, a laziness in Paul's thought which fits perfectly Sanders's view of the unsystematic nature of Paul's thought on the law. An alternative view of the reason why Paul's thought runs from solution to plight will be presented in Chapters 5 and 6 but it is important now to see how not discriminating clearly between 'under the law' and 'under sin' leads Sanders to his conclusion that Romans 2 is not part of Paul's thought.

In the passage above and on several other occasions, Sanders talks of Romans 3:9 as the conclusion of the passage. There Paul says that 'we have already charged that all, both Jews and Greeks, are under the power of sin', however, 'all are under the power of sin' is a point already made ('we have already charged that ...') as he moves towards his main conclusion. Sanders does also make reference to the true climax of the argument (*PLJP*, 82):

> The full ambiguity of Paul's way of describing the human plight comes to expression in Rom 3:19: "We know that whatever the law says it speaks *to those who are under the law*, so that *every mouth* may be stopped, and *the whole world* may be held accountable to God. For *no human being* will be righteoused in his sight by works of the law...."

And he goes on to say that (*PLJP*, 82):

> [Paul] offers no explanation of how what the law says to those under it (the Jews) also applies to "the whole world."

But just before the passage above Sanders has himself commented on Paul's 'explanation' of how Gentiles were 'under the law' like Jews (*PLJP*, 82):

> The explanation on the basis of natural law in Romans 2 is striking because it is not otherwise employed.

The problem for Sanders seems to be, not that Paul does not provide an explanation – as the main text argues and as Dunn implies above, that is precisely what Paul is doing in Romans 1:18-2:29 – but that the 'striking' explanation that Paul offers does not fit with other aspects of Paul's theology as perceived by Sanders.

Sanders is clear about the fundamental difficulty that he has with Romans 2 (*PLJP*, 129, 132):

> The question throughout Chapter 2 is whether or not one does the Jewish law, not as the result of being in Christ, but as the sole determinant of salvation. ... It stands out because it deals directly with salvation and makes salvation dependent on obedience to the law. ... What is said about the law in Romans 2 cannot be fitted into a category otherwise known from Paul's letters ....

This difficulty is so acute for Sanders that he does not regard the material as coming from Paul (*PLJP*, 123):

> I think that in Rom 1:18-2:29 Paul takes over to an unusual degree homiletical material from Diaspora Judaism, that he alters it in only insubstantial ways, and that consequently the treatment of the law in Chapter 2 cannot be harmonized with any of the diverse things which Paul says about the law elsewhere.

The two substantial points to be made in response to this both illustrate the importance of the issues of translation that have been made in this and the previous chapter. There we examined the important section of Galatians 3-4 where Paul uses the noun *stoicheia*. The common situation of Jews and Gentiles prior to the coming of faith is the subject of Galatians 3-4 and Sanders finds the same inconsistency in Galatians 3-4 as he finds in Romans 1:18-2:29. Although, as we saw, it is difficult to find a neat English translation, when Paul says that before the coming of faith both Jew and Gentile are enslaved under the *stoicheia*, it was argued that his meaning is that all are under religious directions for behaviour. Because he defines *stoicheia* as 'pagan deities', Sanders here finds further strong evidence for Paul's 'illogical' thought and links this with the artificial argument of Romans 1:18-2:29 (*PLJP*, 151):

> [Paul] puts all humanity equally under the law. He can hardly have come to this position by analyzing the human condition, and few parts of his letters are more illogical than those in which he equates the status of Jew and Gentile prior to faith. Thus we observed that in Galatians 3-4 he says both that "we" were under the law (3:23) and that "we" were slaves of the *stoicheia* (4:3) ['pagan deities']. This sort of simple equation is explicable as coming from his conviction that everyone equally needs to be saved by faith in Christ, but it is hardly descriptive of the actual condition of Jews and Gentiles prior to faith ... Similarly the labored attempt to make Jews and Gentiles equally guilty in Rom 1:18-2:29 is best seen as springing from the need to lead up to the conclusion in Rom 3:9 ... "all are under sin" ...

The 'simple equation' in Galatians 3-4 in the situation of Jew and Gentile prior to faith is not explicable for Sanders because he interprets 'law' as 'Jewish law' and *stoicheia* as 'pagan deities'. But there is a vast difference if *stoicheia* are 'religious directions for behaviour' and 'law' is not identified with 'Jewish law': then it can make sense to say 'all – Jew and Gentile – are under the *stoicheia*', 'all are under the law'.

This same expansive interpretation of *nomos,* wide enough to contain Gentiles under the law, is absolutely vital in the argument of Romans. In later chapters it will become clear why in Romans, Paul's gospel that faith is for both Jew and Gentile is tied together with the idea that both Jew and Gentile share the same plight of being 'under the law'. This, as the main text indicates, is exactly what Paul is seeking to establish in Romans 2. Yet in *Paul, the Law and the Jewish People* (pp. 123-132), Sanders relegates his consideration of Romans 2 to an appendix, a very overt way of indicating his view that Romans 2 does not contain Paul's distinctive teaching (*PLJP*, 129):

> I think that the best way to read 1:18-2:29 is as a synagogue sermon. ... Christians are not in mind, the Christian viewpoint plays no role, and the entire chapter is written from a Jewish perspective.

This is a very drastic conclusion to come to particularly as Sanders has to create a completely hypothetical source for this text (*PLJP*, 130f):

> We do not have a corpus of Diaspora synagogue sermons with which to compare Romans 2, and thus we can adduce no proof that 2:12-15 [where Paul states, 'the doers of the law will be righteoused'] is a non-Christian Jewish theme. Nevertheless, I regard that as more likely than the view that Paul composed it.

Even more telling against Sanders's case is that he does indeed acknowledge that there is a problem with interpreting *nomos* as 'Jewish law' as traditionally understood in Romans 2 but only considers this difficulty once he has separated this text from Paul and established it in his own mind as a sermon from the Jewish diaspora (*PLJP*, 130):

> ... we must admit that we do not know the contents of "the law" in the original setting of the passage. One might speculate that in a homiletical presentation the question might be left vague. The law which Gentiles are to obey, and which is ascertainable by nature, cannot be the same as the Torah *if* one thinks concretely and in detail. People do not always think that way, however, and we may also assume that not every Jewish sermon would maintain the careful rabbinic distinction between laws which Gentiles might reasonably be expected to follow and those which require revelation and special instruction.

Sanders's central problem with this passage arises out of giving *nomos* a 'hard' or 'rigid' interpretation as 'Jewish law' which prevents him seeing that Paul is presenting a subtle argument exploiting the different meanings that there are in the word to expand its meaning to include Gentiles 'under the law'. To retain the rigid definition, Sanders has to reject Paul's authorship of the passage, produce an almost completely hypothetical source for the material (a Jewish diaspora sermon) and then explain the imprecise way the material in that hypothetical context speaks of the Jewish law being obeyed by Gentiles!

As we shall see (Chapter 5), Paul's argument that 'all have knowledge of the law' is a distinct element for Paul in establishing the nature of the human plight and subsuming this element under the idea that 'all are under the power of sin' makes it impossible to proceed with an analysis which brings real clarity to Paul's understanding of the human condition both before and after the coming of faith. Far from being an irrelevant and misleading section of Paul's thought, Romans 2 contains a vital point, reflected in its position at the beginning of the letter to the Romans, the most systematic presentation of his theology.

Concluding observation

The main text argued for a flexible interpretation of *nomos* in which four different meanings all operate in a subtle relationship, just as can happen in the use of the English word, law. It was possible to do this in a brief span. Just as in the case of the three scholars that we have been examining in this section, that assessment was made on the basis of the relationship between *nomos* and the overall view of Paul's theology. Although some points of connection were indicated in the main text, presenting that overall view is the still unfolding purpose of the whole of the book. Ziesler's interpretation of *nomos* is in line with that of the main text; limitations in his overall picture have already been pointed out and will continue to emerge as the presentation continues. The major consequence of the issues of translation and interpretation that have been considered in this section is that the judgments made by Dunn and Sanders on the meaning of *nomos* make it impossible for them to construct a coherent theology of Paul.

Sanders is explicit about this impossibility; he blames Paul. Returning to the dry-stone wall as an image for Pauline scholarship, Sanders's view that Paul is unsystematic means that, having taken apart the wall to show how it has been built upon an unsteady foundation stone, Sanders has come to the view that Paul puts together sections of wall to serve particular short term purposes but does not align them together to make one coherent structure. Given that Paul is not concerned to join the parts of wall together, it is not such a radical move to discard a small section of wall that seems to organize the stones according to a different pattern (Romans 2). For Sanders, it is clear that Paul has imported this section of wall from another structure and it is wiser to acknowledge that and not strain to make it fit with the rest.

Dunn stridently opposes Sanders's view that Paul is incoherent but on scrutinizing his wall it is clear that there is at least one place near the base of the wall where the stones do not fit together neatly (law of faith equals the Torah reinterpreted in the light of faith) and where a substantial push is liable to bring the whole structure down. Committed to the view that Paul is building one strong wall and that following Sanders's demolition job it is a question of reconstruction with more carefully placed foundation stones, Dunn misses the fact that the peculiar shaped pieces that he is working with belong to a dramatically different structure. The systematic approach of his *Theology of Paul* does not come close to the realignment of the elements of Paul's theology necessary to see the extraordinary nature of what Paul speaks of, not a heavy stone wall but a soaring arch.

Why then the law?

In Jewish understanding, God had made a covenant with Israel which included the gift of the law. Central to this covenant was the demand from God that the people of Israel be holy, understood as 'separate' or 'set apart':

> Now therefore, if you obey my voice and keep my covenant, you shall be my treasured possession out of all the peoples. Indeed, the whole earth is mine, but you shall be for me a priestly kingdom and a holy nation. (Ex 19:5f)

While much practical elaboration of this central injunction had occurred by Paul's time, this call to be separate contained in and demanded by the law remained essential. In Paul's understanding, along with that of his fellow Jews, God had called Israel in particular, making a covenant with her which gave her special favour as long as she stayed true to the law which God had revealed:

> They are descendants of Israel, chosen to be God's sons; theirs is the glory of the divine presence, theirs the covenants, the law, the temple worship, and the promises. The patriarchs are theirs, and from them by natural descent came the Messiah. (Rom 9:4f, REB)

Given this powerful affirmation of God's choice of the Jews, now that Gentiles are also receiving particular blessings from God, Paul has to have an answer for a question that can be put in a variety of ways, 'What has God been doing? Is God now being unfaithful? Is God now being untrue to the covenants and promises? Has God's will for his people failed?'. The question that sums up the issue that Paul must deal with is:

> Why then the law? (Gal 3:19)

Given that Gentiles are experiencing the new life of faith, what was the purpose of the law, both as a way of knowing what God requires and as the central part of the covenant between God and Israel.

The law as a 'childminder'

An important part of the answer that Paul gives in the letter to the Galatians for the question 'why then the law?' is distorted by weaknesses in translation. This can best be seen in the RSV although there is a similar distortion of meaning in the NRSV. Once the changes in translation are made, a clear image emerges in Paul's thought, which significantly clarifies his understanding of the law. The three italicized words in the following brief passage will be examined with the attempt to discover the meaning each one carries and how that meaning is affected by the context in which they are used:

> Now before faith came, we were *confined* under the law, *kept under restraint* until faith should be revealed. So that the law was our *custodian* until Christ came, that we might be justified by faith. But now that faith has come, we are no longer under a *custodian*; for in Christ Jesus you are all sons of God through faith. (Gal 3:23-25, RSV)

The word translated 'custodian' is the Greek word *paidagōgos* which has a very vivid and precise meaning: 'literally, boy-leader, the man, usually a slave whose duty it was to conduct the boy or youth to and from school and to superintend his conduct generally; he was not a "teacher" (BAGD)'. This shows that the word is describing a very particular task. The problem in translating it lies in the fact that there is no precise equivalent task in the contemporary English world. Following the above definition, it is clear that 'schoolmaster' (AV), and 'a kind of tutor' (NEB) are misleading translations; the role that Paul is ascribing to the law is not educational although it is directed towards a child. 'Custodian' is a good translation if it is taken to mean 'one who keeps safe, protects, a guardian' but this English word also carries the meaning of 'an officer of the justice who keeps in confinement or imprisonment' and this is a long way from the sense in the Greek. One modern role that does have similarities to the figure Paul is evoking from his contemporary world is 'childminder'. While not entirely adequate, it does carry the important sense of guiding care for a child which is not primarily educational which is there in the image that Paul has chosen.

Other translations define the figure evoked here as a custodian in the sense of an imprisoning jailor. This comes about because it is judged that *paidagōgos* as defined above is not the key image in the passage. That judgment is made on a prior assessment of how Paul understands the law. The NIV is a good example:

> Before this faith came we were *held prisoners* by the law, *locked up* until the faith should be revealed. So the law was *put in charge* to lead us to Christ that we might be justified by faith. Now that faith has come, we are no longer *under the supervision* of the law. (Gal 3:23-25, NIV)

In this translation, the problem of defining *paidagōgos* is solved by turning the noun into two different verbs: 'to be put in charge', and 'to supervise'. It is true that these are appropriate words for aspects of the role Paul is referring to but the sharp clarity of the image, and with it, the understanding of the law that it evokes, has disappeared altogether. The decision has been made that the image of the *paidagōgos* leading the child to school is not the image of the law that Paul is seeking to relay. The words translated 'held prisoners' (*phroureō*) and 'locked up' (*sugkleiō*) have been made the carriers of the primary image and the image of the *paidagōgos* has been regarded as secondary and dispensable. The elements of the role of the *paidagōgos* of 'being in charge' and 'supervision' have been separated from the role itself and instead of being related to the figure of a childminder have been employed to present the law in the image of a jailor.

So attention needs to turn to the Greek word, *sugkleiō*, which, in the NIV translation, is considered to be shaping the context and is translated 'to lock up' in the NIV and 'to keep under restraint' in the RSV. The one other use of this exact word in the New Testament is in a gospel description of fishing: 'they *enclosed* a great shoal of fish' (Luke 5:6). However, it is closely related to the word for 'to shut' (*kleiō*), normally used with 'door' and in one passage a 'prison door', but also with 'heaven' and 'heart'. From these uses, a consistent idea can be seen operating behind the word, that of 'closing' and also of 'restraint', with an additional component of 'all around' (*sun*). These observations prove nothing except to strongly suggest that the association of the word with 'imprisonment', although possible, is not a necessary one. The word can be used in a variety of contexts to indicate 'restraint' or 'enclosing'. This is not a clinching argument for a particular translation but gives an awareness of the issues involved in coming to an accurate translation, sensitive to the nuances in Paul's thought and the range of meaning carried by the word.

It is important to remember at this stage that behind these subtle matters of definition, there is a substantive issue: it matters a great deal in appreciating Paul's answer to the question about the purpose of the law if his conception of the law is more accurately represented by a jailor or a childminder.

The third word can be dealt with quickly before moving on. The issue here is more straightforward. The verb, *phroureō* comes from the noun, 'a guard' (*phrouros*), consequently there is no problem in seeing how the image of imprisonment can be found here. However there are two sides to the English word, 'to guard', which are also in the Greek. 'To guard' is not only used of keeping prisoners restrained but is also used meaning 'to protect'. So, as with the previous word, while there is clearly the potential for this word also to be used of the restraint associated with imprisonment, this is not its only meaning.

The argument leads to the following important conclusion: the meaning of *paidagōgos* indicates that, to clarify the function of the law, Paul is using the image of the protective restraint of a wandering child rather than, as is usual in modern translations, the custodial restraint of an offending adult. *Sugkleiō* and *phroureō* both have a range of meaning and can comfortably carry the sense of protective restraint from danger just as easily as that of imprisonment. *Sugkleiō* can mean 'to restrain' just as well as 'to lock up'; *phroureō* can mean 'to protect' just as easily as 'to guard'. The interpretation hinges on the meaning of *paidagōgos*:

> Now before faith came, we were *restrained* under the law, *protected* until faith should be revealed. So that the law was our *childminder* until Christ came, that we might be justified by faith. But now that faith has come, we are no longer under a *childminder*; for in Christ Jesus you are all sons of God, through faith. (Gal 3:23-26, adapted RSV)

Clear confirmation for this interpretation comes in following Paul's argument a little further. He continues to contrast being a child or minor (NRSV) with coming of age or full sonship:

> I mean that the heir, as long as he is a child, is no better than a slave, though he is owner of all the estate; but he is under guardians and trustees until the date set by the father. So with us; when we were children, we were slaves under the worldly *stoicheia* (things that 'keep aligned'/'give direction for behaviour'). But when the time had fully come, God sent forth his Son, born of woman, born under the law, so that we might receive adoption as sons. (Gal 4:1-5, adapted RSV)

Right through this passage from the letter to the Galatians, Paul is speaking of the law in connection with the image of childhood. Childhood is the time 'before faith came' (Gal 3:23); law has been a *paidagōgos* 'until Christ came' (Gal 3:24). 'But when the time had fully come' (Gal 4:4), the time of faith, childhood is over and the external guidance of the law, the earthbound *stoicheia* (directions for behaviour) are no longer needed. All this is powerfully consistent with the argument above that *paidagōgos* is rightly understood as chosen by Paul to make clear the purpose of the law because it refers to a particular role in relation to a child – a role concerned with restraint but not imprisonment.

Section conclusion

It is worth developing Paul's image of the wandering infant while returning to the first response which Paul makes to his own question, 'Why then the law?'. What he says is this, 'It was added because of transgressions...' (Gal 3:19). Once a baby becomes a toddler, parents have to be vigilant in ensuring that the child, which does not understand danger, does not wander where it might come to harm. The law was added because of 'wandering', which is what the word translated 'transgression' (*parabasis*) literally means. The young child being taken upon the road to school is inclined to wander into danger and one purpose of the *paidagōgos* is to restrain the child within the safe boundaries of the path. So, in Paul's conception, law has a clear, positive function: it was given to infants to prevent their wandering, their transgression. He is not working with an image of the law as an imprisoning jailor, but rather as a childminder to keep the wandering infant safe until maturity comes and the law is no longer needed.

Conclusion

Paul has a major problem in wanting to affirm that there is a new intimacy with God, a new and better way of knowing what God requires and receiving empowerment to do it. If this is true, what does this say about the past, specifically, about God's covenant relationship with the people of Israel? Does this not inevitably undermine any idea of God's consistency and faithfulness, God's integrity? Two elements that form part of Paul's answer to that question have occupied this chapter: (a) that he conceived of all people, Jews and Gentiles, as under the law before the coming of faith; (b) that the law had a positive but temporary function.

In much of his discussion of the law, the Torah of the Jews is clearly uppermost in Paul's mind but, as the interpretation of *stoicheia* in the last chapter indicated, he is concerned to establish that the religious observances of the Gentiles have a similar purpose to the practice of the Torah. In the letter to the Romans, Paul makes further connections between the religious state of Jews and Gentiles. Even though they do not have the Torah, certain Gentiles indicate by their actions that they have awareness of the commands of God revealed to them through their consciences and through their observation of the world around them.

The question 'why then the law?' has received only a preliminary response. An introduction has been made to the important idea that Paul understands the law to have been given by God as operative for a limited period, a period he identifies as a kind of childhood. Just as a *paidagōgos*, a childminder or guardian, gives protection to a child so that it does not wander into danger, so law gives protection to a people. God's guidance is given in a clear external form. Doing what is right is determined by consulting the written law. When faith comes, doing what is right is determined by the inwardly revealed word – the prophetic word. For Paul, it is the real experience of this inwardly revealed word that now provides the right direction for action.

The image Paul uses for this new situation is a subtle one. The movement from childhood to adulthood involves a real change. The external word of the parent must become the word inwardly established and revealed within the individual. Without this fundamental shift within, the law provides essential guidance and protection.

Once the shift has occurred, the law is no longer required. Going back to the external word of the law makes no sense once the inwardly experienced responsibility of adulthood is reached. The real and obvious change from childhood to adulthood terminates the need for the external authority of the law just as coming to maturity involves a new life of independence from the parent.

While this image is a simple and universal one, it is usually obscured in interpretation. A long 'discussion section' was needed in the middle of this chapter for, on the question of Paul and the law, the confusion and complexity offered by commentators can already be overwhelming and paralyse the ability to go further. Only from the simplicity of the position on law and faith presented in the whole of Part One can a coherent interpretation of Paul begin to be constructed. In Part Two, the image of the child in relation to adulthood will give further help as we explore the condition that the law existed to contain and from which, according to Paul, liberation was needed. Moving forward with a clear understanding of Paul and the relationship between law and faith, there is much more to be discovered which, as well as revealing the subtlety of Paul's theology, will also confirm the accurate placing of these early stages of the argument, the foundation stones at the base of the arch.

PART TWO
The Exposure of Sin

Chapter 5

Childhood and Sin

The last chapter examined Paul's answer to the question: 'why then the law?' and argued that Paul is working with an understanding of 'law' as:

(a) something of which all people – both Jew and Gentile – have some knowledge and
(b) having a positive purpose but only for a limited time.

That positive purpose was seen to be a protective one, keeping humankind on the right path in preparation for the life of faith.

But Paul has other things to say on the law in which it is not simply a protection. Early in Romans, having stated that 'all, both Jews and Greeks, are under the power of sin' (Rom 3:9), he supports that view with a sequence of texts from the Hebrew scriptures which speak of the reality of sin (Rom 3:10-18 quoting Ps 14:1-3; 53:1-3; 5:9; 140:3; 10:7; Isa 59:7-8) and then affirms that 'every mouth' and 'the whole world' are 'accountable to God' before climaxing this section in a highly significant statement about the law in relation to sin:

> For 'no human being will be justified in his sight' by deeds prescribed by the law,
> for *through the law comes the knowledge of sin.* (Rom 3:20)

The purpose of this chapter is to explore precisely what Paul means by the phrase 'through the law comes the knowledge of sin' and how it can be reconciled with Paul's view that the law has a positive God-given protective role.

What makes this investigation a central one in establishing the powerful coherence in Paul's theology is the fact that to investigate Paul's understanding of the purpose of the law is also to approach the idea that Paul has a conception of the purpose of sin. Given that Paul considered that 'through the law comes knowledge of sin' and that God gave the law, the question is raised as to whether the 'knowledge of sin' is a necessary consequence of the law and therefore something 'meant' by God.

To pursue this exploration, our attention will be focused on Romans 7:7-25, one of the most famous, if difficult, passages in the Bible. We will first look at ways in which the account of the creation of humankind in Genesis is informing Paul's thought. This will provide one key to understanding this passage. The second key was introduced in the last chapter. There we saw how, in Galatians, to illuminate the positive purpose of the law, Paul uses the metaphor of the supervision given to a child to protect that child from wandering into danger. In a way never done before, these two images – the creation of humankind in Genesis and the relationship of adult and child – will both be brought to bear on Paul's meaning in Romans 7:7-25.

Adam, Eve and sin

Before turning to Romans 7, it is necessary to consider briefly how the Genesis story of the creation of humankind is functioning in Paul's thought. In different ways, Paul links Jesus and Adam. He describes Adam as 'a type of the one who was to come' (Rom 5:14); he says further:

> Therefore just as one man's trespass led to condemnation for all, so one man's act of righteousness leads to justification (absolution) and life for all. For just as by the one man's disobedience the many were made sinners, so by the one man's obedience the many will be made righteous (absolved). (Rom 5:18f)

This is an important text which will be returned to in the next chapter. These explicit references to Adam and to his 'disobedience' are the most obvious indication that the Genesis account of the fall of humankind from paradise into sin is informing the thought of Paul in a significant way. Further evidence is easy to find.

The following section from early in Romans can be understood as Paul's own presentation of the fall:

> Ever since the creation of the world [God's] eternal power and divine nature, invisible though they are, have been understood and seen through the things he has made. So they are without excuse; for though they knew God, they did not honour him as God or give thanks to him, but they became futile in their thinking, and their senseless minds were darkened. Claiming to be wise, they became fools; and they exchanged the glory of the immortal God for images resembling a mortal human being or birds or four-footed animals or reptiles.
>
> Therefore God gave them up in the lusts of their hearts to impurity, to the degrading of their bodies among themselves, because they exchanged the truth about God for a lie and worshipped and served the creature rather than the Creator, who is blessed for ever! Amen. (Rom 1:20-25)

Unlike the Genesis account, Paul is describing the fall in a 'realistic' rather than 'mythical' way. It is worth making the connections explicit, not only to show the common ground of the two passages, but also as a reminder of the elements of the Genesis story, which form the background for the rest of the chapter.

Just as Genesis begins with the description of the goodness of God's creation, so Paul states how 'ever since the creation of the world [God's] eternal power and divine nature, invisible though they are, have been understood and seen through the things he has made' (Rom 1:20). Genesis describes how the woman saw that 'the tree was to be desired to make one wise' (Gen 3:6); Paul states that 'claiming to be wise, they became fools' (Rom 1:22). In Genesis, God says: '"Let us make humankind in our image, according to our likeness; and let them have dominion over the fish of the sea, and over the birds of the air, and over the cattle, and over all the wild animals of the earth, and over every creeping thing that creeps upon the earth'" (Gen 1:26); in Paul's account of the distortion of the created order after the fall, humankind 'exchanged the glory of the immortal God for an imitation [a likeness], for the image of a mortal human being, or of birds, or animals, or crawling things' (Rom 1:23, NJB). In Genesis, the serpent is the one who deceives (Gen 3:13); in Paul's account, people 'exchanged the truth about God for a lie' (Rom 1:25).

In the Genesis account there are two immediate consequences of disobeying God. The first is the loss of sexual innocence: 'Then the eyes of both were opened, and they knew that they were naked; and they sewed fig leaves together and made loincloths for themselves' (Gen 3:7). The second consequence is a kind of divisive isolation. It is first stated that 'the man and his wife hid themselves from the presence of the Lord God...' (Gen 3:8) and then when the Lord God asks the man if he has eaten from the forbidden tree he immediately blames the woman and God together, '"The woman whom you gave to be with me, she gave me fruit from the tree, and I ate"' (Gen 3:12). Similarly, Paul states that sexual depravity and enmity follow from worshipping the creature rather than the Creator: 'For this reason God gave them up to degrading passions ... And since they did not see fit to acknowledge God, God gave them up to a debased mind and to things that should not be done. They were filled with every kind of wickedness, evil, covetousness, malice ...' (Rom 1:26, 28f), and Paul then lists similar evils.

This brief comparison of the accounts of the fall in Genesis and Paul demonstrates how the Genesis story is functioning in Paul's thought in the opening of the letter to the Romans. It has been presented to support the legitimacy of turning to the Genesis story as an interpretative key to open up the central section of Paul's letter to the Romans. As stated in the introduction, this key will be used along with the image of childhood under the law presented by Paul in the letter to the Galatians. The aim will be to get inside the thought of Paul. The fact that we have two different ways used by Paul of illuminating to others the function and purpose of the law gives a particular opportunity to discover the coherent view which Paul was presenting: what single conception did he have that could enable him to express himself in these two different ways? To answer this will involve unfolding the implications of the images that Paul uses. It is important to remember the argument of the last chapter that 'the law' is not simply the Torah of the Jews but something universally discernible. We now turn to Romans 7:7-25. Smoothness is sacrificed in the translation in order to translate the words in Paul's Greek consistently throughout. The passage is one continuous argument but will be presented in three sections to facilitate comment.

The knowledge of good and evil

Is the law sin?

> 7₇What then shall we say? Is the law sin? Certainly not. But I had not known
> sin, except through law; for I had not known desire, except the law said, 'You
> will not desire'. 8For the sin, receiving a foothold through the commandment,
> worked in me every desire; for without law sin is dead. 9For I once lived
> without the law, but when the commandment came, the sin came to life and
> I died, 10and the commandment which was to be life was found to be death to
> me. 11For the sin, receiving a foothold through the commandment, deceived
> me and, through it, killed me. 12So the law is holy, and the commandment is
> holy and righteous and good. (Rom 7:7-12, author's translation used here and
> throughout the section)

The question Paul is answering here is similar to that in the letter to the Galatians
already examined, 'Why then the law?' (Gal 3:19), but taken a stage further. It can
be paraphrased: how can the law be from God, that is, how can it be good, if it is so
bound up with sin? If 'through the law comes the knowledge of sin' is the law not
then itself sinful? This question is particularly pressing in the letter to the Romans
for Paul has already stated a further view of the law which can be taken in a negative
way: 'Law came in, to increase the trespass' (Rom 5:20, RSV).

Paul now begins a sustained answer in the first person singular. This feature in
itself marks this passage out as peculiar but Paul is speaking in a way familiar among
Jews. In the context of ritual, the usual distinctions between the individual and the
whole people and between the past and the present disappeared. In the Passover
meal, the sense is that each individual Jew was present at the liberation from Egypt
by God. At the meal there is the instruction:

> You shall tell your child on that day, "It is because of what the Lord did for *me*
> when *I* came out of Egypt." (Ex 13:8)

In the Romans passage, Paul is using the first person singular in this same way but
the context indicates that Paul is not simply speaking as a representative Jew, but as a
representative of humankind for, as we shall see as the passage unfolds, the primary
background for what Paul says is the banishment of humankind from the garden of
Eden. When Paul speaks in the first person he can be understood as speaking of the
development and struggle of the whole of humankind.

Paul's first response to his own question, 'Is the law sin?', has precisely the same
sense as 'through the law comes knowledge of sin' but is expressed in this distinctive,
personal way: 'I had not known sin, except through law' (Rom 7:7). What follows
is an elaboration of that statement. Paul's explanation continues: '... for I had not
known desire except the law said, "You shall not desire"' (Rom 7:7). Here is the first
vivid echo of the Genesis story: 'And the Lord God commanded the man, "You may
freely eat of every tree of the garden; but of the tree of the knowledge of good and

evil you shall not eat, for in the day that you eat of it you shall die"' (Gen 2:16f), but then 'the woman saw ... that the tree was to be *desired* to make one wise ...' (Gen 3:6). The one tree is singled out for prohibition and, while there is freedom to eat of every other tree, this is the one that is 'desired'.

It is worth pausing a moment to consider the very precise significance of this prohibition. This is the point at which it is helpful to turn to the Galatians image of the infant in relationship to law. The young child is hungry for knowledge. As soon as any of its senses develop, it is eager to use them for enquiry, whether it is the ability to grasp, to crawl, to walk, to speak. The parents of the child encourage all of this, providing toys, space, games and conversation to encourage and feed this natural desire. Except in one respect: when the child encounters a situation that is dangerous and destructive in a way that is beyond its capacity to understand, the parent simply prohibits. To put this another way, where something that is of value for adult life is in danger of being destroyed through the actions of the child, the parents stop the child. This is most obviously true of situations where the child's life is in danger. To appreciate adult life, the child must survive its childhood! The natural desire of the child for knowledge, which, in every other way, the parent encourages as essential and good, is thwarted. Despite the best intentions of the parents, a certain amount of conflict is the inevitable result. The desire for knowledge in the child is, in the child's mind, even though unarticulated, an absolute good which is not limited to only those things that are not dangerous. The desire to protect the child's life is, in the parent's mind, also an absolute good for the parent can see that knowledge is no use without life. So the unlimited desire for knowledge in the child is restrained by the prohibitions of the parents. Thus from the moment that the child is able, by its own strength, to get itself into situations which endanger its future adult life, it is confronted with a fundamental inconsistency in the way that it is treated by its parents which the child is unable to understand and that leads inevitably to conflict.

Now the point of all this is that in the Genesis account there is a similar fundamental inconsistency in the way that God treats Adam and Eve:

> So God created humankind in his image, in the image of God he created him; male and female he created them. God blessed them, and God said to them, 'Be fruitful and multiply, and fill the earth and subdue it; and have dominion over the fish of the sea and over the birds of the air and over every living thing that moves upon the earth.' God said, 'See, I have given you every plant yielding seed that is upon the face of all the earth, and every tree with seed in its fruit; you shall have them for food. ...' (Gen 1:27-29)

It is well known that there are two different accounts of creation mixed together in the first three chapters of Genesis and scholars today are adept at disentangling them, but to appreciate how Paul understood these chapters it is necessary to take the account as a unity. The inconsistency of God is soon revealed in a passage we have already referred to:

> And the Lord God commanded the man, saying, 'You may freely eat of every tree
> of the garden; but of the tree of the knowledge of good and evil you shall not eat,
> for in the day that you eat of it you shall die.' (Gen 2:16)

How is it that human beings created in the image of God, given dominion over all things, then have placed upon them a limitation which seems to undermine the promise of their creation? In the example of the child and the parent already described, there is a most curious inevitability at work. For the child to be true to the desire for knowledge encouraged within it by the parents, it has to assert itself against the parents. What is more extraordinary is that there is exactly the same tension in the Genesis story. *For humankind to be true to the gift of dominion given to it by God, there is an inevitability to its assertion of itself against the authority of God.* Is there a way to make sense of this?

Paul continues: 'For the sin, receiving a foothold through the commandment, worked in me every desire' (Rom 7:8). 'The sin' is an active player here as the serpent is personified in Genesis. The first thing that the serpent does to the woman is achieve a foothold through the commandment: 'Did God say, "You shall not eat from any tree in the garden"?' (Gen 3:1). Paul sees the law as essential for the sin to arise: 'For without law sin is dead' (Rom 7:8). It is necessary to face directly an obvious but uncomfortable consequence of this last statement which is consistent with the argument above. In Paul's understanding, God gave the law, knowing that sin would arise, just as a parent prohibits the child, even though this will bring a certain rebellion in the child. But just as the parent prohibits the child because he or she can see a greater good for the child – the development towards adulthood – so it is possible to see a similar purpose in Paul's understanding of God's giving of the law. As a consequence of prohibition the sin inevitably arises, but this only makes sense because God has a greater good in view. We are now approaching Paul's subtle understanding of the nature of sin.

The child lives for a while without needing any prohibition but, with the first prohibition, there is this rebellion. It is worth looking closely at this stage in the development Paul describes: 'For I once lived without the law, but the commandment coming, the sin came to life and I died' (Rom 7:9). The structure of Paul's thought in this sentence is that 'the sin' actually takes the place of the 'I'. The 'I' lived without the law but then dies when the commandment comes and 'the sin' comes to life. To elaborate using Paul's analogy of the development of the child. A separate individual emerges when the child, the 'I', naturally hungry for knowledge, is limited by prohibition and asserts itself over against the parents. It is this separate assertiveness in the individual that Paul calls 'the sin'. At that point the child that exists wholly united in will with the parent dies. 'For the sin, receiving a foothold through the commandment, deceived me and, through it, killed me' (Rom 7:11).

In answering the question, 'Is the law sin?', Paul presents the fall of humankind and of each individual human being as a drama in which the key elements play different roles. While the law is an essential player in that drama it is good and cannot be identified with the sin: 'the law is holy, and the commandment is holy and righteous and good' (Rom 7:1). Similarly the created human being, as represented by the child is also good. Note again the echoes of Genesis where the woman tells God: 'the serpent tricked me, and I ate' (Gen 3:13). There is no reason to doubt that the image of being 'tricked' accurately reflects the meaning in both Paul and Genesis; 'to be tricked' is not necessarily to be culpable. One who is trusting and honest can be tricked. The problem still is: how and why did the sin come about, given that God's creation of both humankind and the law is good? From the analysis so far there is a significant pointer. Both parent and child are pursuing things that are good in an absolute sense. The difference which leads directly to conflict, is that the parent sees more than the child. The parent, while encouraging the pursuit of knowledge by the child, limits that pursuit where the child is in danger. This is because the parent can see a greater good. That good is the future adult life of the child. If the child dies it will be this future of which it will be deprived and all its exploration will have come to nothing.

The assertion of the child

> 13Then did the good become death to me? Certainly not. But the sin, in order that it might be revealed as sin, was working death in me through that which is good, in order that sin, through the commandment, might become overwhelmingly sinful. 14For we know that the law is spiritual; but I, having been sold as a slave under sin, am fleshly. 15For I do not understand what I bring about; for I do not practise what I will, but I do what I hate. 16But if I do what I do not will, I agree that the law is good; 17so now I no longer bring this about but the sin dwelling in me. 18For I know that good does not dwell in me, that is, in my flesh, for to will the good is present to me but to bring about the good is not. 19For I do not do the good which I will, but the evil I do not will, this I practise; 20but if I do what I do not will, I no longer work this but the sin dwelling in me. (Rom 7:13-20, author's translation used here and throughout the section.)

This difficult section can also be understood through developing the metaphor of the parent and child. To recapitulate a little: before a certain age, there is no limitation placed upon the child; it is incapable of doing serious damage to itself. When that certain age comes, the parent prohibits the child from getting into dangerous situations. The child cannot see the reason for the prohibitions and its unlimited will for knowledge meets the will of the parent for its safety and survival. From that point, where previously there was a unity of will between parent and child, there are now two wills. For this picture to make sense it must be noted that the parent stands in the place of God; the will of the parent is totally for the good. The sin, that assertion of individuality over against the parent established in the child, although it arose from the good desire for knowledge, cannot itself do good. It is, of its very nature, hostile to the will of the parent which is totally for good including the good of the child. However, a will for good still struggles in the child even though there is no possibility of good actually dwelling in the child without the child coming into line with the will of the parent.

The further implication of Paul's opening point in this section is that the separation of wills – the assertion which is 'the sin' – was for a purpose. Paul says that the sin was working death in me, *'in order that it might be revealed as sin'*. Taking the analogy of the parent and child once again, the implication is that it is through the self-assertion of the child that it comes to have the knowledge of the destructive nature of this assertion – it's nature as sin.

The bold but necessary inference must now be drawn. God's creation of humankind is good; the desire in humankind for dominion over creation is God given and therefore good. The particular tension present in the Genesis account has a curiously inevitable consequence: God makes a creature in God's image, that is, unlimited, and then places upon it a limitation; the creature, being true to its unlimited nature must resist, but this means opposing the very Creator. It is this opposition which is 'the sin'. But it is also in this opposition that the creature comes to understand the nature of sin. It is this knowledge that Paul now vividly describes.

Paul states that the very fact of acting against one's own will, which recognizes the goodness of the law, indicates that there is truly a separate force dwelling within; the 'I' is not the doer: 'I no longer bring this about but the sin dwelling in me' (Rom 7:1). There is an 'I' that wills the good and recognizes that the law is good but it struggles against the sin dwelling within. The connection with the Genesis account at this point is dramatic and confirms significantly the above assessment of the purpose of the sin. Paul is indicating that at least half of the serpent's prediction of what would happen when Adam and Eve ate from the prohibited tree has come true: '"... your eyes will be opened, ... knowing good and evil"' (Gen 3:5). His description has been an acknowledgement of just this situation with a tragic twist: the knowledge of good and evil has become knowing the good and doing the evil, 'For I do not do the good which I will, but the evil I do not will, this I practise' (Rom 7:19). There is more on this as Paul continues.

The limitation that brings painful knowledge

> 21I find then the law to be that to me, one willing to do good, evil is present; 22for I rejoice in the law of God according to the inner person, 23but I see another law in my members fighting against the law of my reason and taking me captive in the law of sin existing in my members. 24O wretched man that I am, who will deliver me from the body of this death? 25Thanks be to God through Jesus Christ our Lord. So then, I myself with the reason serve the law of God, but with the flesh the law of sin. (Rom 7:21-25, author's translation here and throughout this section)

In this section we need to remember the point made in the last chapter about the way Paul uses the concept of the law with a number of meanings contained within it. Here the first use of the word law is equivalent to one of the common uses in English, namely, something which is observed to occur consistently in certain circumstances. To put what Paul is saying another way: 'I find that when I wish to do good, evil is always present'. There is a similar sense of law drawn from observation when Paul speaks of 'the law of my reason, or mind' and 'the law of my flesh'. Paul is referring to an observable, consistent pattern that he has seen at work in himself, in his reason and in his members. He is here connecting these laws which he has observed in himself – those of reason and of his members – with two objective sources of law, 'the law of God' and 'the law of sin': 'So then, I myself with the reason serve the law of God, but with the flesh the law of sin' (Rom 7:25). Given the parallel use of these two phrases, 'the law of God' and 'the law of sin', it is clear that Paul is not speaking, in either case, of a collection of commandments but, rather, the consistent way in which the 'will' of God and the 'will' of the sin are revealed within him.

These preliminary observations should not be allowed to obscure the primary sense of the passage. There is no common ground between 'the law of God' and 'the law of sin'; they must, by definition, have no points of contact. Yet, from what Paul is saying, they are both operative in the human being. What the logic of these two observations indicates is that Paul considered there to be a radical split in each person: 'For I rejoice in the law of God according to the inner man, but I see another law in my members fighting against the law of my reason and taking me captive in the law of sin existing in my members' (Rom 7:22f). The 'law of God' is operative in the 'inner man' or 'reason' and the 'law of sin' is operative in 'the flesh' or 'members'. Good and evil could not be known more intimately because they operate in conflict in each human being. This is 'the knowledge of good and evil' promised by God as a consequence of that assertion of will against God in taking from the tree. God's word to Adam and Eve has proved true. This is the situation which evokes the human cry of anguish: 'O wretched man that I am! Who will deliver me from the body of this death?' (Rom 7:24). This is the cry of the unlimited creature hemmed in by limitation.

Conclusion

The central section of the letter to the Romans has been examined in the light of the Genesis account of the creation of humankind and the image of the law as protective restraint for childhood. This has made it possible to see some major and long-standing difficulties in interpreting Paul from a completely new perspective. A substantial and coherent reason has been given which makes sense of how Paul could consider the God-given law to be both a check to transgression and, at the same time, crucially involved in the coming into being of sin. What is necessary is to acknowledge the scale of Paul's conception: he is concerned with nothing less than the Genesis picture of humankind being made in God's image and likeness. The radical conclusion that he has faced is that being in God's image has to include the knowledge of good and evil. So Paul has come to view the God-given law as instrumental in bringing about a radical split in each human being leading to an infirmity of purpose: even though what is good is known, what is evil continues to be done. This, in the terms of the Genesis account, is the knowledge of good and evil which comes as a consequence of disobeying God. Further, Paul does not avoid the fact that this disobedience is inevitable. Just as the disobedience of the child towards the supervision of the parent is inevitable, so is the disobedience of humankind towards God.

The focus in this chapter has been on the 'childhood' of humankind, a time of immaturity in which, because, from the perspective of childhood, the future adult life can only be understood in a limited way, guidance is needed. Crucial to the coherence of this picture is the fact that the passage that has been examined in this chapter does not end at this point. Paul goes on to speak of a setting free from the law of sin and death. We will see in Chapter 8 how Paul envisages a transition to adulthood for humankind, a 'coming of age'. Just as the individual child becomes an adult after adolescence, a relatively short period of transition, so it will be for humankind. From that new maturity everything, including the past, is seen from a new perspective.

The theme of this new life will be returned to in Chapter 7 but the need in the next chapter is to further investigate the plight which, for Paul, is the experience of all humankind. Once we have gained further clarity on the nature of the slavery in which Paul believes all humankind is trapped we can then move to his understanding of the liberation that is the heart of his gospel. That clarity is particularly important because, as we shall see in later chapters, it is in the nature of humankind under the power of sin that there is a dulling of perception which includes a blindness to the state of enslavement and the need for liberation. Only in the light of the transformation that Paul claims to be experiencing is the need for liberation exposed.

Chapter 6

Sin and Flesh

Paul's view of the human plight – trapped in a struggle between good and evil – is not the end of the story. Romans 8 begins with a confident affirmation that the struggle is over. 'I have been set free.' In order to be clear about the nature of this affirmation, this liberation, we still have further work to do on the nature of the plight, in particular, what Paul means by 'the flesh'.

This is especially the case because it can seem that Paul sees the flesh as a force for evil. This is a misinterpretation but one that has had a lasting impact with Paul's words providing grounds for the denigration of the body and physical existence that has recurred throughout the Christian era. To get an alternative view it is necessary to look with more care than is usually done at precisely how Paul writes about the flesh and its connection with sin.

The first half of the chapter is concerned with how the flesh is related to three key ideas: individuality, selfish assertion and mortality. Paul has a subtle understanding of what happens when an individual is identified with the flesh understood as their separate physical existence. The second part of the chapter involves giving some detailed attention to two important texts from Romans both of which are concerned with the nature of condemnation and liberation. By carefully tackling two issues of translation in 5:18f, and by combining what emerges with the subtle understanding of flesh discovered in the first half of the chapter, we will be in a position to understand what Paul is saying at the climax of the Romans 7 text examined in the last chapter: 'There is now no condemnation for those who are in Christ Jesus. … You have been set free. … God has condemned sin in the flesh …' (Rom 8:1-4). What all our work to this point will enable us to see with clarity for the first time is that the state of being trapped in a struggle between good and evil which Paul is expressing in Romans 7:7-25 is precisely the 'condemnation' spoken of at the beginning of Romans 8. The selfishness that is the consequence of being 'identified with the flesh' is precisely the 'plight' of humankind. The limited perception that inevitably arises from a self-centred point of view makes it impossible to even see, yet alone to live, the liberated and completely unselfish life of the Spirit.

Flesh

The flesh and individuality

The climax of the creation account in Genesis is the creation of woman:

> Then the man said, 'This at last is bone of my bones and flesh of my flesh ...'
> (Gen 2:23)

It is through the gift of a creature of the same flesh that Adam receives the companionship that comes through diversity:

> Then the Lord God said, 'It is not good that the man should be alone; I will make him a helper as his partner.' (Gen 2:18)

Yet the sameness of their flesh makes possible a unity:

> Therefore a man leaves his father and his mother and clings to his wife, and they become one flesh. (Gen 2:24)

This combination of real unity and real diversity in flesh is vividly evoked:

> And the man and his wife were both naked, and were not ashamed. (Gen 2:25)

Immediately at this point in the Genesis account of creation the serpent appears, powerfully connecting the creation of separate fleshly identity with the entry of sin. The consequence of believing the serpent and disobeying God is that the God-given unity and diversity in the flesh gives way to division and isolation:

> Then the eyes of both were opened, and they knew that they were naked; and they sewed fig leaves together and made loincloths for themselves. They heard the sound of the Lord God walking in the garden at the time of the evening breeze, and the man and his wife hid themselves from the presence of the Lord God among the trees of the garden. (Gen 3:7f)

This separation of man from woman and both from God is driven home in the description of the human fear and unrepentance when faced by God with this disobedience; as was noted in Chapter 5, the man blames the woman and by implication God who gave the woman; the woman blames the serpent (Gen 3:11-13).

Flesh, law, sin, death: these ideas are closely linked together in the thought of Paul. It is important to see how they are also closely linked together in the Genesis story of humankind and the coming of sin. In the Genesis account, there is nothing negative about God's creation of individual difference – 'flesh of my flesh' has a thoroughly positive meaning. But it is followed immediately by the coming of the sin ('the serpent'), which was described in Chapter 5 as the assertion against God. As has been proposed, the consequence of this assertion against God's will is the knowledge of good and evil. A further consequence is that death enters the picture; in the terms of Romans 7, the 'I' dies and 'the sin' comes to life. Paul is working in a creative and subtle way with the key elements of the Genesis story. How he understands the place of death in this story needs our attention but it is first necessary to focus still more sharply on his understanding of 'flesh'.

The flesh and selfish assertion

> For what the flesh desires is opposed to the Spirit, and what the Spirit desires is opposed to the flesh; for these are opposed to each other, to prevent you from doing what you want. ... Now the works of the flesh are obvious: fornication, impurity, licentiousness, idolatry, sorcery, enmities, strife, jealousy, anger, quarrels, dissensions, factions, envy, drunkenness, carousing, and things like these. I am warning you, as I warned you before: those who do such things will not inherit the kingdom of God. (Gal 5:17,19-21)

It is not difficult to establish that 'the flesh', in Paul's understanding, is set against the Spirit.

> By contrast, the fruit of the Spirit is love, joy, peace, patience, kindness, generosity, faithfulness, gentleness, and self-control. (Gal 5:22f)

The Spirit is shorthand for the Spirit of God and one central manifestation of its work is the power of God that works in and through the individual. Given this understanding of the Spirit, 'the flesh' can be understood as directly opposed to the Spirit of God, that is, as the moving force in each individual of any striving against God. The following verse from the letter to the Romans is emphatic:

> [T]he mind that is set on the flesh is hostile to God; it does not submit to God's law – indeed it cannot, and those who are in the flesh cannot please God. (Rom 8:7f)

Wherever there is friction between people, that is clear evidence that people are being motivated by 'the flesh'. Paul says to the Corinthians that anyone being jealous towards or striving against another person, let alone striving against God, must, by definition, be living 'in the flesh':

> And so, brothers and sisters, I could not speak to you as spiritual people, but rather as people of the flesh, as infants in Christ. I fed you with milk, not solid food, for you were not ready for solid food. Even now you are still not ready, for you are still of the flesh. For as long as there is jealousy and quarreling among you, are you not of the flesh, and behaving according to human inclinations? For when one says, 'I belong to Paul', and another, 'I belong to Apollos', are you not merely human? (1 Cor 3:1-4)

For Paul, the flesh, the focus of our individual difference, our 'individuality', is also the locus of selfish assertion against others and against God.

The flesh and mortality

There is an important point to be made about the relationship between Paul's use of the words 'flesh' and 'body'. Paul does not always use the word 'flesh' with negative connotations. Notably he uses the phrase, 'according to the flesh' to designate a line of descent:

> ... the gospel concerning [God's] Son, who was descended from David according to the flesh ... (Rom 1:3)

In a similarly unloaded way, Paul can be found to speak of 'in the flesh' with the same meaning as 'in the body':

> For even when we were come into Macedonia, our flesh had no relief, but we were afflicted on every side ... (2 Cor 7:5, RV)

In one passage of the letter to the Philippians, Paul moves easily from speaking of life 'in my body' to life 'in the flesh' with no change of meaning:

> ... Christ will be exalted now as always in my body, whether by life or by death. ... If I am to live in the flesh, that means fruitful labour for me. ... [T]o remain in the flesh is more necessary for you. (Phil 1:20, 22, 24)

Similarly Paul, on one clear occasion, uses the word 'body' with the same negative sense that he usually reserves for the word, 'flesh':

> ... [F]or if you live according to the flesh, you will die; but if by the Spirit you put to death the deeds of the body, you will live. (Rom 8:13)

As can be seen from even a superficial reading of Paul, he generally uses the word 'flesh' to indicate something morally destructive and almost always uses the word 'body' in a morally neutral sense. However, because Paul occasionally uses the words 'flesh' and 'body' interchangeably, it allows us to get a clear picture of a vital aspect of his understanding of 'the flesh': the precise way in which it is connected with death.

'The flesh', like 'the body', is mortal:

> For while we live, we are always being given up to death for Jesus' sake, so that the life of Jesus may be made visible in our mortal flesh. (2 Cor 4:11)

When Paul describes the flesh as mortal this is not a morally loaded statement; Paul uses the parallel phrase, 'visible in our bodies', immediately before the above verse, indicating that by 'mortal flesh' he simply means 'body'. But it is this connection of the flesh with death that leads to the characteristic sharpness of Paul's thinking revealed in the next passage (the traditional language of the Authorized Version is helpful in order to see the important final point of this section):

> Now this I say, brethren, that flesh and blood cannot inherit the kingdom of God; neither doth corruption inherit incorruption. ... For this corruptible must put on incorruption, and this mortal must put on immortality. So when this corruptible shall have put on incorruption, and this mortal shall have put on immortality,

> then shall be brought to pass the saying that is written, Death is swallowed up in
> victory. (1 Cor 15:50, 53f, AV)

In Paul's understanding, flesh and blood logically *cannot* inherit the kingdom of
God, because what is mortal and corruptible cannot inherit what is immortal and
incorruptible and flesh and blood is always mortal and corruptible.

It is the understanding of the mortality and corruptibility of the flesh that underlies
Paul speaking of 'the infirmity of the flesh':

> Ye know how through infirmity of the flesh I preached the gospel unto you at the
> first. (Gal 4:13, AV)

Here Paul is speaking of a 'bodily ailment' (RSV) or 'physical infirmity' (NRSV)
which led to him visiting the community in Galatia. What is at first sight surprising
but illuminating for understanding Paul is that he uses this very same phrase, 'the
infirmity of the flesh', to describe the limitation in understanding of those to whom
he is writing:

> I speak after the manner of men because of the infirmity of your flesh ... (Rom
> 6:19, AV)

This indicates the tight connection in Paul's thought between the corruptibility of
the body and the corruptibility of human understanding: just as 'flesh and blood' is
always mortal and corruptible (that is its nature), so is human understanding that is
'according to the flesh'.

Individuality, selfish assertion and mortality

There is no doubt that Paul believed that all are sinners; we have seen this already
(pp. 7-9) and he states it clearly:

> For there is no distinction; since all have sinned and fall short of the glory of God
> ... (Rom 3:22f)

The way that the three aspects of Paul's understanding of 'the flesh' – 'individuality,
selfish assertion and mortality, – are bound up with this universal state of sin in
Paul's thinking needs careful teasing out.

We have seen that, for Paul, 'the flesh' is not automatically morally negative. Yet
he does speak of 'the flesh', regularly, and without qualification, as a negative force.
Two phrases from Romans 8 can help us understand why. In this section Paul speaks
of how people live 'according to the flesh' (Rom 8:5) and 'set their minds on the
things of the flesh' (Rom 8:5-7) and contrasts this with what it is to live 'according to
the Spirit' and 'to set the mind on the Spirit'. Given the conclusions from the sections
above, 'to set the mind on the flesh' is to set the mind on 'our individual difference,
our "individuality"', 'the locus of selfish assertion against others and against God'.
The phrases in English, 'according to the flesh' or 'to set the mind on the flesh' do not

capture the force of what Paul is saying at this point. To make sense of Paul's many statements on the relationship of individuals to 'the flesh', it is necessary to see that, in the state Paul is describing, a person is actually identified with his or her separate fleshly existence. Existence is falsely identified with the assertive striving of the flesh apparently now separate from God. More than that, the assertive striving of the flesh is, for Paul, the source of all striving against God, so that this identification with the flesh is a way of speaking of the fundamental state of sin. This is a different way of expressing what was seen in Romans 7. Instead of the 'I' in line with God being at the heart of human identity, the 'I' has identified itself with the individual, separate flesh, and life is seen from the perspective of its needs.

A further step can be made: because 'flesh' is 'mortal and corruptible' so is 'the mind that is set on the flesh'; human understanding that is 'according to the flesh' or 'based on the flesh' is prone to infirmity as the flesh is prone to infirmity. It is important to remember the observation of the last chapter that what is being described here is a way of being that, Paul says, is not usually seen. This is how existence is and the invisibility of the fact that it is 'wrong', in the sense that it is not human existence as willed by God, is a central part of the 'infirmity' of human understanding based on the flesh. Paul is not describing a conventional notion of selfishness where people make their decisions based upon their 'fleshly' desires. Self-centred decision making is an inevitable part of what Paul is describing but its motivation, according to Paul, is much more deeply rooted. People are experientially identified with their mortal fleshly individuality in such a way that conceiving of a fundamentally different way of experiencing human existence is barely possible.

It is important to remember that, in Paul's understanding, all have made this identification. It is precisely because all have identified their existence with the individual mortal flesh that 'all have sinned and fall short of the glory of God'. There is a completely closed circle in which sin, flesh and death operate. However great the striving to be free, that struggle is always doomed to failure because of the 'infirm' or 'corruptible' nature of human understanding – 'infirm' or 'corruptible' as a consequence of this identification with the mortal flesh which is, in its nature, 'infirm' or 'corruptible'.

From this point, it is possible to see why Paul argues that the law, even the law of Moses – 'the embodiment of knowledge and truth' (Rom 2:20) – cannot deal with sin. It can, as we have seen, provide a restraint – this is its role as a childminder (pp. 81-84) – and it gives 'knowledge of sin' (Rom 3:20) but it is not able to bring sin to an end. So that even among those seeking to fulfil God's law, just as Peter and Paul had been before they came to faith, there is always a corruption or infirmity of purpose in living out that law, this because the flesh with which the individual identity is now falsely bound up is mortal and corruptible.

Flesh: summary sentence and discussion

All human individuals have identified their existence with the flesh, with the body, the locus of individuality, and because the flesh is mortal and always subject to infirmity and corruption, then the mind set on the flesh is similarly subject to infirmity and corruption, a central fact of which is the inability to perceive the wrongness of this state.

In his commentary on Romans, Ziesler provides a helpful set of observations relevant to Paul's use of *sarx* (flesh). Having acknowledged that Paul can use it in a neutral way of 'human descent' and 'the physical stuff of which we are made' (*Romans*, 60f), he goes into greater depth on Paul's negative use, noting first that, 'in its negative sense "flesh" (*sarx*) is not particularly and certainly not exclusively physical. "The works of the flesh" in Galatians 5:19-21 include physical sins, but also religious and above all social sins.' This is supportive of the main text where it was argued that when Paul talks of living 'according to the flesh' he is indicating a life rooted in individual selfishness which inevitably leads to social sins. *Sarx* can be used by Paul to describe simple 'immorality' (*Pauline Christianity*, 78) or 'libertinism, of doing what pleases us, because in the satisfaction of our desires and in our self-interest we find the centre and sufficiency of our life' (78f).

Ziesler notes how (*Romans*, 61)

> In crucial passages, especially Rom 8 and Gal 5, being in the flesh, or living according to the flesh, is bad and hostile to God, while being in the Spirit, or living according to the Spirit, is good and means commitment and obedience to God. The opposition is not between physical and non-physical, but between life centered in something other than God, and life centered in God.

He detects a wide range of meaning in the word as used by Paul and a still wider range of use in Paul's contemporary context. The interpretation that Ziesler favours reflects the weakness of an approach which involves finding a definition that embraces as much as possible of that wide range of meanings. What he comes up with is broad but consequently bland and imprecise: as noted in the previous paragraph, he identifies living 'according to the flesh' as 'living for something other than God' (*Romans*, 176). Having helpfully clarified that 'the *sarx*-Spirit dualism in Paul is not a body-soul dualism', he presents his alternative view (*Pauline Christianity*, 79):

> [It is] a 'life under God;' – 'life under anything else' dualism. To live by the Spirit is to live by God, and to live by the *sarx* is to live by what is not God, whether in itself it is good (like the Law) or bad (like self-gratification).

While it is obviously true that living by 'what is not God' contains life 'according to the flesh' much greater precision on Paul's meaning can be obtained, as the main text has shown, from focusing carefully on how the different elements of Paul's theology fit coherently together. Flesh has a particular place in Paul's view of the human plight and without getting clear about this, Ziesler's understanding of both plight and solution is severely limited.

Particularly unhelpful is that, owing to the broadness of his definition, Ziesler is able to also identify *sarx* as a demonic power (78):

> [*Sarx*] is not merely an error, but a demonic enslaving power. It is anything other than God in Christ in which we put our final trust.

Ziesler is concerned to make clear that, according to Paul, living with 'the mind set on the flesh' is not something from which we have the power to liberate ourselves. An alternative power is needed. This inability of humankind to effect its own escape from the plight was emphasized in the main text. But the reason for this is not that humanity is trapped by 'flesh' conceived of as a demonic power but for the significantly more subtle reason that individuals are trapped in a false notion about the nature of their existence, in particular, its rootedness in the individual identity which is powerfully expressed in fleshly difference, a belief which is blind to the radically different understanding which we will investigate when we look in more detail at life in the Spirit.

Sanders also tends to present Paul's understanding of flesh as an enemy power (35f/43):

> Paul sometimes uses [the flesh] to mean 'the physical body', but in [Romans 5-7] it often refers to the state of humanity when it opposes God. Thus, strikingly, Romans 7:5f.: 'while we were living in the Flesh … But now we are discharged from the law … so that we serve not under the old written code but in the new life of the Spirit.' The 'we' refers to Paul and other Christians. They are no longer 'in the Flesh', though they are still in their skins with their body tissue intact. As Paul puts it in Romans 8:9, 'You are not in the Flesh, you are in the Spirit', and the contrast of Flesh and Spirit continues (8:9-13). My guess is that we see here the explanation of why Paul uses 'Flesh' to mean 'humanity in the state of opposition to God': it is simply the word which is opposite 'Spirit', which in turn denotes the divine power. This is, at any rate, the best way to decide when to capitalize Flesh, so that it points not to humanity as physical, but to humanity under an enemy power. It is the latter when there is a clear contrast between it and the Spirit of God. Then flesh becomes Flesh.

As we have seen in earlier sections (pp. 53, 76-80), Sanders gives up on trying to discover coherence or consistency in Paul's description of the human plight. After much detailed analysis, Sanders is convinced of 'the unsystematic character of Paul's thought on the law' (*PLJP*, 145). Given how other elements of Paul's thought on the human plight – sin, flesh, death – are directly bound up with Paul's understanding of the law, and, on the surface, present much less possibility of discovering coherent and consistent meanings, it is perhaps not surprising that Sanders does not investigate in any detail Paul's use of 'flesh'. In contrast to his careful analysis of Paul at other points, on this issue as we see above, Sanders is happy to 'guess' that Paul simply uses 'Flesh' as 'the word which is opposite "Spirit"'.

Unlike Ziesler and Sanders, Dunn is clear that 'flesh' is not helpfully regarded as an enslaving power (*Romans*, 364):

> *Sarx*, however, should not be characterized simply as a "power" like sin, death or even law …, since in contrast to these three, Paul never says *hupo sarka* [under the flesh] …

He defines 'the flesh' as (*Galatians*, 287):

> the human condition in its belongingness to this world – that is, the weakness of the human being in contrast to the power of the divine, the dependency of the creature on the satisfaction of bodily appetites, and the tendency of the body to decay and corruption.

Several of his observations are absolutely in line with points made in the main text. He notes that in Chapter 8 of Romans 'flesh' can readily be interchanged with 'body' qualified by a negative adjective or phrase (*Romans*, 301):

> With chap. 8 sin and law quickly fade into the background in turn, and the role of chief negative factor is taken by flesh, with "body," qualified by a negative adjective or phrase ("body of sin," "mortal body," "body of death," "dead body," "deeds of the body") providing a near synonym.

Dunn also highlights the links we have seen between mortality and the infirmity of both body and spirit (*Romans*, 273):

> As in the broader sweep of Jewish thought also, there is no suggestion of a distinction between "spiritual" and "physical" death: human weakness (5:6), the corruptibility of the flesh…, and death are all of a piece in that they characterize the whole sweep of creaturely alienation from the Creator …

The significance for Paul of the link between the corruptibility of the flesh and both spiritual and physical weakness is pursued further in a section where Dunn observes the vital point made in the main text that integral to this state is a blindness not only to the truth of God but to the nature of 'creatureliness'. Commenting on Paul's words in 6:19, 'I speak in human terms on account of the weakness of your flesh', he says (*Romans*, 345):

> "The weakness of the flesh" characterizes Paul's understanding of the human condition: man as "flesh" is by definition "weak," mortal, corruptible, subject to his all too human desires, blind to the truth of God and of his own creatureliness, etc. A clear disjunction should not be made between moral defect and the inadequacy of human perception; in Paul's use of *sarx* the two senses run into each other ...

Despite these very important points of connection in his interpretation of Paul, Dunn does not uncover the radical identification of humankind with 'the flesh' that has been presented in the main text. This extended extract of his interpretation of Paul's use of 'flesh' in Galatians 5:13 has many telling observations including the fact that by 'flesh' Paul is not referring to an 'innate sinfulness' in the human condition but a kind of 'egocentrism' even as Paul is also saying that this human condition cannot be escaped. But Dunn does not spot that the source of this 'egocentrism' in Paul's understanding is the precise and crucial element of identification with individual physical existence (*Galatians*, 287):

> By 'flesh', as usual, Paul means the human condition in its belongingness to this world – that is, the weakness of the human being in contrast to the power of the divine, the dependency of the creature on the satisfaction of bodily appetites, and tendency of the physical body to decay and corruption. Translations like 'lower/ unspiritual nature' (NEB/REB) lose the wholeness of the concept, and 'sinful nature' (NIV ...) implies an innate sinfulness of the human condition rather than a propensity towards what is sinful or weakness before the power of sin (Rom vii.14-25); 'flesh' needs to be retained as an important theological concept … Paul did not think that this human condition can be escaped (ii.20; iv.14). His fear was rather that life would be lived solely on that level, that satisfaction of bodily appetites (self-indulgence in all its forms) would become the chief factor in living, that result in a casting off of all restraint. It is a sad commentary on the

human condition that what is human weakness regularly becomes the dominant factor in determining life-style. That 'egocentrism' ... is in view is also indicated by the antithetical 'serve one another'. The continuity of his thought is confirmed when we recall that Paul also saw his fellow Jewish opponents as also putting too much on the stress on the flesh ...: too much dependence on a priority of the flesh either way (ethnic identity, or self-indulgence) were dangers equally to be avoided. ...

In this subtle presentation of Paul's view of the 'flesh' Dunn speaks of individuals demonstrating in their lives a 'dependency on the satisfaction of bodily appetites' or a 'belongingness to this world' or 'a propensity towards what is sinful' or 'weakness before the power of sin' . All of these observations are helpful and perceptive expressions of the *symptoms* of humankind 'in the flesh' but they do not capture the way Paul is pointing to identification with individual physical existence as a more fundamental root *cause* of all these outward signs and inward struggles. What Dunn identifies here are all elements of the human condition that are recognized sources of struggle whereas what the main text argues is that what Dunn describes in an earlier quotation above as the 'blindness to the truth of God and his own creatureliness' is the identification of individuals with their separate physical existence. Paul is saying that, in the liberation that he claims is taking effect, this fundamental 'sin' is what is being exposed. The closest Dunn comes to seeing the point made in the main text is in this description of 'focusing on' or 'clinging to' the flesh (*Theology*, 72):

> For Paul, ... the negative factor was not simply bodily existence itself, but the ephemeral character of human existence as existence in desiring, decaying flesh which, as it is focused on and clung to, subverts that existence as existence before and for God.

Condemned to mortality; set free to do right

In the first few verses of Romans 8 Paul is clearly speaking of the nature and effectiveness of God's solution to the plight of humankind. Just as these verses are central to the letter to the Romans they are central to his thought and in the light of all that we have explored in both parts of the book so far can now be fundamentally reappraised and significant steps made in coming to a clear and sharp meaning. For, of course, Paul is not just speaking of the closed circle of sin, flesh and death but of how that circle has been broken.

The rest of the book will explore in more detail what this breaking of the closed circle has brought about and how this has happened. The purpose of the rest of this chapter is to get clear about what the meaning of 'condemnation' when Paul says that 'there is now no condemnation for those who are in Christ Jesus' (8:1). While, once again, the task in examining details of translation is akin to picking away at a knot, the matters under consideration here are central to Paul's thought and the conclusion that emerges at the end of this chapter is of real significance, for it is only through gaining new clarity about the 'plight' of humankind that the full impact of what Paul means by liberation can be realized.

Right action

In order to gain a precise sense of what Paul is saying in Romans 8:1-4, it is necessary to turn to an earlier section of the letter. In Romans 5:16-18, – not an easy passage – Paul is again contrasting Adam and Jesus Christ:

> And the free gift is not like the effect of the one man's sin. For the judgement following one trespass brought *condemnation*, but the free gift following many trespasses brings *justification*. … Therefore just as one man's trespass led to *condemnation* for all, so one man's *act of righteousness* leads to *justification* and life for all. (Rom 5:16, 18)

To get clear about Paul's meaning here it is necessary to spend some time on the translation of three Greek words. Two occur both here and in Romans 8:1-4: *katakrima*, translated as 'condemnation' above and *dikaiōma*, used twice above, first translated 'justification' and then 'act of righteousness'. The third word is *dikaiōsis* which, confusingly, is also translated 'justification' in the NRSV above and only occurs one other time in Paul:

> … [Jesus] was raised for our justification. (Rom 4:25)

This particular word is not especially problematical. It can be rendered 'the act of pronouncing righteous, justification, acquital' (BAGD). Our work in Chapter 1 argued that this 'pronouncing righteous' is well interpreted as 'absolution', a real 'setting free from sin into a state of righteousness'. Balancing the 'condemnation for all' that follows Adam's trespass, 'absolution and life for all' follow from 'one man's act of righteousness'.

Dikaiōma is difficult to render into English. It is a word which, in the NRSV and other versions, receives significantly different translations on the five occasions when Paul uses it: decree (1:32); requirement (2:26); justification (5:16); act of righteousness (5:18); just requirement (8:4). The -*ōma* ending tends to denote the 'outward expression' of something and this simple point is helpful with *dikaiōma*, giving the clumsy but accurate sense of an 'outward expression of righteousness'. The first two and the last of the NRSV translations above, define this 'outward expression of righteousness' as an element of the law: decree, requirement and just requirement. The two translations in Romans 5 present the 'outward expression of righteousness' as 'right actions' with the first of these referring to the specific 'right action' of God that is 'justification' or, as proposed, 'absolution', and the second referring to Jesus' 'act of righteousness' in accepting death. This range of translations needs looking at in more detail to see how, in fact, Paul's use of this word reveals a consistent meaning running through them all. The careful interpretation of this point of detail has major consequences for seeing the coherence in Paul's theology.

The first use speaks of God's *dikaiōma* (1:32):

> They ['those who by their wickedness suppress the truth'] know God's *decree*, that those who practise such things deserve to die ...

The second use in Romans (2:26) combines it with the law:

> So, if those who are uncircumcised keep the *requirements* of the law, will not their uncircumcision be regarded as circumcision?

These first two can be used to support the view that the outward righteous expression that *dikaiōma* refers to is some element or form of the law. This simple definition is not sustainable in the next use (5:16):

> For the judgment following one trespass brought condemnation, but the free gift following many trespasses brings *justification*.

The phrase that ends with *dikaiōma* is clearly meant to parallel the phrase that ends with 'condemnation' and the translation reflects that. 'Condemnation' and 'justification' both serve as dramatic consequences, of 'judgement following one trespass' on the one side and 'the free gift following many trespasses' on the other. This needs further comment which will be made after examining the fourth use only two verses later (5:18):

> Therefore just as one man's trespass led to condemnation for all, so one man's *act of righteousness* leads to justification and life for all.

Note that *dikaiōma* in Romans 5:16-18 is a further example of a text where a single Greek word used twice in a short but important section is commonly given different translations for each use: in verse 16, the NRSV renders it 'justification'; in verse 18, an 'act of righteousness'. Yet with just a slight change this latter translation can be used in both places and can be seen to make very clear sense of what Paul is saying. The slight but significant change is to replace 'act of righteousness', which can only refer to a single act, with 'right action' which can also refer to a continuous state. This gives us a consistent translation for the uses in 5:16 and 5:18 bringing a sharp focus to Paul's meaning but flexible enough to embrace both a continuous state for the first phrase – '... the free gift following many trespasses brings *right action* ...' – and a single act for the second – '... one man's *right action* leads to justification and life for all':

> And the free gift is not like the effect of the one man's sin. For the judgement following one trespass brought condemnation, but the free gift following many trespasses brings *right action*. ... Therefore just as one man's trespass led to *condemnation* for all, so one man's *right action* leads to justification (*absolution*) and life for all. (Rom 5:16, 18, adapted NRSV)

It can be seen how 'right action' as the 'outward expression' of righteousness makes good and consistent sense in this passage. Further support for this interpretation comes when we return to the two early uses in Romans quoted above which speak of the wicked who 'know God's *decree*' and the uncircumcised who keep 'the *requirements* of the law'. God's 'decree' and the 'requirements' of the law are not as appropriate and obvious as they seem at first. Both come in the middle of the long section of Romans we have already referred to (pp. 65-6 and pp. 76-80) where Paul is arguing that there are Gentiles who, by definition, do not know the law, but who, nevertheless, act righteously according to the law. 'They know God's decree' is misleading. What 'they' know, and Paul has in view here Jews before Moses and the Torah as well as Gentiles, is what Paul has spoken of earlier as God's 'eternal power and divine nature … understood and seen through the things he has made' (Rom 1:20). It is this that can be appropriately described as knowledge of God's 'right action' – how God's way of acting rightly can be seen in the created world. Similarly, in the second use in Romans, the 'uncircumcised' do not know and therefore are not in a position to keep 'the requirements of the law' (2:26). But Paul has been saying of those Gentiles 'who do not have the law' but 'do instinctively what the law requires' that they show that 'what the law requires is written on their hearts' (Rom 2:14f). Without knowing the Torah, they know the 'right actions' God requires and that the law also points to.

Having identified the translation 'right action' for *dikaiōma*, we can see the parallel intended by Paul's Greek in Romans 5:16-18. 'The free gift' that is the 'right action' of the one man is 'absolution (or justification) and life for all'. That life being spoken of here is the life of 'right action' or 'acting rightly' that flows from the absolution, the liberation from sin, that is the effect of the 'free gift of the one man'. In the first chapter on 'doing what is right' it was argued that 'righteousness' (*dikaiōsunē*) carries the sense of 'a state/manner of existing which subsists in a way of doing what is right'. The connection is simple and obvious: one who has come to 'righteousness' (*dikaiōsunē*) through being 'righteoused' (*dikaioō*) does 'right action' (*dikaiōma)*.

As well as confirming the use of 'right action' in the Romans 5 passage, the clarity that emerges from this consistent interpretation of *dikaiōma* argues convincingly for the translation of *dikaiōma* as 'right action' in the important statement in Romans 8:1-4:

> … so that the law's *right action* might be fulfilled in us, who walk not according to the flesh but according to the Spirit.

As will see when we focus on this passage shortly, this also is referring not to the 'decree' or 'requirement' of the law but to the 'right action' that the law points to.

Mortality

In the Romans 5 passage the word that parallels *dikaiōma* ('right action') is *katakrima* (usually translated 'condemnation'); it also is used in Romans 8:1-4. It is necessary to now get clear about the translation of *katakrima* before the full significance of the consistent translation of *dikaiōma* in both Romans 5:16, 18 and Romans 8:1-4 can be seen.

In both passages 'condemnation' is associated with 'death'. This can lead to a simple but crucial confusion. The word 'death' in English usually describes a single event; there is a death after which, we say, a person has died. The important observation about Paul's understanding is that he has a conception of death as a continuous state.

This does not seem possible to capture in English in a clear single word; 'a state of deadness' is a phrase which clumsily relays Paul's meaning. This has real significance when it comes to interpreting what Paul means when he says that the consequence of the sin of Adam was 'condemnation' for all.

This preliminary point enables an examination of the parallel that Paul presents:

> For the judgement followed one trespass bringing condemnation, but the free gift followed many trespasses bringing right action. (Rom 5:16, author's translation)

The meaning here is simple but usually obscured in translation; the NRSV will provide a contrast:

> For the judgement following one trespass brought condemnation, but the free gift following many trespasses brings justification. (Rom 5:16, NRSV)

The point is this: Paul is describing the consequences of the single actions of Adam (the 'one trespass') on the one hand and Christ ('the free gift') on the other. In the NRSV translation the impression is given that the consequences are also single events: 'condemnation' and 'justification'. This sense is not dictated by the Greek; both *dikaiōma* and *katakrima* can be used for single actions or continuing states. We have seen how in the second half of the sentence when Paul uses *dikaiōma* his meaning is 'right action'. He is saying that what God has done is to give the way of doing what is right by which 'right action' is now possible. What can be misleading in the other side of the equation is that, because Paul associates this condemnation with death (5:12, 17, 21), an English translation tends to evoke in the reader's mind the absolute end implied by the phrase 'condemned to death'. But this, of course, is not the only sense of condemnation; a person may be 'condemned to imprisonment' and this is a helpful indication of Paul's meaning. What Paul says is that the consequence of death coming into the world through the sin of one man is a continuous state in which death now 'reigns' or has 'dominion':

> ... [B]ecause of the one man's trespass, death exercised dominion through that one ... (Rom 5:17)

Once it is seen that Paul means *dikaiōma* to be understood as the continuing state of right action or right conduct, so it becomes clear that Paul means *katakrima* to be understood as a continuing state – a state of deadness or a condemnation to mortality. *It is crucial to accurate interpretation that Paul's understanding of the consequence of Adam's trespass can be conceived of as a sentence of imprisonment in mortality rather than a once for all destruction.* The significance of this observation will be seen as we turn to the opening of Romans 8.

It is worth noting that the chapters and verses of the Bible were added long after the texts had been written so there is no special significance in the fact that Chapter 8 of the letter to the Romans begins at this point. It can be considered as continuing from the Romans 7 passage examined in Chapter 5 in which Paul speaks in the first person as a representative of all humankind. This is the primary argument for following the early version of the Greek text which reads 'set me free' in verse 2 [RSV, AV, RV, NIV, TEV] as opposed to the alternative which reads 'set you free' [NRSV, NJB, JB, REB, NEB]. This liberation that Paul speaks of is also described by him as the ending of 'condemnation'. We are now in a position to see precisely what he means by this.

In the first part of this chapter, it was argued that Paul understands the fundamental sin as the identification which each human person makes with their separate, mortal, fleshly existence. Just as the flesh is always subject to infirmity so the mind that is set on the flesh is similarly infirm. The point was made that any assertive striving of humankind identified with the flesh is doomed to frustration because of the mortality and infirmity of the flesh. In Romans 7 where, as we have seen, Paul is elaborating upon the story of Adam's sin, Paul speaks of being 'sold into slavery under sin' (7:14), and of the law in his members making him captive (7:23). It is this sense of captivity which Paul has been describing when he says that '... I can will what is right, but I cannot do it'. (7:18) and that makes him cry out: 'Who will rescue me from this body of death?' (7:24). A clear connection can now be made: the judgement following the one trespass of Adam brings 'condemnation'; this condemnation is better understood as a continuous state ('condemned to mortality' rather than 'condemned to death'); this 'condemnation' follows directly upon the trespass. *What makes perfectly coherent sense is that it is precisely the 'slavery' and 'captivity' Paul has been describing in Romans 7:7-25 that are the condemnation.* To put this another way, the consequence of Adam's sin is a condemnation to death but death understood as an identification with the mortal flesh. This identification with what is mortal brings about a continuing infirmity of purpose – 'I can will what is right, but I cannot do it'. In this description the law only intensifies the struggle. To bring this struggle to an end was 'what the law, weakened by the flesh, could not do'. What this means is that when Paul exclaims: 'There is therefore now no condemnation for those who are in Christ Jesus' (Rom 8:1), he is claiming that for those in Christ, the 'slavery' or 'captivity' is over, that is, the struggle to do what is right has come to an end:

> For the law of the Spirit of life in Christ Jesus set me free from the law of sin and death. (Rom 8:2, author's translation)

Paul is not using 'law' here of a written code but with the sense of a 'consistent way or pattern' that we encountered in Chapter 5 (pp. 96-7). Just as in Romans 7:21-23 Paul contrasts 'the law of God' with 'the law of sin' with this sense of two different, consistent 'ways' so here he is speaking of the liberation of 'the way of the Spirit of life in Christ Jesus' that ends the condemnation of 'the way of sin and death'.

The simplicity of what follows is a good indication of the accuracy of the above interpretation. In the last phrase of the Romans 8 passage Paul says that God has acted

> ... in order that the right action of the law might be fulfilled in us, those who do not walk according to the flesh but according to the Spirit. (Rom 8:4; author's translation)

Paul is contrasting living by flesh and living by Spirit according to the ability they give to do what the law says it is right to do. While the law indicates what right action is, it does not give the power to fulfil it; even the most rigorous follower of the law will know the struggle involved. This was the point made in the last section; the best efforts of those in the flesh are doomed to frustration because of the mortality – the infirmity – of the flesh. However, now, through the Spirit, Paul says that to do the right action prescribed by the law is possible. Paul is referring to the new source of motivation that is life in the Spirit. It is a life that, Paul says, has replaced the old, which gave knowledge of sin but could not set free – 'absolve' – from sin.

In Romans 8:1-4, which is the climax of the presentation of Rom 7:7-25, a number of elements of Paul's theology are brought together in a short span. In this important section *dikaiōma* is almost always translated with the sense of 'just requirement' but, with the clarity we have gained on Paul's understanding of the nature of the transformation he believes is taking place, translating *to dikaiōma tou nomou* as 'the law's right action' or 'the right action prescribed by the law' makes excellent sense:

> There is therefore now no *condemnation* for those who are in Christ Jesus. For the law of the Spirit of life in Christ Jesus has set me free from the law of sin and of death. For God has done what the law, weakened by the flesh, could not do: by sending his own Son in the likeness of human flesh, and to deal with sin, he condemned sin in the flesh, so that the law's *right action* might be fulfilled in us, who walk not according to the flesh but according to the Spirit.

Paul is describing two human 'states' or 'conditions'. On the one side is the state of condemnation Paul has been evoking in the distinctive first person account in Romans 7:7-25 – humankind blindly and almost helplessly identified with the 'flesh'; on the other is the 'right action' that the law points to but has not the power to make happen, but which can now be 'fulfilled' in those 'who walk', who conduct their lives, who 'keep aligned', 'not according to the flesh but according to the Spirit'. What Paul says in Romans 5:16-18 is that it is a 'right action' – the one 'right action' of the one man Jesus Christ that now makes possible 'right action' for all.

Condemned to mortality; set free to do right: summary sentence and discussion

In the light of the new life of liberation that Paul says has now come about in which he and others are empowered to act rightly, Paul perceives that, in the radical identification of humankind with 'the flesh' which is infirm and dies, all come under the power of death, experienced, not only as a deeply rooted sense that death comes when the physical body dies, but, as a 'state of deadness', the universal condition of limited perception and understanding described in Romans 7:7-25 which is characterized by an inability to know what is right and act consistently in line with that knowledge.

Mortality, sin and Adam

Dunn confirms one major element of the main text when he comes to the same assessment of death as a continuing state (*Romans*, 431):

> *Nekros* denotes a state of deadness (so also with its most frequent use in Paul: *hoi nekroi* – those who have died and are in the state of death, that is, in a state from which they can be made alive again ...).

In commenting on Romans 5:12-21, Dunn describes Paul as characterizing the age of Adam as the 'universal reign of death' (*Romans*, 281) and states that '[Paul's] theme is original *death* more than original *sin*' (*Romans*, 273). All these ideas – the 'state of deadness', the 'universal reign of death', 'original death' – are helpful phrases to describe that continuous state which the main text suggests is the state of 'condemnation' in which humankind is trapped.

Even though the precise sense of the cause of this state of deadness in the identification of each person with their physical existence is not seen by Dunn, his analysis of the phrase 'to set the mind on the flesh is death' (Romans 8:6) or, as he translates it, 'the flesh's way of thinking is death', indicates clearly the way in which this identification has consequences in both a continuing inability to live above self-centredness and a life that ends in death as the body dies (*Romans*, 442):

> Flesh ends in death; it can look forward to nothing beyond decay and corruption, ending in destruction. ... Those who live at the level of the perishable and corruptible perish with the perishable. Those whose aspiration and striving does not rise above merely human concerns die with the death of that in which they were alone concerned.

Every person has made this identification, a kind of death which is entry into the state of mortality, coming under the sway of death. Commenting on the brief phrase 'and I died' in Rom 7:10, Dunn says (*Romans*, 383):

> This is simply another way of saying ...: I = Adam = humankind = everyman passed under the sway of death, both as expulsion from the presence of God (and the tree of life) and as its inevitable end in physical and moral corruption to death.

Ziesler also explores in some depth the way Paul uses Adam in his theology. He clearly identifies the universal nature of the condemnation. He identifies 'Adam's sin', not as an action in the past which has then been passed on 'by some infection or transmission' but, rather, 'arising from Adam's role as Everyman. He is not just someone who lived long ago;

he is everyone, and his bondage to sin and death is the bondage of everyone (55).' And in speculating on the precise relationship in Paul's mind between sin and death Ziesler uses the helpful phrase 'death-in-life' to describe this universal state (55):

> Sin and death cannot be separated. Paul uses them almost interchangeably, perhaps because one inevitably results in the other, or perhaps because sin means death in relation to God. Indeed we cannot be sure how far he means physical death or 'spiritual' death (as in Rom 8: 10) or both together, so that sin in effect *is* death-in-life, with the awful threat that it will one day be made absolute.

Consistent with what we have seen in earlier chapters, Sanders is dismissive of Paul's observations on the 'plight', or, in other words, the state of condemnation of humankind. In the view of Sanders, Paul's concern and focus is on the fact that liberation has come. The condemnation is simply the alternative human state to being saved and Paul is not thought through or consistent in how he describes this 'plight'. Sanders believes Paul has simply come to the conclusion that 'the world must have been condemned' based on his absolute conviction that 'God sent Christ to save the world' (41/48). This means that Sanders acknowledges in Paul an absolute contrast between life 'in the flesh' and life 'in the Spirit'; because all need the liberation Christ brings, the state of bondage is universal and cannot be escaped by any other means (*PLJP*, 99):

> In the flesh one cannot do the good which the law demands (7:18-22; 8:5a, 7-8); those in the Spirit fulfill the law (8:4). ... Those in the flesh, despite their best efforts, which Paul does not criticize, cannot do what the law requires; those in the Spirit can and do.

But when it comes to analysing Paul's statements in Romans 5 on the universality of sin and its connection with the figure of Adam, Sanders finds Paul reduced to making simple assertions (37/44f):

> Adam, he states, sinned, and this introduced sin and its consequence, death, into the world ... His anthropology (unlike Augustine's) did not include the conception of inherited sin, and thus he had no logical way of 'proving' universal condemnation by appeal to Adam. He simply asserted it ...

Dunn and Ziesler's important point that, when Paul speaks of 'Adam' he can be understood as referring to 'humankind' or 'Everyman' is missing here.

Missing or ignoring the link between Romans 8:1-4 and 5:12-21

The accurate translation of *dikaiōma* and interpretation of *katakrima* depend upon acknowledging and making use of the link between Romans 8:1-4 and 5:12-21. There are two simple related arguments for seeing a link between these two texts. Firstly, *katakrima* is only used three times by Paul (Rom 5:16, 18; 8:1); *dikaiōma* is only used five times (Rom 1:32; 2:26; 5:16, 18; 8:4). As can be seen, apart from two uses of *dikaiōma*, all the uses of these two words occur in these two passages. Secondly, there are close parallels in the subject matter. Both are sharply contrasting the situations before and after Christ. The 'before' situation is characterized by powerlessness in relation to sin and death which is explicitly linked with the figure of Adam in Romans 5 and implicitly so in Romans 8 which continues the argument of Romans 7:7-25 which, as we have seen, draws on the Adam story from Genesis. The 'after' situation is a transformed state of liberation to do right brought about by God through Jesus Christ.

Even in his commentary on Romans, Ziesler makes no link between Romans 5:12-21 and 8:1-4. Sanders makes a passing reference, noting on 8:1 that 'the term "condemnation" seems to refer back to the discussion in 5:16-21' (*PPJ*, 459f). In his comments on Romans 8:1, Dunn picks up more strongly on Paul's earlier use of *katakrima* (*Romans*, 415):

> *Katakrima* likewise recalls the thought to the great climax of 5:12-21 ... It is the black and white contrast between the epochs (Adam and Christ) marked out so decisively in 5:12-21 to which Paul here reverts ...

However, while he notes the broad connection, he does not use the passages together to clarify the definitions of *katakrima* and *dikaiōma* which, as we saw in the main text, dramatically illuminates Paul's meaning.

The translation of *dikaiōma*

The translation of *dikaiōma* in Romans 5:16 and 18 provides a particularly good example of the importance of the approach to translation taken in the main argument as a whole. All our scholars take care over the interrelationships of the words used by Paul in the passage. For both Ziesler and Dunn the fact that *dikaiōma* is used in direct contrast to *katakrima* helps determine its meaning; this fact is also acknowledged and built upon in the main text. But, in contrast to the main text, *katakrima* in 5:16 is interpreted by Ziesler and Dunn with the almost exclusive emphasis on the act or event of condemnation rather than its continuing effect, and, consequently, *dikaiōma* is translated as an act or event. This is Ziesler's interpretation (*Romans*, 149):

> ... the word here is *dikaiōma*, which can have more than one meaning (cf. v. 18), but is here in parallel with *katakrima*, condemnation, and so means God's justification, his free acceptance or acquittal.

Dunn concurs (*Romans*, 281):

> *Dikaiōma* normally means "regulation, requirement" (*BAGD*). But here is chosen obviously as yet another *–ma* word [along with *charisma* (gift) and *katakrima*]. As such it has to be taken as the opposite of "condemnation", so "justification, acquittal".

All three scholars support the view that at this point Paul's thought is primarily being shaped in legalistic categories: God is the judge who can issue condemnation or acquittal. Sanders states this clearly in a comment on v. 18 (*Paul*, 47/56):

> The *dikai-* word group not infrequently has the expected judicial meaning in Paul's letters. Thus, for example, Romans 5: 18: 'Then as one man's trespass led to condemnation for all men, so one man's act of righteousness (*dikaiōma*) leads to rightness (*dikaiōsis*) and life for all men.' Here *dikaiōsis* is often and accurately translated 'acquittal': it is the reverse of condemnation, and the entire sentence is couched in terms of legal guilt or innocence.

It is important to note how when Sanders approves 'acquittal' as the translation for *dikaiōsis* it is because it contrasts easily and directly *katakrima*, understood as carrying the 'once-for-all' sense of 'condemnation'. *Dikaiōsis* does indeed comfortably carry a once-for-all sense; in the main text it was indicated that this word can be well understood as 'liberation' or 'absolution'. What also needs to be seen is the significance of the generally accepted change in the translation of *dikaiōma* from 'justification' in v. 16 to something like 'act of righteousness' in v. 18.

> And the free gift is not like the effect of the one man's sin. For the judgement following one trespass brought *condemnation* (*katakrima*), but the free gift following many trespasses brings *justification* (*dikaiōma*). ... Therefore just as one man's trespass led to *condemnation* (*katakrima*) for all, so one man's *act of righteousness* (*dikaiōma*) leads to *justification* (*dikaiōsis*) and life for all. (Rom 5:16,18, NRSV)

Both Ziesler and Dunn subscribe to this apparently insignificant shift in meaning. Ziesler comments on v. 18 that having rendered *dikaiōma* as 'justification' in v. 16 'it can hardly mean that here' (Ziesler, *Romans*, 151). Dunn also notes no difficulty in offering a different translation so soon after the previous use of the word but offers some useful background information to his translation in v. 18 which is strongly supportive of the argument of the main text (Dunn, *Romans*, 283):

> *Dikaiōma* normally means "regulation", "requirement" ...; but the sense of "righteous act" is attested by Aristotle and the LXX, and that clearly fits best here ...

As was noted in the main text, words with the *-ma* ending tend to carry the meaning of the outward expression of something. 'Regulations' and 'requirements' are a kind of outward expression of 'righteousness' but in every context in which Paul uses *dikaiōma* it can without strain carry a different sense of the outward expression of 'righteousness', that of 'right action', whether that 'right action' is one specific 'right action' of one person or the general 'right action' of many. Dunn's reference quoted above to Aristotle and the Septuagint provides telling support for this translation.

The discussion of the translation of this one word is of relevance to the whole approach to translation taken in the main argument. What is being proposed throughout the work and very clearly in this particular example is not an unrealistically rigid understanding of how language works. The simple argument being made is that it is not acceptable, as Dunn and Ziesler do, to suggest that the one word, *dikaiōma*, is used by Paul with two different meanings within a couple of verses. What is necessary for a precise translation is to find an English word or phrase that can, as far as is possible, replace the Greek word used by Paul, an English word or phrase that has both an equivalent core meaning but also an equivalent *flexibility* to enable its use in the same contexts where it is placed by Paul. This can only be done by systematically seeking a word or phrase that is applicable in the variety of contexts in which Paul uses it. In the case of *dikaiōma*, 'right action' is a simple and easily understandable English translation that, remarkably, accurately replicates both the substantial core meaning and the flexibility in Paul's Greek. It fits readily and comfortably in all the contexts in which Paul uses *dikaiōma*. It can refer to the one 'right action' of the one man, Jesus (5:18) or the consequent continous 'right action' of many that follows from this 'free gift' (5:16). It can refer to the 'right action' that the law requires (8:4) or the 'right action' perceived to flow from an understanding of how God is active in the created order (1:32; 2:26). The context determines precisely what it is referring to without any need for the translation to be altered. Once this work is done rigorously, it may be appropriate for translators to use different English words in order to make a clear and flowing translation but that task must follow after determining the consistent meaning in the word.

Dunn on Romans 8:1-4, liberation and the law

Serious attention was given to Dunn's interpretation of Paul on the law in Chapters 3 and 4. As we consider Dunn's interpretation of Romans 8:1-4 and the place of *dikaiōma tou nomou* in the argument these earlier observations will be recalled. It is of particular importance to consider Dunn's position in some detail because at key points it is closely aligned with the arguments of the main text and yet at others there are sharp and crucial differences.

Dunn notes the intensity of feeling with which Paul expresses the view that 'justification by faith means *liberty*' (*Theology*, 388). And Dunn goes on to make clear that this experience of liberation leads Paul to see his previous life under the law as a kind of slavery (388):

> ... Paul experienced his coming to faith in Christ as one of liberation. The practice of the law, which had previously been his delight, he now regarded as a kind of slavery, the slavery of the spiritually immature ([Gal] 4:1-3).

This echoes strongly the main text and the argument that Paul comes to view his old life under the law in a negative way as part of his new experience of the 'adult life' of faith. In presenting this negative view of the law, Dunn also affirms that the law had a temporary value and contrasts unfavourably with the new direct guidance that faith gives (143f):

> The first point which stands out is Paul's argument in Galatians 3-4 that Israel's special relation under the law was only temporary. ... Israel no longer needed the special protection of the law, no longer needed the law as its guardian angel. It was time once again for an immediacy between the promiser and those for whom the promise had been given (3.6-9, 15-18, 25-29), without the intervention of the law (3.19-24). It was time for the heirs to enter upon their inheritance, to leave behind the slavelike status of the underage child (4.1-7). In contrast, their clinging to the law was a clinging to an underprivileged status.

And there are many occasions when Dunn clarifies the nature of the 'immediacy' he speaks of above including his comments on the meaning of 'the law of the Spirit' in Romans 8:2 where he asks (647):

> And what does this mean in practice for Paul? Paul presumably had in mind a conduct informed and enabled out of a direct and immediate apprehension of the divine will. This is already implied in his earliest letter: "you yourselves are being taught by God to love one another" (1 Thes 4.9).

These powerfully stated points offer strong support for positions established in the argument of the main text. Yet at other points in his argument, including other things he writes on Romans 8:1-4, Dunn presents interpretations of Paul on the law that, put at its most positive, do not easily cohere with the points made above, and therefore introduce an unsteadiness into his argument on the law that destabilizes his presentation of Paul's theology. Arguably, Dunn's overall presentation can be charged with the same weakness with which Sanders targets Paul, that various lines of interpretation are followed through to powerfully stated conclusions which are not then reconciled with each other.

So, while we have noted Dunn's view that Paul sees the law as having a temporary role, at other points he states just as powerfully that, provided that it serves faith, it has a continuing place (641):

> The law for Paul retained its function as a measure of righteousness.

One significant aspect of this view is that Dunn argues forcefully that, in Romans 8:2, 'the law of the Spirit' which liberates and 'the law of sin and death' which enslaves are both referring to the Torah (see p. 71). According to Dunn, by 'the law of the Spirit' Paul means the Torah now correctly understood and lived through faith. In commenting on 'the law of the Spirit' and 'the law of sin and death' in Romans 8:2, it is clear that Dunn himself feels the difficulty in sustaining this point of view (*Romans*, 436):

> Paul tries to squeeze so much into two compact phrases that he runs some risk of confusing his readers. Does he still mean the law here, the law given to Israel? How could the Paul who warned his Galatian converts so passionately against submitting to the slavery of the law (Gal 4:1-11; 5:1-4) speak of the same law as liberating? Yet readers who had time to reflect on the course of the argument would probably soon find themselves driven to the surprising conclusion that Paul must mean the same law in both phrases, the law given to Israel.

This is special pleading. There are very few 'readers who have had time to reflect on the course of the argument' who have come to this 'surprising conclusion'. Dunn continues to note the difficulties of his argument in 8:2 (*Romans*, 436):

> [T]he impression that Paul has caught himself in contradiction is hard to shake off. ... It is the exhilarating sense of being liberated which marks out v. 2 so clearly; ... Paul certainly recalled his conversion to faith in Jesus Messiah as an expression of liberation ... and thought of return to his old lifestyle of obedience to the law as a return to slavery (Gal 4-5). The "Spirit" ... he clearly experienced as a power whose transforming effects marked his own ministry in no uncertain manner ..., in some distinction from the law ... How then could he link the law with the Spirit and describe it as that very same liberating power?

The simple response to Dunn is that Paul did not. As has been argued in some detail (pp. 63-8), Paul is using the word 'law' in a flexible way. 'The law of the Spirit' is not the Torah interpreted through faith or even, as Dunn says in a neat summary phrase for his position, 'the law understood as guidelines for Spirit-directed conduct' (*Theology*, 647). The argument of the main text is that 'the law of the Spirit' is the direct guidance that the Spirit provides in contrast to the indirect guidance of the law. Paul is saying that these are two different sources of motivation, even if there may often be a correspondence in what they require, particularly in moral standards. The Torah served a God-given purpose for a time, to protect and guide the people of Israel until the time of faith came, but, for Paul, that time has now come and a new, more intimate relationship with God has opened up. In the light of that new experience, the old is seen as a kind of slavery, and it is towards those who wish to hold people back as slaves that Paul is at his most fiercely confrontational.

Dunn considers directly the key question that his approach raises, 'how could the law be both the enslaving and liberating power?'. He answers it by referring to Paul's interpretation of a brief section of Jeremiah's description of a 'new covenant' (Jer 31:33):

But this is the covenant that I will make with the house of Israel after those days,
says the Lord: I will put my law within them, and I will write it on their hearts ...

It is helpful to return to Dunn's interpretation of these significant words. Dunn offers what he
knows is not the 'popular' interpretation (644):

> [I]t is important to recall that the hope which Paul saw as ... fulfilled in the Spirit
> was not hope for another law or a different Torah. ... On the contrary, the hope
> was for a means to a more effective keeping of the law. Only a circumcision of
> the heart would enable an adequate keeping of the law (Deut 30.8-10). Contrary
> to popular opinion, the promise of a new covenant in Jeremiah is not of a new
> or different law. The promise is plain: "I will put my law within them, and I will
> write it on their hearts" (Jer 31.33).

This view is taken up in his commentary on Romans 8:2 (*Romans*, 436f):

> The point is that for Paul the power of the new covenant is not so different from
> or discontinuous with the rule of God over Israel exercised through the law; on
> the contrary, the two are in direct continuity ("my law"). Yet they are different,
> since the new covenant is a matter of inner power ("upon their hearts"), not of
> external constraint ..., and consequently it transcends the national and ethnic
> restrictiveness which inevitably focuses so much and depends so much on the
> distinctive identity markers of outward ritual which Paul now found so irksome.

Here we find again this central theme in Dunn's interpretation. When the Torah is interpreted
through faith, those elements which mark out the Jews as a distinctive people recede and
can be dispensed with, particularly the ritual elements of the law which serve as boundary
markers.

Intriguingly and revealingly, the potential confusion in the way in which, in Dunn's
interpretation, Paul speaks of the Torah as both positive ('law of the Spirit') and negative
('law of sin and death') in Romans 8:1-4 arises, according to Dunn, because of an acute
psychological tension between 'continuity and discontinuity with his Jewish heritage' in Paul
himself (*Romans*, 437):

> It is this sense of both continuity and discontinuity with his Jewish heritage to
> which Paul must cling; otherwise his own self-identity would begin to disintegrate.
> But it sets up a sometimes agonizing tension which comes to one of its sharpest
> expressions in this whole section.

This observation at the heart of Dunn's interpretation provides us with a way to identify
clearly the central point of difference between Dunn's view of Paul and the law and that of the
main text. For Dunn the crucial discontinuity between Paul's past and his present attitude to
the law lies in his rejection of those elements of the law that serve as boundary markers. It is
these which provide sinful nature with a toehold from which pride springs up. Without them
the law can serve its universal purpose of bringing about complete dependence upon God,
the life of faith, manifested by Abraham and the true attitude to God for all people – Jew and
Gentile. So when Dunn interprets the climax of Paul's presentation on the law at the beginning
of Romans (3:20), 'for by works of the law shall no flesh be justified before him (Dunn's
translation [*Romans*, 145])', he sums it up like this (*Romans*, 184):

> ... God's justifying does not operate by reference to those requirements of the law
> which mark out Jewish identity ...

In other words, God's transforming power does not operate through those aspects of the law which mark out the people of Israel and, by implication, that power *does* work through other aspects of the law, now identified and clarified as serving the real purpose of the law, to bring about the complete dependence upon God that is the proper understanding of faith. But a little careful attention provides a radically different meaning for this important summary phrase, 'for by works of the law shall no flesh be justified before him'.

As Dunn himself notes, Paul is quoting here from Psalm 143:2, 'for no one living is righteous before you', but deliberately changes 'no one living' to 'no flesh'. Paul's use of 'flesh' at this point is deliberate and suggestive. The first half of the main text of this chapter set out Paul's understanding of 'flesh' as the source of individual, separate existence with which each human being is falsely identified. With that interpretation, the point being made here is that no human being in that false state wholly identified with separate fleshly existence can be liberated. Indeed, it is precisely the sense of separate existence that is the slavery or 'childish' state from which liberation is required. Law is that God-given source of guidance for this limited time of childhood but also the instrument by which humankind as a whole and each individual comes to that direct experience of good and evil which is essential to adult life. So, in sharp contrast to Dunn's interpretation of Paul's need to shore up his own threatened self-identity, the interpretation of 'flesh' in this chapter indicates that *it is precisely a disintegration of Paul's own false self-identity that is at the heart of the change he has been through*. It is hard to imagine a more powerful image of radical discontinuity than what Paul says in Galatians (2:19f):

> For through the law I died to the law, so that I might live to God. I have been
> crucified with Christ; and it is no longer I who live, but it is Christ who lives in
> me.

The law has indeed played a positive part in Paul's understanding – 'through the law' – but even that positive role is explicitly said by Paul to be discontinued – 'through the law I died to the law'.

Dunn seeks to hold together an understanding of the law as both given for a limited time but also having a continuing purpose. Despite his arguments that the law that continues is the law properly understood through faith and modified in the light of that understanding, this is a rocky foundation stone that Dunn's interpretation places at the heart of Paul's theology. The instability of this foundation stone is strikingly evident in the interpretation of statements like that of Romans 8:4 that those 'in Christ' fulfil the law. We have already seen (pp. 74-6) the difficulties Dunn gets into by interpreting 'fulfilling the law' as 'keeping' or 'observing' the law. Dunn has to acknowledge that Paul is clearly stating that the whole law is 'fulfilled' not just an edited version of the law, but, as we were reminded above, Dunn openly acknowledges that the law is reduced in order to be placed at the service of faith. This is what Dunn says on 'the requirement (*dikaiōma*) of the law might be fulfilled (*plērōthē*) in us' in Romans 8:4 (*Romans*, 423):

> In its sense of "requirement" or "claim", he has in mind something more or other
> than the requirements his fellow Jews would normally focus on as part of their
> distinctive self-definition (circumcision, sabbath, food laws, etc. ...). *Plēroō* in
> the sense of "fulfill" a commandment is well enough known ..., but still imprecise
> enough to leave open the question, "Fulfill in what sense?" *Plērōthē* here cannot
> mean "fulfill" in a one-to-one sense, an item by item correlation. It must mean

"fulfill" in a more profound sense – the essential requirement ... which lies behind the individual requirements, the character and purpose which the individual requirements are intended to bring to expression.

This definition of 'fulfil' is absolutely in line with the argument of the main text but it is a nuanced interpretation that easily disappears at other points when Dunn is discussing Paul on the law. For example, note how Dunn interprets Romans 8:4 in his *Theology* (646):

Perhaps most striking of all, the purpose for which God sent his Son is explicitly stated as to bring about the fulfilment of the law's requirement (8.4). For Paul, the objective of God's saving action in Christ was to make possible the keeping of the law!

The final exclamation mark suggests that Dunn is making a significant point here but the subtle interpretation of 'fulfil' above is relegated to a footnote. In order to sustain the view that there is a continuing place for the law in Paul's understanding of faith, Dunn has to adopt a very loose approach to the meaning of 'keeping' or 'observing' the 'whole' law, which changes significantly at different points in his interpretation and obscures the fact that he interprets Paul's statements on the law in widely different if not contradictory ways.

The fundamental disagreement between Dunn on the law and the position of the main text can be focused in the experience at the heart of Paul's message.

1. For Dunn:
    (a) the essential insight of faith is the universality of the life of the Spirit; the life of the Spirit is compatible with living by the law;
    (b) what is exposed as wrong is the law hijacked for limited ethnic identity and pride;
    (c) the life of the Spirit involves a new kind of empowerment to do what the law requires including a clarity about those elements of the law which corrupted its real purpose.

2. In the argument of the main text:
    (a) faith is an experience of liberation, a liberation into Spirit-led right action;
    (b) what is exposed as wrong is the nature of human slavery in a false identification with separate mortal fleshly existence;
    (c) the liberation that the Spirit brings:
        (i) reveals the value of the law for guidance in the past life, life that was a kind of slavery even though it was not perceived of as such;
        (ii) transcends the law in that the law has no purpose for those who live by faith, doing what is right guided and empowered by the Spirit, and, indeed, can become destructive in providing a focus for resisting the new right action of God.

Conclusion

It has been shown that Paul is working with an understanding of the flesh that is informed by the Genesis account of creation. Just as in Genesis the flesh is associated with the creation of individuality, so, in Paul's understanding, the flesh is associated with individual selfish assertiveness. The identification of existence with the flesh leads to an assertion by the individual against God and others. This is the fundamental 'sin'. Because the flesh is mortal and corruptible, an understanding of existence as based upon the individual 'flesh' is always 'infirm' – it is always mortal and corruptible. Humankind, identified with perishable, mortal, fleshly existence, cannot inherit the imperishable kingdom of God. A significant part of that infirmity is that humankind is unable to see what is wrong, to see the nature of the identification with fleshly individuality. This Paul describes as a state of slavery or imprisonment. This is the condemnation which is being exposed and, from which, Paul is claiming, God is bringing liberation.

For humankind trapped in this state, the law is protective, in that it guides people in how to act rightly, but it also has a role in intensifying the sense of sin as humankind consistently tries and fails to do what is right. It is easy to see how the protective function of the law sits easily with it being given by God, but we have also seen in Chapter 5 how the way that the law intensifies the state of sin has a necessary and positive effect in humankind in that it is through this struggle that humankind comes to the knowledge of good and evil which is necessary for maturity, for being the conscious instruments of God, the true image of God in creation.

Romans 8:1-4 is a powerful summary statement in which a number of key elements of Paul's theology come together: the law, the Spirit, liberation, the flesh, sin, death, the sending of the Son, 'in Christ', condemnation, 'right action'. Part Three of the book will be concerned to clarify what Paul is speaking of when he speaks of the Spirit and what it means to be 'in Christ'. Part Four will tackle what Paul means by 'the sending of the Son to deal with sin'. The argument of the book so far has revealed how Paul is concerned with a central fact of human experience which is recognizable today – the struggle to know and do what is right. Paul speaks with a confidence that the struggle is over. Liberation has come. Although only affecting a small group, he claims that the way to know and do what is right is established in humankind. And from this perspective, he describes the previous lot of humankind as a condemnation, an entrapment in a kind of slavery – humankind unable to know clearly what is right and act consistently in line with that knowledge. And it has been argued that Paul has a subtle understanding of the source of that condition as arising from an identification of existence with our physical state. Identified with our individual physical bodies, our understanding is limited in a false understanding of what we are created to be. Our focus in the next part of the book is the fact that Paul does not limit his conception of what is taking place to his own liberation or even to that of the first Christians but that the movement from childhood to adulthood embraces 'all' – the whole of humankind.

PART THREE
From Childhood to Adulthood

Chapter 7

Infants in Christ

The last chapter gave attention to the nature of the plight of humankind and established that it can be understood as an identification with the flesh, with the locus of separate individual existence. Because the flesh is mortal, so the person who identifies themselves with the flesh, lives with the expectation that he or she will die when the flesh dies. This reality shapes and limits their life.

What Paul sets in opposition to the flesh is the Spirit. As we have seen (pp. 20-22) the Spirit is from God but comes to guide and empower individuals and communities, working in them in such a way that God's work can be done through them. In this chapter and the next we will explore in more detail Paul's understanding of the relationship between the Spirit and the individuals and communities to which it comes. Crucial to getting a clear idea of how the Spirit is involved in human transformation is appreciating that Paul's conception of the Spirit is always bound together with a sense of a universal transformation that is to come in the future. Manifestations of the Spirit are signs of this future total transformation. Indeed we will see clearly how Paul consistently describes them as not only 'signs' of this future change but already part of it.

Also essential for an accurate interpretation of Paul's understanding of the Spirit is to see that while there are texts where Spirit is clearly set in opposition to flesh, the most consistent image for the relationship between flesh and Spirit in the new life is that flesh does not come to an end but is covered over by Spirit. This is crucial when we realise how Paul's view of the setting right of what went wrong in the fall is a true reconciliation of Spirit and flesh. In the next three chapters, we will come to see how life in the Spirit according to Paul is a transformed experience of physical life, in other words, life on earth, not a non-physical spiritual future.

This chapter will focus on the way in which the present real experience of transformation for individuals and relatively small groups of people is seen by Paul as an anticipation of what is to come for all. Dramatic as that experience is, it is still a kind of 'infancy'.

The 'alive-making' Spirit

When Paul is speaking of transformation of an individual, he consistently speaks of it as a kind of dying. A person must go through such a death in order to be transformed and enter a new life:

I want to know Christ and the power of his resurrection and the sharing of his
sufferings by becoming like him in his death. (Phil 3:10)

Paul regularly associates this dying with baptism which clearly describes a point of
transition, a point of discontinuity between the old life and the new:

Do you not know that all of us who have been baptized into Christ Jesus were
baptized into his death? Therefore we have been buried with him by baptism into
death, so that, just as Christ was raised from the dead by the glory of the Father,
so we too might walk in newness of life. For if we have been united with him in
a death like his, we will certainly be united with him in a resurrection like his.
(Rom 6:3-5)

Although Paul considers this dying to be a radical change it is clearly not the end
of a person's natural life. So it is important to establish as clearly as we can what
it is that dies, what continues and how that is related to what has gone before. The
image of dying for the transition emphasizes as powerfully as any image could the
discontinuity between the old life and the new but this is not the only image that Paul
uses and we will see now how he manages to retain the sense of radical change in the
context of a continuing existence.

Swallowed up by life; clothed with the Spirit

We will look first at two passages that both work with the same image for the
transformation with which Paul is concerned. In this first passage, Paul is talking of
mortal life, describing it as an 'earthly tent' and relating it to the 'heavenly dwelling'
to come:

Now we know that if the earthly tent we live in is destroyed, we have a building
from God, an eternal house in heaven, not built by human hands. ... For while
we are in this tent, we groan and are burdened, because we do not wish to be
unclothed but to be clothed with our heavenly dwelling, so that what is mortal
may be swallowed up by life. (2 Cor 5:1, 4, NIV)

The main purpose in presenting this passage here is to give an awareness of the shape
of Paul's thought on the relationship between mortality and immortality. The NIV has
been used for several of the quotations in this section because of the consistency of
its translation of the passages under consideration but one aspect of this consistency
is obscured in the above translation: 'to be clothed' in the phrase 'to be clothed with
our heavenly dwelling' should contain an element which other translations render in
various ways to indicate the sense in simple English, 'to put on over the top of' ('to
be further clothed' [NRSV, RSV], 'to be clothed upon' [AV, RV], 'longing to put on
our heavenly home over the present one' [NJB]). It is this sense that Paul emphasizes
in the last phrase, 'so that what is mortal may be swallowed up by life'. The image
is of 'immortal life' being put on over the top of 'mortal life'. Paul says, 'we do not

wish to be unclothed' with the sense that 'we do not wish to lose our mortal life' but rather that the mortal life be further clothed with immortal life.

In this next passage, in which he is elaborating on the theme of the 'resurrection of the dead', Paul uses very similar language:

> For the perishable must clothe itself with the imperishable, and the mortal with immortality. When the perishable has been clothed with the imperishable, and the mortal with immortality, then the saying that is written will come true: 'Death has been swallowed up in victory.' (1 Cor 15:53f, NIV)

In this image of 'clothing over' or 'swallowing up' the old life with the new, there can be seen the continuity between life before and after the 'death' that was referred to above: the new life is 'put on over' the old.

The same image of 'clothing over what is mortal' is used of the Spirit which will now become the focus of the chapter. Attention will be given first to Paul's use of the simple Greek word, *zōopoieō*, which is used to describe the Spirit. This word is made up of two Greek words, 'to make' (*poieō*) and 'alive' (*zōos*), hence it is translated into English as 'to make alive' or 'to give life'. There is no difficulty over the translation of this word and it is used consistently by Paul. He uses it in a straightforward way to describe the working of the Spirit over against the law:

> ... [T]he letter kills, but the Spirit *gives life*. (2 Cor 3:6)

Paul's use of the word in the letter to the Galatians implies the same inability on the part of the law:

> ... [I]f a law had been given which could *make alive*, then righteousness would indeed come through the law. (Gal 3:21)

In an important verse in Romans 8, Paul uses the word in the future tense:

> If the Spirit of him who raised Jesus from the dead dwells in you, he who raised Christ from the dead *will give life* to your mortal bodies also through his Spirit who dwells in you. (Rom 8:11)

Note that in this verse it is God who is the one who 'gives life'. It is the same in this next example which comes in a passage on the faith of Abraham:

> ... God ... *gives life* to the dead and calls into existence the things that do not exist. (Rom 4:17)

What the above texts indicate is the straightforward consistency with which Paul uses this word: on the one hand, the law cannot give life; on the other, God or the Spirit or God through the Spirit give life to what is dead or mortal. It is vital to note that all the references above are speaking of a 'making alive of what was dead' that relates to ordinary existence, not life after the death of the physical body. They provide appropriate examples of the point made earlier that when Paul is speaking of what is 'mortal' or, indeed 'dead', he is referring to 'a state of deadness' that, for Paul, is the lot of humankind alive in the flesh (pp. 111-114).

The image of what is mortal being swallowed up or clothed over with life or the Spirit is not the only image of continuity between the old life and the new life used by Paul. Chapter 15 of the first letter to the Corinthians is concerned with the raising of Christ from the dead and the consequence of this for believers. In two main sections of this chapter Paul is contrasting Adam and Christ and in both sections he uses the word *zōopoieō* as part of the contrast. Paul uses this word in an analogy from plant life:

> What you sow *does not come to life [is not made alive]* unless it dies. And as for what you sow, you do not sow the body that is to be, but a bare seed, perhaps of wheat or of some other grain. But God gives it a body as he has chosen, and to each kind of seed its own body. (1 Cor 15:36-38)

In the passage from which this text comes, Paul manages to indicate both the continuity and the discontinuity between life before and after the transformation: continuity because the transformation which resurrection speaks of arises out of and is subsequent to the life we know; discontinuity because there has to be a death of the life we know before this transformation can come about. The really important use of this word comes as part of the development of Paul's presentation of this issue. This is how his comment on the above analogy continues:

> So it is with the resurrection of the dead. What is sown is perishable, what is raised is imperishable. It is sown in dishonour, it is raised in glory. It is sown in weakness, it is raised in power. It is sown a physical body (*sōma psuchikōn*), it is raised a spiritual body (*sōma pneumatikōn*). If there is a physical body (*sōma psuchikōn*), there is also a spiritual body (*pneumatikōn*). Thus it is written, 'The first man, Adam, became a living being (*psuchen zōsan*)'; the last Adam became a life-giving spirit (*pneuma zōopoioun*). (1 Cor 15:42-45)

The Greek transliterations have been included so that the precise distinctions Paul is making can be seen. Paul is not offering a contrast between life in the spirit (*pneuma*) and life in the body (*sōma*) but between two different kinds of 'bodily' existence: *sōma pneumatikōn* ('[S]piritual body') and *sōma psuchikōn* ('physical' or 'natural body'). The point that Paul leads up to is a contrast between the kind of life in Adam and Christ. The life that was transmitted through Adam is that of the 'physical' or 'natural'; Jesus, in contrast, becomes a Spirit that makes alive. (Whether to capitalize 'spirit' or 'spiritual' is a decision that rests with the translator.)

Just as the climax of the Genesis account of creation is the making of Adam and Eve, through whom 'natural', 'physical' life comes to all, so now Paul speaks of the last Adam bringing a new kind of life to all:

> For since death came by a human being, the resurrection of the dead has also come by a human being; for as all die in Adam, so *all will be made alive* in Christ. (1 Cor 15:21f)

Note again that it is not necessary in order to make sense of what Paul is saying to think of the contrast that he is making as one between a 'physical' and a 'Spiritual' existence. As this chapter and the concluding chapters of the book unfold, further support will be provided for the view that, while Paul considers the change that the Spirit brings to be a radical transformation of the natural life, he carefully presents his understanding, as in the case of the image of the seed and the plant, to indicate that this transformed life arises out of or, perhaps more accurately, contains within it the old.

Clothed over with Christ

We are now well placed to see and understand Paul's use of the image of clothing over the former life with the new life in a passage on baptism:

> You are all sons of God through faith in Christ Jesus [RSV 'in Christ Jesus you are all sons of God'], for all of you who were baptised into Christ have clothed yourselves with Christ. (Gal 3:26f, NIV)

Note once again that the image that Paul is using does not indicate an end to fleshly life but rather its transformation by being enveloped in Christ. While there is a remarkable similarity between Paul's thought in this passage and the previous section there is the revealing difference that the agent of transformation is Christ. Whereas there, the mortal being is swallowed up by life and the individual clothed with the Spirit, here the baptized are clothed with Christ. Just as Paul's statement that 'the last Adam became an "alive-making" Spirit' (1 Cor 15:45) indicates, there does not seem to be any substantial difference for Paul in speaking of the Spirit that 'makes alive' or Christ who 'makes alive'.

So Paul describes the individual's transformation from old life in Adam to the new life in Christ as a dying. Because the identification of existence with the flesh is the reality of life as people experience it then, just as the physical death of the body is feared as the end of existence, so the end of existence identified with the body is described by Paul as going through a kind of dying. Paul also affirms the continuity of the new life with the old when he uses the image of mortal existence being clothed over with the 'alive-making' Spirit or Christ.

In Christ; reversing the fall

The previous two chapters have given attention to the way the thought of Paul is connected with the account of the fall in the book of Genesis. It can be simply noted that the consequences of the wilful disobedience of God by the fleshly individual are reversed in Paul's description of life in the Spirit. When Paul speaks of having the 'mind of the Spirit' he describes the actions that flow from this as 'the fruit of the Spirit'; They are a demonstration that the assertion against God described by Paul in Romans 7 as 'the sin' – 'the sin' replacing the 'I' – is now itself replaced by the activity of the Spirit so that action is performed according to the will of God. This is confirmed by the way Paul presents the Spirit as indwelling the believer, thus ousting 'the sin' and ending the hostility to God:

> [T]he mind that is set on the flesh is hostile to God; it does not submit to God's law – indeed it cannot, and those who are in the flesh cannot please God. But you are not in the flesh; you are in the Spirit, since the Spirit of God dwells in you. (Rom 8:7-9)

As well as ending hostility to God, this experience of being led by the Spirit also ends hostility to others. This is clear in Paul's presentation of the life of a community guided by the Spirit. Life in the Spirit is essentially corporate. Paul describes the community of those who have been 'clothed over in Christ' as 'the body of Christ'. Its members are 'in Christ' and, in the way Paul describes how they live, the hostility brought about by the fall is at an end.

> [A]ll of you are one in Christ Jesus. (Gal 3:28)

To see how consistent this image of being clothed over by a new kind of life is and how, in Paul's description of this new life, being 'in Christ' or 'in the Spirit' are bound together we need to look at another distinctive word Paul uses.

The 'giving of sonship' Spirit

In contrast to the associations of the flesh with selfish, divisive individuality explored in the last chapter, the Spirit is associated with unity, but unity perceived of by Paul in a distinctive way. Taking his statements at face value, Paul understands the baptized to have access to the same kind of relationship with God as Jesus Christ had; as Jesus was the Son of God, so the faithful become the sons of God. Unfortunately, in English we do not have a non-'gender specific' word to include both sons and daughters and reflect the fact that for Paul, there is no male or female in the unity in Christ Jesus. One of the earliest titles for Jesus was indeed 'child of God' (Acts 4:27, 30) and then those who follow him can be referred to as 'children' but, unfortunately, replacing 'sons' with 'children', as the NRSV does, loses the sharpness in indicating that a change to a new relationship is involved. A clumsy way of expressing what Paul means is that Jesus was the one who had 'a relationship with God like that of a son or daughter to a parent' and others can enter a similar relationship. So, in the texts we will consider, becoming 'sons' of God as Paul intends it embraces both adult and child and male and female. The NRSV with its inclusive language will be used where possible but other translations are sometimes more helpful and, where appropriate, the literal translation of the Greek will be added in brackets so that the sense of what Paul is expressing can be clearly seen.

We have already referred to the first part of the following text which speaks of how the baptized are 'clothed with Christ' but the connection with Christ is stronger still:

> You are all sons of God through faith in Christ Jesus [RSV 'in Christ Jesus you are all sons of God, through faith'], for all of you who were baptised into Christ have clothed yourselves with Christ. There is neither Jew nor Greek, slave nor free, male nor female, for you are all one in Christ Jesus. (Gal 3:26-28, NIV)

As well as saying 'you have clothed yourselves in Christ', Paul says that 'you were baptised *into* Christ'. And one of his most common ways of speaking about faith is to use the phrase 'in Christ' or 'in the Lord'. As he goes on to say above:

> … [Y]ou are all one *in Christ Jesus*. (Gal 3:28, NIV)

So, not only does Paul work with an image of the baptized as clothed in the Spirit or clothed in Christ, he confirms and strengthens that image by saying that, in some sense, the baptized enter into Christ to become sons and daughters of God as he was Son of God. Instrumental in this is the Spirit:

> So then, brothers and sisters, we are debtors, not to the flesh, to live according to the flesh – for if you live according to the flesh you will die; but if by the Spirit you put to death the deeds of the body, you will live. For all who are led by the Spirit of God are children [Gk 'sons'] of God. (Rom 8:12-14)

Paul then elaborates on that last sentence in a way that is important but not easy to translate. Two modern translations provide examples of the two main options. This is what is in the NIV:

> For you did not receive a spirit that makes you a slave again to fear, but you received the Spirit of sonship. And by him we cry, 'Abba, Father.' (Rom 8:15, NIV)

The REB offers this alternative:

> The Spirit you have received is not a spirit of slavery, ... but a Spirit of adoption, enabling us to cry, 'Abba! Father!' (Rom 8:15, REB)

The Greek word translated, 'of sonship' or 'of adoption' (*huiothesia*) is qualifying or describing the kind of Spirit that has been given. The sense would be clearer if in English there were a single word that could be inserted before the word Spirit to indicate the nature of the Spirit that has been given but no one word exists; it is, literally, a 'giving of sonship' Spirit. What the concluding phrase which speaks of crying, 'Abba! Father!' confirms and which both translations seek to express is that the effect of the coming of the Spirit is to establish the recipient as a son or daughter in relation to God. It is not obvious what Paul means when he says that the Spirit enables the cry, 'Abba! Father!', but it is clearly meant as a reference to this new state of 'sonship' that will be readily understood by his readers. There is precisely the same combination of the 'giving of sonship' and the giving of the Spirit in the letter to the Galatians:

> But when the fullness of time had come, God sent his Son ... in order to redeem
> those who were under the law, so that we might receive adoption as children
> [Gk 'the gift of sonship']. And because you are children (sons), God has sent the
> Spirit of his Son into our hearts, crying, 'Abba! Father!' (Gal 4:4-6)

In both of these passages, from Romans and Galatians, Paul goes on to draw out a
further consequence of 'sonship': the recipients, as a consequence of being given
sonship, also become heirs. The importance of this will be examined after exploring
one further way Paul speaks of the experience of being 'in Christ'.

The body of Christ

In the first part of the book the view was presented that Paul understands the Spirit
as being experienced as both objective and subjective. Paul has a familiar way of
speaking about the Spirit that successfully maintains this tension in the way he
understands the experience of the Spirit as being both 'from outside' and, at the
same time, 'within': he uses the analogy of the spirit and body of a person. Just as
an individual has a spirit which penetrates every part of him or her, so it is with God.
Paul says that

> ... the depths of a man can only be known by his own spirit, not by any other man,
> and in the same way the depths of God can only be known by the Spirit of God.
> (1 Cor 2:11, JB)

This quotation is taken from a passage where Paul is describing how those who have
been chosen by God and have received God's Spirit are therefore privy to God's
purposes. As the spirit of a person communicates the will of that person to each part
of the body, so, Paul claims, the Spirit communicates the will of God to members of
the body of Christ:

> But, as it is written, "What no eye has seen, nor ear heard, nor the heart of man
> conceived, what God has prepared for those who love him," God has revealed to
> us through the Spirit; for the Spirit searches everything, even the depths of God.
> For what person knows a man's thoughts except the spirit of the man which is
> in him? So also no one comprehends the thoughts of God except the Spirit of
> God. Now we have received not the spirit of the world, but the Spirit which is
> from God, that we might understand the gifts bestowed upon us by God. (1 Cor
> 2:9-12, RSV)

The two aspects of the experience of the Spirit – that the Spirit is always 'other',
from outside, and that the Spirit is 'within' – come together in Paul's thought to form
one simple, vivid idea. The individual who has been baptized becomes a member – a
hand, an eye, an ear – of the body of Christ. As a hand has a particular function that
cannot be performed by any other part of the body, so the baptized individual retains
a separate identity and has a particular calling within the community. Similarly, as
a hand cannot perform its particular function apart from the body, so the baptized

individual is animated by the life flowing through the body. In Paul's conception, as the spirit of a person animates and directs the hand, so the Spirit animates and directs the community of the baptized. The spirit of a person is both from outside the hand but within the hand; analogously, the Spirit is both outside the baptized individuals and within them. After listing for the Corinthians a variety of gifts, Paul says:

> All these are activated by one and the same Spirit, who allots to each one individually just as the Spirit chooses. For just as the body is one and has many members, and all the members of the body, though many, are one body, so it is with Christ. For in the one Spirit we were all baptized into one body... (1 Cor 12:11-13)

The important thing to note from this is the fact that by this metaphor Paul is able to hold together both sides of the combination noted above without blurring them together. The Spirit, in this metaphor, is both 'other' – from outside – and 'within'. Each individual, while retaining a distinctive identity, is animated from the same source. Just as, in the Genesis account, before the fall, the creation of fleshly individuality is the source of unity and diversity, so now that same combination of unity and diversity is brought about anew through the Spirit:

> Now there are varieties of gifts, but the same Spirit ... To each is given the manifestation of the Spirit for the common good. (1 Cor 12:4, 7)

Individuality, no longer falsely identified with the flesh, is restored to unity in the Spirit without losing its variety.

The implication of what Paul is saying is that the same Spirit that animated Jesus Christ is now animating those who come after him, who are 'clothed with him', who are 'in him'. With the death of the individual assertiveness that arises through identification of existence with the flesh, all are united in the one Spirit that was in Christ. Recalling the material of Chapter 2 (pp. 17-23), the Spirit is bound together with the coming of the prophetic word. Where there were once many individuals acting, at best, in separation from each other and, at worst, in open hostility to each other, there is now one body where the activities of the individual members are guided by the prophetic word, co-ordinated by the same Spirit that was in Jesus Christ.

The 'first instalment' of the Spirit

The analysis of Part Two of the book showed how the Genesis account of the creation and fall of humankind is informing the thought of Paul. The last section was entitled 'In Christ: reversing the fall' and indicated how Paul considers that whereas life based in the flesh brings about mortality and sin, life based in the Spirit brings about immortality and the way of doing what is right from God. This is the extraordinary claim that Paul makes for life lived according to the Spirit:

> So I say, live by the Spirit, and you will not gratify the desires of the sinful nature
> [Gk 'flesh']. (Gal 5:16, NIV)

As we have seen, the phrase 'you will not' is emphatic in the Greek – 'you will definitely not' (p. 39).

Given this presentation of life in the Spirit as a reversal of the fall then there is an obvious problem which must be examined for the integrity of Paul's claims to be sustained. If Paul is stating that when a person lives by the Spirit the desires of the flesh are definitely not gratified and that this is the fundamental change that liberates the individual from the need for the law, why is there so much evidence of continued sin among the baptized? If the gift of the Spirit has brought about a reversal of the fall, a transformation for all humankind, where is the evidence?

In Part One of the book it was claimed that when he speaks of living by faith rather than the law Paul was indicating a life directed by the Spirit with the same clarity as direction given by the law; with the immediacy of this guidance, the need for law disappears. Yet there are plenty of ethical instructions in Paul's letters that indicate that he recognized the need among the early Christians for guidance and for continued exhortation to depart from sin. The opening section of 1 Corinthians is a clear condemnation of 'strife' and 'party spirit', two of the 'works of the flesh' that Paul lists:

> Now I appeal to you, brothers and sisters, by the name of our Lord Jesus Christ, that all of you should be in agreement and that there should be no divisions among you, but that you should be united in the same mind and the same purpose. For it has been reported to me by Chloe's people that there are quarrels among you, my brothers and sisters. (1 Cor 1:10f)

Here what Paul says contrasts sharply with the simplicity of that statement made to the Galatians, 'live by the Spirit, and you will definitely not gratify the desires of the flesh'. Making sense of this will enable us to see how, while Paul has a conception and experience of real change in the present, that change is fundamentally oriented to the future.

Still in the flesh

It was pointed out in the last chapter that Paul considers baptism to effect a real change in the baptized but a change that primarily looks forward to the future when there will be a further transformation – the baptized become sons and daughters as Jesus was son in relation to God and, as sons and daughters, heirs of a future inheritance. This section introduces a vital distinction which can be discerned in Paul's thought: for Paul 'living by the Spirit' is not equivalent to 'living by faith'. It will be argued in what follows that it is because this distinction is operating in his thinking that Paul can affirm the genuinely liberated life that flows from being clothed in the Spirit even as he continues to provide exhortation and guidance about the avoidance of sin in the life of faith.

Paul allows no overlap between 'faith' and 'works of the law'. If someone, having begun a life of faith, begins to go back to the works of the law, Paul's condemnation is unequivocal:

> Listen! I, Paul, am telling you that if you let yourselves be circumcised, Christ will be of no benefit to you. ... You who want to be justified (liberated/absolved) by the law have cut yourselves off from Christ; you have fallen away from grace. (Gal 5:2, 4)

It has already been seen that there is a similar absolute opposition in Paul's thought between 'the Spirit' and 'the flesh':

> For what the flesh desires is opposed to the Spirit, and what the Spirit desires is opposed to the flesh; for these are opposed to each other... (Gal 5:17f)

Having noted these two sets of opposites – 'faith' and 'works of law', 'the Spirit' and 'the flesh' – we can now consider the relationship between them in Paul's thought.

> [I]f you are led by the Spirit, you are not subject to the law. (Gal 5:18)

This straightforward statement makes an interesting start to establishing how 'faith' and 'law', 'Spirit' and 'flesh' are related. A suggestion consistent with the above statement would be to conclude that there is a congruity between the two sets of opposites: being 'led by the Spirit' would then be equivalent to the life of faith and 'being under the law' would be equivalent to living according to the flesh.

flesh	Spirit
Law	faith
	in Christ

coming
of Christ

There is further support for this view in the letter to the Romans:

> While we were living in the flesh, our sinful passions, aroused by the law, were at work in our members to bear fruit for death. But now we are discharged from the law, dead to that which held us captive, so that we are slaves not under the old written code but in the new life of the Spirit. (Rom 7:5f)

The opposition between flesh and the law on the one side and 'the new life of the Spirit' on the other is clear. Although on the basis of these texts the two sets of opposites may be congruous, there is an alternative.

Before taking the next step in the argument it is necessary to remember that Paul speaks of being liberated/absolved (justified) by faith as a single event:

> Do you not know that wrongdoers will not inherit the kingdom of God? ... And
> this is what some of you used to be. But you were washed, you were sanctified,
> you were justified (liberated/absolved) in the name of the Lord Jesus Christ and
> in the Spirit of our God. (1 Cor 6:11)

As has already been mentioned, at the beginning of 1 Corinthians, Paul is addressing the fact that there are divisions in the community, and after giving a description of 'those who are Spiritual' (1 Cor 2:15), those who have 'the Spirit that is from God' (1 Cor 2:12), those who 'have the mind of Christ' (1 Cor 2:16), Paul continues:

> And so, brothers and sisters, I could not speak to you as spiritual people, but
> rather as people of the flesh, as infants in Christ. I fed you with milk, not solid
> food, for you were not ready for solid food. Even now you are still not ready, for
> you are still of the flesh. For as long as there is jealousy and quarrelling among
> you, are you not of the flesh, and behaving according to human inclinations? (1
> Cor 3:1-3)

In this passage, Paul is referring to those 'in Christ' – members of the body of Christ – who have undoubtedly been liberated/absolved (justified) by faith but who are clearly also not 'Spiritual' but rather 'still of the flesh'. The congruity of faith and Spirit over against law and flesh breaks down. This gives an indication that, in Paul's understanding, after liberation/absolution (justification) by faith there continues to be a real struggle between flesh and Spirit for those in Christ. Those under the law are still in the flesh; those living according to the Spirit are liberated/absolved by faith; but there are those in Christ who, while freed from the law and living by faith, are still drawn to live according to the flesh.

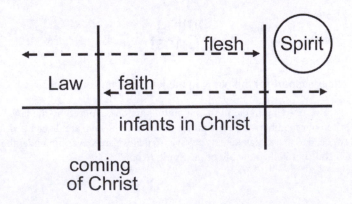

Yet Paul has no doubt that the Spirit has been given to those in Christ. It is active in baptism:

> For in the one Spirit we were all baptized into one body – Jews or Greeks, slaves
> or free – and we were all made to drink of one Spirit. (1 Cor 12:13)

The entry of the Spirit into the believer is unequivocally affirmed by Paul:

> ... God has sent the Spirit of his Son into our hearts, crying, 'Abba! Father!' (Gal
> 4:6)

> ... God's love has been poured into our hearts through the Holy Spirit that has
> been given to us. (Rom 5:5)

Given this unequivocal nature of Paul's affirmation of the giving and indwelling of the Spirit, and that, in Paul's words, those who live by the Spirit will definitely not gratify the desires of the flesh, how does Paul reconcile these statements with the continuing existence of 'jealousy and quarrelling'?

The Spirit is particularly associated with a future hope of transformation; it is the gift of the Spirit that establishes those who are baptized as children of God, looking forward to the future inheritance. We have seen how Paul can describe the Spirit in extremely powerful ways as 'alive-making' and as 'giving-sonship'. There are, however, a significant number of descriptions of the gift of the Spirit that are qualified in a specific way, the clarity and consistency of which disappears in most modern translations. It is helpful to begin with the memorable phrase from the Authorized Version, 'the earnest of the Spirit':

> Now he which stablisheth us with you in Christ, and hath anointed us, is God;
> who hath also sealed us, and given the earnest of the Spirit in our hearts. (2 Cor
> 1:21f, AV)

While 'earnest' is not now in common usage it very accurately expresses in English the meaning of *arrabōna*, the Greek word that Paul is using:

> Money in part-payment, especially for the purpose of binding a bargain. Also
> figuratively a foretaste, instalment, pledge, of what is to come. (SOED)

In order to relay this concept of 'earnest' for a modern readership, the NRSV has translated the word in two different ways: 'first instalment' and 'guarantee'. It can be seen that these accurately pick up on the figurative sense of 'earnest' defined above, 'an instalment of what is to come' or 'a pledge of what is to come for the purpose of binding an agreement'. These are well chosen words to replace 'earnest' and do not give a problem. Distortion of Paul's Greek comes because of the way a particular interpretation of his meaning shapes the way that these new translations are used and completely obscures the meaning proposed in this section.

The NRSV interpretation, reflecting the almost universal view of scholars on this matter, is that when Paul speaks of 'the earnest of the Spirit', this 'first instalment' or 'guarantee', he is referring to the gift of the Spirit that Christians have now received, the existence of which is the 'first instalment' of the coming of the Spirit to all humankind, indeed, to the whole of creation in the future. That Christians have the fullness of the Spirit now is a 'guarantee' of its future outpouring on others. So the NRSV does not simply replace the AV reading that God gives 'the earnest of the Spirit in our hearts' with 'the first instalment of the Spirit in our hearts' but rather God gives us 'his Spirit in our hearts as a first instalment'. This simple change removes for the reader in English an alternative interpretation that is present in the Greek: that the 'first instalment of the Spirit' is not the gift of the Spirit given *fully* to Christians now as a guarantee that it will come for others in the future but, rather, *the first instalment of the full gift of the Spirit given to Christians as a guarantee of the full outpouring that is to come in the future as much upon Christians as upon others.*

The second use in the letter confirms the view that what Paul is referring to is the experience of those 'in Christ' who, though they have truly received the Spirit of God and can witness to the gifts of the Spirit among them have, as yet, only received this gift 'in part'. It comes at the end of 2 Corinthians where Paul is giving sustained attention to the contrast between the present struggle and the future hope:

> So we do not lose heart. Even though our outer nature is wasting away, our inner nature is being renewed day by day. For this slight momentary affliction is preparing us for an eternal weight of glory beyond all measure ... (2 Cor 4:16f)

And we then come to words of Paul that we have already considered which lead into his use of *ton arrabōna tou pneumatos*:

> For while we are still in this tent, we groan under our burden, because we wish not to be unclothed, but to be further clothed, so that what is mortal may be swallowed up by life. He who has prepared us for this very thing is God, who has given us the Spirit as a guarantee. (2 Cor 5:4f)

The AV at this point has the phrase 'the earnest of the Spirit'. In the NRSV, despite the fact that tension between the present 'affliction' and future 'glory' of those 'in Christ' is the focus, the possibility that Paul is speaking of a part gift of the Spirit to those in Christ, given as a guarantee that the full gift of the Spirit is to come in the future, has disappeared. Only one interpretation is possible in reading the NRSV translation: in the midst of their struggle, Christians have received the fullness of the Spirit which provides them with a guarantee of future glory. In this simple change in translation, the coherence in Paul's thought disappears. The easily seen coherence is this:

(a) the one who lives by the fullness of the Spirit, will definitely not sin;
(b) sin continues to be a reality in the Christian communities;
(c) yet the Spirit is a reality in the Christian communities;
(d) hence the Spirit is only known in part in the present situation;
(e) that present partial experience of the Spirit is an 'earnest' or 'first instalment' or 'guarantee' of the fullness of the Spirit to come in the future.

There is further support for this interpretation in Paul's use of two similar qualifications in describing the present experience of the Spirit which can be interpreted in precisely the same way. In this next verse, Paul is explaining the purpose of the death of Christ to the Galatians:

> ... that in Christ Jesus the blessing of Abraham might come to the Gentiles, so that we might receive the promise of the Spirit through faith. (Gal 3:14)

'The promise of the Spirit' is open to the same interpretation as 'the earnest/first instalment of the Spirit'.

The second phrase is even more supportive of the proposed interpretation:

> We know that the whole creation has been groaning in labour pains until now; and not only the creation, but we ourselves, who have the first fruits of the Spirit, groan inwardly while we wait for ... the redemption of our bodies. (Rom 8:23)

As with 'the earnest/first of the Spirit', the phrase – 'the first fruits (*aparchēn*) of the Spirit' – is usually understood as referring to the gift of the Spirit which has been given to those in Christ – 'we ourselves' – and will come to all in the future. 'The first fruits of the Spirit' is held to be the Spirit in its fullness that has been given to those in Christ as the initial part of the fullness of life that is to come to the whole of creation. Our alternative interpretation is arguably the more natural interpretation. Just as with *arrabōna*, the gift that has been received is part of the gift to come, so the gift of 'firstfruits' is a gift of part of something as a sign of the willingness to give the whole of it. Because they have received this initial part of the coming gift those in Christ can be certain of receiving the full gift in the future but they still await their future inheritance. There is no grammatical reason for preferring the former interpretation to the latter. As with other words and concepts that have been considered, our decision as to which interpretation is accurate is shaped by our effort to discover the consistency and coherence in Paul's thought.

If what has been given by God is an earnest of the fullness of the Spirit that is to come then this clarifies how Paul can both claim that those who live by the Spirit will definitely not gratify the desires of the flesh and yet continue, without contradicting this basic assertion, to provide realistic moral exhortation for the early communities. Paul can affirm the gift from God of the indwelling Spirit and the efficacy of the Spirit in living free from sin but, simultaneously in his exhortations and instructions, clearly acknowledge that Christians still 'live in the flesh'. Until their future hope is realized and the Spirit is given in its fullness, Christians have the earnest of the Spirit, truly the gift of the Spirit, but still only a foretaste; the struggle in the mortal flesh continues. Even when Paul does not use one of the qualifying words presented above when speaking of the gift of the Spirit, the sense argued for here is still present. The present experience of the Spirit is always only part of what is to come in the future. It is 'earnest', 'first instalment', 'firstfruits' of what is to come. So the present experience is always looking forward to its future fulfilment. Just as becoming an 'heir' is a real change but one that, in the very concept used, is always bound together with the future hope of 'inheritance', so receiving 'the first instalment' of the Spirit is a real gift but one that, in the very concept used, is always bound together with a future transformation, when, 'what is mortal may be swallowed up by life' (2 Cor 5:5).

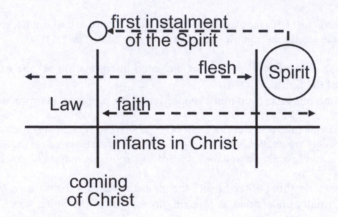

The 'first instalment' of the Spirit: summary sentence and discussion

> Those 'in Christ' have received the 'first instalment' of the Spirit, the beginning of the liberating power of the Spirit that will be fully given in the future.

All three scholars draw attention to the life of the Spirit as bound together with the 'End' or 'New Age' or 'life of heaven' or 'full transformation at the return of the Lord or resurrection' or 'God's final rule' or 'the wholeness of salvation'. Each of them interprets 'the first instalment of the Spirit' as 'the Spirit' in its fullness that is given now to those in Christ as a guarantee of the transformation that is to come to all at the 'End'. 'In passing', Dunn rejects the interpretation offered in the main text (470):

> We should note in passing the more or less universal agreement among commentators, that by "the gift of the Spirit" Paul and his fellow first-century Christians certainly meant the Spirit itself as the gift. Paul did not think of the *arrabōna* and *aparchē* as only part of the Spirit. Nor did he think of the process of salvation as gaining or receiving an ever larger share of the Spirit. Rather, the Spirit was itself the *arrabōna* and *aparchē*, and the full "payment" or "harvest" was the wholeness of salvation which the Spirit thus given would work in and through the individual.

Note that this very firm statement rests on the 'more or less universal agreement among commentators' *and nothing else.*

Conclusion

This chapter began by introducing the idea that Paul conceived of the Spirit as bringing a transformation of natural, physical life. While he speaks of a dying that is gone through in baptism, emphasizing the discontinuity between the old life and the new, Paul also speaks of the new immortal life being put on over the old mortal existence. He speaks of the mortal being 'clothed over' with either the life-giving Spirit or the risen Christ without any apparent difference in meaning.

This change is the effective reversal of the fall. Identification with 'the flesh' – individual physical existence – is over. Life is identified with 'the Spirit': immortal; of God; empowering each person as Jesus was empowered. Guided by the Spirit, clothed in the Spirit, individuals act in line with the purposes of God but the distinctiveness of each individual is maintained. This life is essentially 'corporate'. Any idea of individual liberation recedes as Paul describes life in the Spirit, life beyond fleshly identity, as bringing about an ideal community. As parts of the same body, individuals are led by the same Spirit in their own individual expression of the life of God.

While it is clear that Paul believed there to be a real change in baptism, it is also clear that he conceives of this change as, essentially, a preparation for a further change in the future. Those who are baptized seek to be animated and guided by the same Spirit that was in Christ. They become sons and daughters in relation to God the Father. But, while children, in the present they remain heirs; the inheritance is still in the future.

The relationship between present transformation and future inheritance was explored further. It was argued that to make coherent sense of what Paul says it is important to see that the life of faith is not equivalent to life in the Spirit. Both describe a life without the law but in the life of faith there is evidence of continuing identification with separate fleshly existence with the propensity to living on the basis of self interest that brings. Friction between people is the consequence and this is clearly in evidence in the Christian communities to which Paul writes indicating that the freedom from sin and consequent unity that flows from life in the Spirit is still not realized among the baptized.

Yet Paul does not deny the reality of work of the Spirit in the communities. Behind Paul's use of the precise terms expressed in English as 'firstfruits' and 'earnest' or 'first instalment' is an important fact which strengthens the coherence of what Paul is claiming. To describe the present activity of the Spirit as a foretaste of the full transformation that the Spirit will bring about in the future is not quite an adequate description. There is no doubt that Paul affirms the real activity and gift of the Spirit among the early faith communities. What is important to see is that Paul does not separate the present gift from the future transformation. This is the precise sense of the images of 'first-fruits' and 'earnest'. They are already the future gift, but given and received before the time for full payment. The modern equivalent is a down-payment: payment has not yet been made but in anticipation of the time when that full payment will be made a suitable amount of that payment is given. The down-payment is part of the future payment and not separate from it. What this image indicates is that when Paul encounters the activity of the Spirit, integral to his experience is a sense of the future event to which the phrase 'earnest of the Spirit' points; this future perspective to the present experience of transformation pervades his thought.

Chapter 8

Coming of Age

Much of the book so far has been examining two sharply contrasted pairs in Paul's way of thinking: 'flesh' and 'Spirit'; 'law' and 'faith'. We have discovered the clarity in Paul's thinking:

(a) 'living by faith' excludes 'living by law';
(b) 'living in the Spirit' brings to an end 'the deeds of the flesh';
(c) 'the law' is no longer needed once 'the deeds of the flesh' are brought to an end;
(d) 'living by faith' is not equivalent to 'living by the Spirit';
(e) at least some, if not most (more precision on this is to come in the following section and in Chapter 11), of those who 'live by faith' are 'infants in Christ' who have 'the first instalment of the Spirit'.

We now need to pursue the relationship in Paul's thought between a further contrasted pair: childhood and maturity.

The 'end' of childhood

It was seen in the last chapter how Paul indicates the importance of the time of the transition when the child becomes treated as 'son/daughter' and heir. The child, 'is under guardians and trustees until the date set by the father' (Gal 4:2), and adoption as 'sons/daughters' happens 'when the fullness of time had come'. Something changes at a particular time. We also considered the text where Paul describes a group of those 'in Christ' who are involved in 'jealousy and quarrelling' as 'infants' (1 Cor 3:1-3). In the extended section leading up to that observation, Paul speaks of the 'mature' (*teleioi*) (1 Cor 2:6). Once again translation can blunt the sharpness of the distinction in Paul's thought. In that the English word 'mature' implies a later stage of development it contrasts well with 'infant' or 'child' but there is a further sense to the contrast that the translation 'mature' obscures.

Other translations indicate an important extra element that is there in the word, *teleioi*. Instead of 'the mature' the AV has 'them that are perfect'. In this translation the contrast with infancy is lost but it does relay something of the sense in the Greek. The root word to which *teleioi* is related is most simply translated 'end' (*telos*). Just like the English word 'end' the Greek word can be used in a number of different ways. 'End' can be used for the termination of a period of time or an activity; it can have therefore the sense of completeness which is closely related to perfection. It can be used for the purpose – the 'end' – for which something was created. Flexible as the meaning of this word is, there is a consistent core meaning within the word of the final point of something – its completeness. The weakness of the translation 'the mature' is that it tends to evoke a picture of gradual development as opposed to a once for all change – an 'end'. The NJB translation gets over this weakness by using the phrase: 'those who have reached maturity'. This captures the meaning of the Greek: 'the mature' here are 'those who have come of age' – those who have reached the transition to adulthood. The simplest word in English meaning 'those who have come of age' is 'adult' and this makes for an image in which there is no blurring. To make the issue clear, it is possible for a child to be mature and an adult to be immature but it is not possible for an adult to be a child; it is the sharpness of the contrast between adult and child that is being conveyed by Paul's use of language.

There is interesting support for this interpretation in the two further occurrences of this word in 1 Corinthians. The first simply makes clear its use by Paul to contrast adult and child:

> Brothers and sisters, do not be children in your thinking; rather, be infants in evil,
> but in thinking be adults (*teleioi*). (1 Cor 14:20)

The second example comes from the most famous passage in the whole of Paul's writing and provides a fascinating example of how translation can blur the sharpness of Paul's images and thus distort his meaning. Its content will also take us a step further in the argument of the book. The subtle but important issue in translating Paul's Greek can be revealed by looking at the RSV translation first before moving on to the AV and the NRSV:

> For our knowledge is imperfect and our prophecy is imperfect; but when the
> perfect comes, the imperfect will pass away. When I was a child, I spoke like a
> child, I thought like a child, I reasoned like a child; when I became a man, I gave
> up childish ways. For now we see in a mirror dimly, but then face to face. Now I
> know in part; then I shall understand fully, even as I have been fully understood.
> (1 Cor 13:9-12, RSV)

There are two layers of distortion here, both easy to point out. Firstly, every time the word 'imperfect' occurs in the first sentence, there is, in fact, the same short Greek phrase (*ek merous*) as is translated 'in part' in the last sentence. The AV translates this consistently:

> For we know in part, and we prophesy in part. But when that which is perfect is
> come, then that which is in part shall be done away with. (1 Cor 13:10, AV)

The NRSV is also consistent in its translation of 'in part' but replaces 'perfect' with 'complete':

> For we know only in part, and we prophesy only in part; but when the complete
> comes, the partial will come to an end. (1 Cor 13:10, NRSV)

Given these translations, 'perfect' and 'complete', it will not be a surprise that they are translating *teleion*, carrying exactly the same range of meaning as *teleios*. The AV accurately conveys the fact that in Greek, 'in part' (*ek merous*) and 'perfect' (*teleion*), while clearly being used to make an important contrast, are not from the same Greek root. Both the RSV and the NRSV seek to bring 'in part' and 'perfect' into line with each other. The RSV takes the 'perfect' translation for *teleion* as the determining factor and translates *ek merous* as 'imperfect'; the NRSV takes the 'in part' translation for *ek merous* as the determining factor and translates *teleion* as 'complete'. Both of these options clumsily and completely empty Paul's simple but profound image of meaning. Whether one opts for 'imperfect' and 'perfect' or 'in part' and 'complete', to suggest that at the climax of this most profound piece of writing Paul is stating the bland and totally obvious fact that the 'perfect' brings to an end the 'imperfect' or the 'complete' brings to an end the 'in part', either option is entirely missing his point.

We have already shown how important the contrast between 'childhood' and 'adulthood' is for Paul. It is this image that Paul is working with in this brief but very significant section. As we have seen in earlier sections (pp. 18-19, 134-5), in 1 Corinthians 12-14, Paul is addressing the present state of the community, in particular, how different gifts of the Spirit operate in harmony in 'the body of Christ'. At this point, he interrupts the flow of his discourse saying 'and I will show you a still more excellent way' (1 Cor 12:31). He then goes on to speak of the primacy of love and, as the section moves to its climax, the fact that, in contrast to other gifts of the Spirit, 'love never ends' (1 Cor 13:8). At this point, Paul has introduced the element of time, of a contrast between present and future. Now, he is saying to his brothers and sisters in the community, our prophecy and our knowledge is 'in part' or 'incomplete'; then, in the future, what is 'in part' will come to an end:

> For now we see in a mirror, dimly, but then we will see face to face. Now I know only in part; then I will know fully, even as I have been fully known. (1 Cor 13:12)

It is of the most profound significance that at this point Paul presents 'love' as the 'gift of the Spirit' that will not come to an end but is available in the present; it is a bridge to the future life. It is this focus on love that makes this passage so universally accessible. But for those engaged on understanding the elements of Paul's theological picture, it is very illuminating to see clearly how, in this passage of central importance, he again uses the universal image of the transition from childhood to adulthood to illustrate the universal change – the movement from 'first instalment' to 'fullness'; from becoming 'heirs' to 'inheritance' – that is still to come, for those 'in Christ' as much as for those on the outside.

Returning now to the section where this image is obscured in translation:

> For we know only in part, and we prophesy only in part; but when the complete (*teleion*) comes, the partial will come to an end. When I was a child, I spoke like

a child, I thought like a child, I reasoned like a child; when I became an adult, I put an end to childish ways. (1 Cor 13:10f, NRSV)

The determining factor for translating *teleion* is not 'in part' but the contrast in the next sentence between 'when I was a child' and 'when I became a man (*aner*)'. The use of the word in the above passage – 'when the complete comes'/'when the perfect comes' – indicates that it is referring here to the *transition* to adulthood – not the *state* of adulthood but the 'coming of age'. With this translation, the sustained image involving childhood, coming of age and adulthood can now be seen clearly:

> For we know only in part, and we prophesy only in part. But at the coming of age, the partial will come to an end. When I was a child, I spoke like a child, I thought like a child, I reasoned like a child: when I became an adult, I put an end to childish ways. For now we see in a mirror, dimly, but then we will see face to face. Now I know only in part; then I will know fully, even as I have been fully known. (1 Cor 13:10-12, adapted NRSV)

It is important to see the sharpness of Paul's image operating both here and elsewhere. There is a separation, between infancy or childhood on the one hand and adulthood on the other, marked by an event, a coming of age. We have seen how Paul uses the image of slaves becoming heirs to indicate the change that has come to those who are baptized; the Spirit brings about the sonship/daughtership of those who were once slaves but, despite this real transformation, the inheritance to which sonship/ daughtership looks still lies in the future. As we saw in the last chapter, the present fruits of the Spirit in the community, though real and transformative, are still only the 'earnest' or 'firstfruits' or 'promise' of the full gift in the future: the gift of the Spirit is, as yet, 'partial'. Now we have seen how Paul uses the image of a change that is part of the experience of every adult: at a certain time, over a relatively brief period, the things of childhood are put away; a stage in maturation is reached which makes the things of childhood redundant. And once again, he uses an image to affirm both that a real change has happened but that it is bound up with, indeed, part of, a change that is still to come. What is present now is 'partial knowledge' and 'partial prophecy'. The 'coming of age' is still future. It is only then that the 'partial' will come to an end.

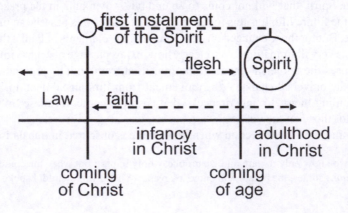

What has already been suggested in the overall argument of this book and will receive further support as the argument proceeds to its conclusion is that Paul is using this image of the transition of a child to adulthood – the 'coming of age' – to communicate his expectation for the whole of humanity. Just as at a certain time the individual becomes an adult so Paul expects a comparable transformation for the whole of humankind. When this time comes, Paul says, the partial knowledge and prophecy of childhood will be at an end and, just as has been claimed for the life of the Spirit, there will be an immediacy about the relationship between God and humankind:

> For now we see through a glass, darkly; but then face to face: now I know in part; but then I shall know even as also I am known. (1 Cor 13:12, AV)

A universal inheritance

The next chapter will draw together earlier themes to explore in depth what Paul believes will happen at the coming of age. This brief section prepares the way for that exploration.

We have now noted how Paul links present transformation with future change. One further significant way in which he does that is by using the idea of inheritance. We have seen how Paul speaks of those who have received the Spirit as 'heirs'.

> When we cry, 'Abba! Father!' it is that very Spirit bearing witness with our spirit that we are children [Gk 'sons'] of God, and if children [Gk 'sons'], then heirs, heirs of God and joint heirs with Christ. (Rom 8:16f)

Paul uses the same image in the letter to the Galatians:

> And because you are children [Gk 'sons'], God has sent the Spirit of his Son into our hearts, crying, 'Abba! Father!' So you are no longer a slave but a child [Gk 'son'], and if a child [Gk 'son'] then also an heir, through God. (Gal 4:6f)

While those who receive the Spirit are no longer slaves but 'children' or 'sons' of God and have experienced a real transformation, they are still only heirs; their full inheritance lies in the future.

On three occasions, Paul links the idea of inheritance with the kingdom of God. Two of them are to indicate who will not 'inherit the kingdom of God': those who do works of the flesh (Gal 5:21) and 'wrongdoers' or 'the unrighteous' (1 Cor 6:9). The third example enables us to see something essential in connection with inheritance:

> What I am saying, brothers and sisters, is this: flesh and blood cannot inherit the kingdom of God, nor does the perishable inherit the imperishable. (1 Cor 15:50)

What Paul means by 'the kingdom of God' will receive attention in Chapter 12 but it is already possible to see how several important ideas are linked together in his thought. A simple but crucial point is being made by Paul in this brief text. At its heart is a crude logical point: what is 'perishable' or 'mortal' cannot inherit what is 'imperishable' or 'immortal'; it simply is not possible. This provides the reason for what Paul says about the kingdom. The kingdom, being of God, is by definition 'eternal' or 'immortal'; it will never die. 'Flesh and blood' are by definition 'mortal'; 'flesh and blood' dies. Therefore, Paul is saying, 'flesh and blood' cannot inherit the 'kingdom of God'.

A superficial interpretation of the implications of this is that humankind in the flesh cannot inherit the kingdom. This would indicate that Paul has in mind some transformation of humankind into a non-physical, spiritual state in which the inheritance of the kingdom would be possible. But what he says a couple of verses later is, in fact, entirely in line with the coherent picture that has been emerging in this part of the book:

> When this perishable body puts on imperishability, and this mortal body puts on immortality, then the saying that is written will be fulfilled: 'Death has been swallowed up in victory.' ... But thanks be to God, who gives us the victory through our Lord Jesus Christ. (1 Cor 15:54, 57)

The image of the perishable body putting on imperishability and the mortal body putting on immortality is clearly not indicating an end to physical existence but rather its being 'swallowed up' by 'victory', that is, by the 'alive-making' Spirit/ Christ.

Linking this material with observations from the first two parts of the book makes powerfully coherent sense. There we talked about the centrality in Paul's thought of real change, a shift in self-perception. This has now become sharpened to suggest a shift in the locus of identity. For, of course, Paul is speaking metaphorically when he speaks of death being swallowed up by victory and of being clothed in Christ. What has been suggested is that it is what a person identifies him or herself with that Paul is referring to. So, as we saw in Chapter 6, while people are identified with the flesh, they are identified with their separate physical existence and, as a consequence, are identified with the death of the body. If the identification shifts to the Spirit, then everything changes. The one who is identified with the Spirit is not under the power of death for the Spirit does not die. Therefore such a one is in a position to inherit the eternal kingdom of God. This, according to Paul, is the condition of those who have been baptized. They have put on Christ, been clothed in the Spirit and have therefore become heirs of the kingdom. As such they look forward to the 'coming of age' when they enter their inheritance.

What that inheritance is we will turn to in the next chapter but one more point needs making at this stage. We have seen how Paul is concerned with the banishment of humankind from Eden and how that situation is being reversed. It is important to note that his idea of inheritance is not simply limited to a few. He envisages that, just as 'all' come under the power of death, 'all' will be affected by the transformation:

[F]or as all die in Adam, so all will be made alive in Christ. (1 Cor 15:21f)

Any sense of personal transformation has a sense of incompleteness without the transformation of all, a complete reversal of the fall. The idea of future transformation that Paul is working with involves nothing less than an end to the power of death:

> And [the Lord of hosts] will destroy ... the shroud that is cast over all peoples, the sheet that is spread over all nations; *he will swallow up death for ever*. Then the Lord God will wipe away the tears from all faces ... (Isaiah 25:7f)

The veil that is spread over 'all peoples', 'all nations' will be taken away and – the implication is – humankind will 'come of age' and enter its inheritance.

Conclusion

We have already seen how Paul uses the idea of 'childhood' and 'adulthood' in Galatians 3:23-4:11 to illuminate the positive nature of the law as a guide for childhood in preparation for the step into greater maturity involved in being guided by faith (pp. 81-4). We have seen too how parallels between the relationship of parent and child on the one side and God and humankind on the other can illuminate the interpretation of Romans 7 (Chapter 5).

The clarity and coherence in Paul's use of the image of 'childhood' and 'adulthood' in relationship to the life of faith and life in the Spirit received further clarification in the examination of 1 Corinthians 13:10-12. Just as in each person's life there is a 'coming of age' when, over a relatively short period of time, the things of childhood are put away, and knowledge which was inaccessible to the child, is now open to the adult, so, for humankind, Paul's vision is of a similar process: there is a childhood for humankind in which the law provides guidance; there will be a coming of age when the fullness of the Spirit comes. The present is a time of transition in which for those who are 'infants in Christ' liberation and the continuing life in the Spirit are still partial.

This future transformation moved to the fore in the final part of the chapter: to describe someone as an 'heir' makes no sense unless there is something to inherit; the present change in status that comes through becoming an heir is entirely directed to the reality of a future inheritance. The child becomes an adult at the right time – the 'coming of age'. It has been suggested that Paul is using the image of the passage from childhood to adulthood of a universal future change for all humankind in keeping with his sense that through the coming of Christ, the reversal of the fall is underway. In the time of inheritance for humankind the fullness of the Spirit will come and 'what is mortal will be swallowed up by life'. The next chapter will explore this future inheritance in more detail. How does Paul conceive of this change? What does he mean when he speaks of 'the inheritance'?

Chapter 9

The Inheritance

Drawing on all the elements of Paul's thought that have been explored so far, this chapter reveals the precise nature of what Paul expected by the idea of 'inheritance'. We have taken seriously Paul's claim that a transformative experience is going on among the first Christian communities. If Paul is claiming that God is restoring what was lost in the fall then this must involve the whole of creation including the whole of humanity. A reformed life for particular individuals, even a large number of individuals living in community, cannot amount to the setting right of what went wrong with humankind. We will see how from his present experience of transformation, Paul draws conclusions about a real change in the future on a universal scale.

Identified with creation

This section shows how at the heart of Paul's account of the fall is a description of a shift in human perception in which the ability to perceive the things of God, the invisible and eternal, is lost. Once again careful work on some details of the text is required to enable Paul's meaning to be seen clearly.

Paul's account of the fall

As we saw in the last chapter, it is clear that the scope of Paul's vision includes the whole of humanity:

> [F]or as all die in Adam, so all will be made alive in Christ. (1 Cor 15:22)

This vision of the whole of humanity is clearly operative when Paul presents his own description of the fall and, as a further examination of his own account will stimulate a number of the reflections in this chapter, it is worth reproducing in full once again:

> Ever since the creation of the world [God's] eternal power and divine nature, invisible though they are, have been understood and seen through the things he has made. So they are without excuse; for though they knew God, they did not honour him as God or give thanks to him, but they became futile in their thinking, and their senseless minds were darkened. Claiming to be wise, they became fools; and they exchanged the glory of the immortal God for images resembling

[Gk 'the likeness of an image of'] a mortal human being or birds or four-footed animals or reptiles. Therefore God gave them up in the lusts of their hearts to impurity, to the degrading of their bodies among themselves, because they exchanged the truth about God for a lie and worshipped and served the creature rather than the Creator, who is blessed for ever! Amen. (Rom 1:20-25)

In the earlier chapter on 'Childhood and Sin', the purpose in presenting this text was to show the points at which it connects with the Genesis account of the fall and to thus help establish the legitimacy of using Genesis 1-3 as an interpretative key for important aspects of Paul's thought. As this chapter proceeds it will now be possible to clarify these connections still further by a careful examination of the thought of this passage in the light of the findings of the intermediate chapters. However, there is a matter of translation to tackle first; the simple shape of Paul's thought in this passage can be easily missed because of the way it is conventionally translated. Two phrases are involved, one at the beginning and one at the end of the passage. The argument is more easily followed if the latter is dealt with first. Paul says of humankind that

> ... they exchanged the truth about God for a lie and worshipped and served the creature rather than the Creator ... (Rom 1:25)

'Creature' and 'Creator' are both related to the root word 'to create' (*ktizō*). The 'creature' is 'that which is created'; the 'Creator' is 'that which creates'. The issue of translation arises over a distinction that is present in English but not in Greek. The word translated here 'creature' (*ktisis*) can also be translated 'creation'. Both of these English words contain the meaning 'that which is created' but have a different sense. In the first place, 'creature' is a word that has come to be used primarily for living things and, in particular, living things other than humans. This is a recent development and not the main point; the word in its simplest meaning can be used of animate or inanimate objects. A classic example of this older way of using the word occurs in the Book of Common Prayer Communion Service where the prayer of consecration speaks of communicants receiving 'these thy creatures of bread and wine'. The bread and wine are specifically described in this way to emphasize that they are part of the created order. However, there is always in English a distinction in the use of the words 'creature' and 'creation', even when the word 'creature' is understood as referring to inanimate objects. The word 'creature', while always having the sense of 'that which is created', can never be used to refer to 'the whole creation'. It always refers to a discrete part of 'the creation'. In the Greek word there is a fluidity that is lost whether the translation 'creature' or 'creation' is used and there simply is not a single English word that reproduces the nuances of the Greek, straightforward though they are.

This can be most clearly seen by trying for a few moments to find an English word to refer to the quality of an object as 'created' that can be used with the definite article and can serve interchangeably for both 'the creation' and 'the creature', each of which carry a more limited meaning than Paul's Greek. It is possible to speak of some distinct piece of work by an explicitly creative individual or team as 'the creation' but this carries ironical connotations. Going to visit Picasso, if you are warned with a smile to avoid tripping over 'the "creation" that is outside the bathroom' you can be certain that it is a sculpture that is being referred to rather than the cat. 'The creation' usually carries the sense of the whole of the created order which cannot be described as 'the creature'.

To sum up this issue of translation, when Paul uses this word, it carries the precise meaning of 'that which is created', 'something that has the quality of having been created', but within that precise meaning it carries a fluidity of meaning covering on the one hand both animate and inanimate objects, and on the other, either one discrete piece of creation, like humankind, or all of that which is created. The phrase at the end of the passage can now be understood as follows:

> ... [They] worshipped and served what is created rather than what creates ... .

The assertion of human wisdom

The full significance of this issue of translation will become clear when, towards the end of the chapter, we turn to one of the most important passages from the letter to the Romans but it is important at this stage of the argument too. For this significance to be seen, the earlier use of the word in the Romans 1 passage must be clarified:

> Ever since the creation of the world [God's] eternal power and divine nature, invisible though they are, have been understood and seen through the things he has made. (Rom 1:20)

'Creation' in this phrase is the same Greek word as in the phrase above only here it is being translated to mean 'the act of creation'. Were this correct then it would be the only instance of Paul using the word in this way. But there are more telling indications that there is an inaccurate translation here. Two steps are necessary to clarify the translation. Firstly, the word translated here 'since' is more simply translated 'from' (AV). Secondly, an entirely legitimate way of translating the phrase 'the creation of the world' is, in fact, 'the world of the creation' (*apo ktiseōs kosmou*). Adding to this the findings of the last paragraph yields the following alternative translation:

> From the world of what is created [God's] eternal power and divine nature, invisible though they are, have been understood and seen through the things he has made. (Rom 1:20, author's translation)

This indicates that Paul is not referring to the fact that the invisible things of God have been evident since the beginning of creation but rather, as the sentence proceeds to say, from being 'understood and seen through the things he has made'. At first sight the sense of this revised translation may not appear dramatically different but a closer examination of the whole passage will confirm the importance of this clarification.

We look first at the relationship between these two phrases because they frame the passage. The implication of the opening phrase is that the very purpose of that which is created is to give knowledge of God which, in turn, leads to glorifying God and giving God thanks. The last phrase indicates that what was created to give knowledge of God has now itself become the object of that service and worship that is due to God. Paul describes this situation as exchanging 'the truth of God for a [Gk 'the'] lie'. That which is created is made precisely for the purpose of giving knowledge of God; the things of God, while invisible, can be clearly perceived through what is made; that which is created is therefore good – that which is created cannot itself be 'the lie'. What Paul says indicates that 'the lie' is involved in the misdirection of worship and service to that which is created rather than the Creator. But what is 'the lie' that could lead to this misdirection? In the Genesis account, 'the lie' is the words of the serpent to the woman, tempting her to eat of the tree:

> 'You will not die; for God knows that when you eat of it your eyes will be opened, and you will be like God, knowing good and evil.' (Gen 3:4f)

Being 'like God, knowing good and evil' is a powerful image of human assertion. There is the assertion of human wisdom at the heart of Paul's account too:

> ... for though they knew God, they did not honour him as God or give thanks to him, but they became futile in their thinking, and their senseless minds were darkened. *Claiming to be wise*, they became fools ... (Rom 1:21f)

This still does not quite take us to an understanding of what precisely 'the lie' is but it does suggest that as well as involving the misdirection of worship and service it also involves the assertion of human wisdom.

To make further progress it is necessary to remember the unique place of humanity in relation to God and in relation to the rest of what is created:

> Then God said, 'Let us make humankind in our image, according to our likeness; and let them have dominion over the fish of the sea, and over the birds of the air, and over the cattle, and over all the wild animals of the earth, and over every creeping thing that creeps upon the earth.' (Gen 1:26)

That humankind is made in the image of God is directly connected with the dominion that humankind is given over the rest of what is created. 'The dominion' is God's creative dominion but this 'creature', made in the image of God, is given the exercise of God's dominion. At the heart of Paul's description of the fall is an 'exchange':

> ... [T]hey exchanged the truth of God for the lie ... (Rom 1:25, author's translation)

This 'exchange' is described in another way directly related to the Genesis text above:

> ... [T]hey exchanged the glory of the immortal God for images resembling [Gk 'the likeness of an image of'] a mortal human being or birds or fourfooted animals or reptiles. (Rom 1:23)

In the Genesis account of the creation, humankind has a unique place, as it were, on the side of God. While part of what is created, humankind is made in the image of God, in Paul's words, sharing in the truth and glory of God, capable of perceiving the invisible things of God and of glorifying and giving thanks to God, and, in particular, exercising God's creative dominion over that which is created. In other words, humankind is not only on the side of that which is created but also on the side of the Creator – 'that which creates'. What is described as 'exchanging the truth of God for the lie' is something going wrong in humanity that affects its relationship with the Creator on the one side and what is created on the other. Having been created in the image of God, the one to be served and worshipped, with dominion over that which is created, humankind comes to serve and worship that which is created instead. And at the heart of what goes wrong Paul places the assertion of human wisdom.

The darkened mind

In Paul's account of the fall, the loss of the appropriate response to God, which Paul says is to honour and give thanks to God, worship and serve God, is tied together with a coarsening of human consciousness – 'they became futile in their thinking, and their senseless minds were darkened' – and a descent into idolatry. The implication of this is important for understanding Paul. The assertion of futile human thinking is tightly linked with the loss of the ability to perceive the invisible things of God. The 'futile thinking' and 'darkened mind' is bound up with a situation in which God is not glorified and thanked and, as a further consequence, is no longer 'known'. Once, according to Paul, the perception of the invisible things of God is lost all that can be perceived is that which is created. The fall, according to Paul, is a change in perception, a loss of the perception of the divine connected with the assertion of futile human thought and a darkening of the heart. The consequence of this is that *humankind can only see clearly the physical and comes to be identified with the physical stuff of human existence. This is 'the lie'.* Having been created to be the image of the Creator in the world of what is created, doing the creative work of the Creator, humankind ends up blind to the invisible things of God and identifying existence with what is created – physical, visible and mortal. And, very importantly, *'the invisible things of God' includes that 'image of God' in humankind itself.*

Exchanging the truth of God for the lie

To further demonstrate the consistency and importance of Paul's understanding of the plight of humankind presented in this early section of the letter to the Romans, several points can be drawn from 2 Corinthians 3-5, an important passage which will be returned to in Chapter 12.

Seeing God's glory

In the first section, Paul is comparing the old law of Moses with the new covenant of the Spirit. Central to his argument is a discussion of the glory that lasts completely overwhelming the fading glory which was present in the giving of the law:

> Now if the ministry of death, chiselled in letters on stone tablets, came in glory so that the people of Israel could not gaze at Moses' face because of the glory of his face, a glory now set aside, how much more will the ministry of the Spirit come in glory? For if there was glory in the ministry of condemnation, much more does the ministry of justification abound in glory! Indeed, what once had glory has lost its glory because of the greater glory; for if what was set aside came through glory, much more has the permanent come in glory! (2 Cor 3:7-11)

Glory is bound up in Paul's thinking with God and consequently with God's eternal nature. The biblical description of the giving of the old law to Moses is an event full of the glory of the eternal God yet that law, according to Paul, is passing away. So Paul says that, in the light of the glory of that which remains, the glory of that which is passing disappears. If the fall involved losing 'the glory of the immortal God' (Rom 1:23), then the law was not, according to Paul, the true recovery of this glory, for the glory of the law was 'passing away'.

Later in the 2 Corinthians passage there is a further occasion where there is this association of 'glory' with what is eternal. In this section there are three other elements that also occur in the Romans 1 passage:

> Yes, everything is for your sake, so that grace, as it extends to more and more people, may increase thanksgiving, to the glory of God. So we do not lose heart. Even though our outward nature [Gk 'outward man'] is wasting away, our inner nature [Gk 'inner man'] is being renewed day by day. For this slight momentary affliction is preparing us for an eternal weight of glory beyond all measure, because we look not at what can be seen but at what cannot be seen; for what can be seen is temporary, but what cannot be seen is eternal. (2 Cor 4:15-18)

In this section Paul is describing the present situation of believers in terms of a process of change: the 'slight momentary affliction' of the present is leading to what he describes as 'an eternal weight of glory'. The first sentence makes a connection with the Romans 1 passage. There Paul presents one of the causes of the human plight as being that, even though people knew God, 'they glorified him not as God, neither gave thanks'. Here in this passage Paul presents one of the purposes of the spreading of the gospel as being to 'increase thanksgiving, to the glory of God'. In itself this would be simply an interesting but not necessarily significant example of Paul using parallel terms. What raises its importance is the last point of the section. Paul says of himself and his fellow believers that 'we look ... at what cannot be seen'. This connects this section much more directly with the thought of the Romans 1 passage for there, as noted above, Paul says that '[God's] eternal power and divine nature, invisible though they are, have been understood and seen through the things he has made'. It is because the invisible things of God are clearly seen that all are without excuse, 'for though they knew God, they did not honour him as God or give thanks to him'. The implication of the above section is that believers now see 'the invisible things of God' and glorify and give thanks to God. Something of what was lost in the banishment from Eden is restored.

Closely related to this is a further important connection. The reason Paul gives for looking at the things that are not seen is that they are 'eternal'. The things which are seen are 'temporary'. Among those things that are seen and are temporary is, what Paul calls, 'our outward man/person'. He says of this that it is 'decaying', a word with the same root as 'corruptible', and it is clear that by the 'outward man/person' Paul is meaning 'the mortal body'. So the 'outward man' or 'flesh' or 'body' is corruptible, temporary, one of those 'things which are seen' unlike the 'invisible things of God' which are incorruptible and eternal. What should be noticed here is that Paul also speaks of the 'inner man/person'. It is presumably the 'inner man/person' who looks 'at the things which are not seen' – the things that are eternal. It is important to note what follows from this: in Paul's thinking, the dividing line between seen and unseen, temporal and eternal, corruptible and incorruptible is drawn within each human being.

Glorying in human wisdom

Further aspects of this emerging picture can now be obtained by giving attention to three more points from the Romans 1 passage. First it should be noted how Paul describes a consequence of the fall as God giving up humanity to 'the lusts of their hearts unto uncleanness, that their bodies should be dishonoured among themselves'. This is very similar to the description of life according to the flesh:

> For what the flesh desires is opposed to the Spirit ... Now the works of the flesh are obvious: fornication, impurity, licentiousness ... (Gal 5:17,19)

There is nothing very surprising in this but, once again, it is only one point in indicating the consistency in the shape of Paul's thought. We have already referred in Chapter 6 (p. 101) to the early part of 1 Corinthians as providing an insight into Paul's understanding of the flesh as the ground for assertiveness against God and against others. Early in the letter there is a noteworthy parallel to the material in Romans 1:

> Do not deceive yourselves. If you think you are wise in this age, you should become fools so that you may become wise. For the wisdom of this world is foolishness with God. For it is written,
> 'He catches the wise in their craftiness',
> and again,
> 'The Lord knows the thoughts of the wise,
> that they are futile.'
> So let no one boast in human leaders [Gk 'men'].
> (1 Cor 3:18-20)

This includes the same reference to the futility of the reasonings of the wise as in the Romans passage, confirming the common pattern of Paul's thought, but what really sharpens the picture comes through comparing the last point about not glorying in men with the Romans passage:

> ... [T]hey became futile in their thinking, and their senseless minds were darkened. Claiming to be wise, they became fools; and they exchanged the glory of the immortal God for images resembling [Gk 'the likeness of an image of'] a mortal human ... (Rom 1:21-23)

The continuation of the above sentence tends to an interpretation of this section as a description by Paul of the descent into religious idolatry as a consequence of not glorifying God; it speaks of the images of 'birds, fourfooted beasts, and creeping things'. That this is part of Paul's meaning is not to be denied but the parallel from the first letter to the Corinthians confirms that there is a more subtle and telling point in Paul's words. The boasting in 'men' described there is not the glorying in any material idol but rather glorying in a particular individual, whether Paul or Apollos or Cephas. The whole point of this section of the letter is clearly expressed by Paul:

> But God chose what is foolish in the world to shame the wise ... that no one [Gk 'flesh'] might boast in the presence of God. (1 Cor 1:27, 29)

What this confirms is that Paul's description of the descent into idolatry in the Romans 1 passage, speaking as it does of exchanging 'the glory of the immortal God for the likeness of an image of mortal man', does not preclude a subtle understanding of idolatry as glorying in the flesh – understood as glorying in any human wisdom.

What this points to is how Paul views the reality of the fall as taking place in each human being. Each human being is made up of both the invisible, creative 'inner person', and the visible, created 'outward person'. That which is created in each human being is 'the flesh' which is 'visible' and 'mortal'. The individual human being, parallel with losing sight of the invisible things of God, comes to serve instead the flesh, losing the perception of that which is of God in him or herself – that which is invisible, glorious and immortal. This is a further clarification of what Paul means by 'exchanging the truth of God for the lie'. This 'exchange' is, for Paul, a matter of human perception. The 'darkened understanding' and 'senseless mind' is a description of humankind having lost sight of the invisible, eternal things of God, including knowledge of being the image of God and therefore, in the terms explored in Chapter 6, identifying existence with the separate, individual flesh.

Exchanging the truth of God for the lie: summary sentence and discussion

As the visible, mortal creation and the invisible, eternal things of the Creator co-exist in each human being, the experience of the fall – exchanging the truth of God for the lie and identifying life with the physical body – is part of the consciousness of each person.

Dunn is helpful in this section in that he explores in some depth the internal human process of turning to what is created but there is a subtle shift in the way he interprets Paul's words which reduces the scale of what is at stake. What follows is a commentary on a summary at the end of a major section headed 'Adam' in which Dunn lays out 'Paul's indictment of humankind'. Dunn starts by stressing the importance of understanding humankind, not just as 'weak and corruptible' but with 'an inescapable dimension of sin, of failure and transgression'. He then goes on to say (101):

> Humans were created for relationship with God, a relationship which is the essence of human life, a relationship which gives humankind fulfilment of being, as creature (in relation to God) and as human (in relation to the rest of the world).

While this might appear unexceptionable – after all, its talk of 'relationship with God' is very characteristic Christian language – it does not do justice to the Genesis account of creation where humans are made in the very image of God. They are not simply 'creature' in relation to God and 'human' in relation to the rest of the world. Rather, this human creature is the very image of God in creation. Dunn goes on (101):

> [Humankind] has turned from God and focused attention exclusively on the world, revolting against its role as creature and thinking to stand as creator in its own right. In consequence humankind has fallen when it thought to rise, has become foolish not wise, baser not superior.

This very much echoes the material in the section above but the next sentence introduces a subtle confusion (101):

> [Humankind] has denied its likeness to God and preferred the likeness of beasts and things.

This sounds neat but the neatness conceals confusion. In the first part of the sentence Dunn has embraced the more radical closeness to God evoked by 'likeness to God' rather than 'relationship to God'. Just as in the main text, Dunn is saying that this is what has been denied. What, Dunn says, has been preferred instead, is 'the likeness of beasts and things'. Despite the parallel use of language, this is describing something different, only a symptom of the inward shift that the first part of the sentence describes. What is it that changes in humankind, corresponding to 'denying its likeness to God', that adequately describes what humankind comes to prefer? The main text argues that it is a turning towards physical, created, visible, mortal existence, symptomatic of which is the turning to idolatry. It is this shift that is related to the loss of consciousness of the things of God, as Dunn goes on to say (101):

[Humankind] has lost its share in the majesty of divinity, and now falls far short of what it might have become. Instead of sharing eternal life, it has become dominated by death, a "sucker" for sin.

Dunn finishes this section with a comment that is designed to speak to his contemporary readers (101):

... [T]he point of Paul's critique remains sharp and continues to probe the conscience of a society in whose ears the subtly deceptive whisper still entices: "You shall be like God."

For Dunn this suggestion is intrinsically deceitful but Paul is in more dangerous territory in which, as we will see in the next section and next chapter, rediscovering the likeness of God, here and now, is precisely what he is concerned with.

The reconciliation of Spirit and flesh

Before proceeding with the argument of this section of the chapter, a section which primarily consists of an examination of one important part of the letter to the Romans, it is worth placing some of the points made in the chapter so far alongside other conclusions reached in Parts Two and Three of the book:

(a) the coarsening of human consciousness and the worship and service of what is created is what Paul means by life according to the flesh (pp. 153-62);

(b) life according to the flesh is life subject to mortality, where death frames reality in a limiting way (pp. 111-14);

(c) life according to the Spirit is a 'clothing over' of fleshly life so that the individual no longer identifies existence with the flesh but with the Spirit (pp. 128-31);

(d) in the Spirit, the division that comes through identifying existence with the flesh gives way to the diversity in unity present before the fall (pp. 132-35);

(e) the falling away of separate existence leads to an experience of unity in the Spirit that is, at present, incomplete but which makes sense as part of a universal transformation to come (pp. 135-43).

Chapter 5 involved an examination of Romans 7:7-25, illuminated by considering the relationship between parent and child. Chapter 6 picked up the continuation of Paul's presentation in 8:1-4, clarifying that Paul is speaking of a true liberation from sin such that the behaviour that the law points to is now flowing naturally from the life in the Spirit. What follows then in Romans 8:5-17 is an examination of 'flesh' and 'Spirit' which Paul finishes by speaking of the baptized becoming 'heirs'; this has been our focus in Chapters 7 and 8. Having made careful points about the translation of 'creation' and Paul's subtle conception of the fall as a loss of perception of the glory of God, we will turn now to Romans 8:18-25 where Paul's vision of what is to come has a vivid universal sense. What this section will establish is how, even though Paul is speaking of a transformation of the whole of creation, the locus of this transformation is humankind, specifically, the human body.

A short passage from 2 Corinthians (5:1-5), which follows directly from the section on the 'outward' and 'inner' man/person examined earlier in the chapter, provides a vital point of connection enabling us to see how individual experience and the expectation of universal change are bound together in Paul's thinking. The RSV gives us the best opportunity to see the parallels between the two passages.

> For we know that if the earthly tent we live in is destroyed, we have a building from God, a house not made with hands, eternal in the heavens. Here indeed we groan, and long to put on our heavenly dwelling, so that by putting it on we may not be found naked. For while we are still in this tent, we sigh with anxiety [Gk 'groan']; not that we would be unclothed, but that we would be further clothed, so that what is mortal may be swallowed up by life. He who has prepared us for this very thing is God, who has given us the Spirit as a guarantee [Gk 'earnest/first instalment of the Spirit']. (2 Cor 5:1-5, RSV)

This first passage was first referred to in Chapter 7 (pp. 128-30). There, the purpose was to note the consistency with which Paul speaks of that which is mortal being swallowed up by or clothed over with immortality and then to go on and connect this image with baptism and the clothing of the baptized with the risen Christ. The second passage will receive detailed examination in the rest of this chapter:

> I consider that the sufferings of this present time are not worth comparing with the glory that is to be revealed to [Gk 'in'] us. For the creation waits with eager longing for the revealing of the sons of God; for the creation was subjected to futility, not of its own will but by the will of him who subjected it in hope; because the creation itself will be set free from its bondage to decay and obtain the glorious liberty of the children of God. We know that the whole creation has been groaning in travail together until now; and not only the creation, but we ourselves, who have the firstfruits of the Spirit, groan inwardly as we wait for adoption as sons, the redemption of our bodies. (Rom 8:18-23, RSV)

Connections between the two passages can be pointed out without difficulty. Both passages are concerned with a present situation that points to a future transformation. The 2 Corinthians passage is immediately preceded by the section speaking of the present 'light affliction, which is for a moment' but which leads to 'an eternal weight of glory' (2 Cor 4:17); the Romans passage begins by speaking of 'present suffering' which is not worth comparing to 'the glory which shall be revealed'. The 2 Corinthians passage speaks of 'what is mortal' being 'swallowed up by life' while the Romans passage uses different terms but is also concerned with the transformation of 'what is created' which will be 'delivered from the bondage of corruption into the glorious liberty of the children of God'. Active in this process is 'the earnest of the Spirit' in 2 Corinthians or 'the firstfruits of the Spirit' in Romans. And, in the immediately following verses, both passages speak in a recognizably similar way of living by what is unseen – faith and hope – rather than by what is seen. The 2 Corinthians passage speaks of walking by faith:

> [F]or we walk by faith, not by sight. (2 Cor 5:7)

And the Romans passage speaks of hope:

> For in hope we were saved. Now hope that is seen is not hope. For who hopes for what is seen? But if we hope for what we do not see, we wait for it with patience. (Rom 8:24f)

The still more vivid parallel in the passages comes in the way Paul speaks four times of the 'groaning' that is involved in waiting expectantly for what is to come:

> For in this tent *we groan*, longing to be clothed with our heavenly dwelling ... For while we are still in this tent, *we groan* under our burden ... (2 Cor 5:2, 4)

> We know that *the whole creation has been groaning* in labour pains until now; and not only the creation, but *we ourselves*, who have the first fruits of the Spirit, *groan* inwardly while we wait for adoption, the redemption of our bodies. (Rom 8:22f)

These are the only occasions when Paul uses *stenazō* which has this sense of 'groaning' (or, perhaps better, 'sighing') in the expectation of something, often in the context of hope for release from suffering of some kind (TDNT). Something that can be easily seen is that while there are vivid points of connection between the two passages, there is a marked difference of focus. Both the uses of *stenazō* in the 2 Corinthians passage concern the situation of believers still burdened with mortality, sighing as they long to be clothed in immortality. The second use in the Romans passage is very similar to this, once again referring to the sighing of believers as they await future transformation. The different picture arises from the first use of the word in the Romans passage for this speaks not of the sighing in expectation of believers but of the whole creation:

> We know that the whole creation has been groaning in travail together until now. (Rom 8:22, RSV)

This idea of the created universe in the pangs of childbirth is prompted by Paul's use of *ōdinō* (translated 'in travail' above), a Greek word whose primary use is for the pains of childbirth. Using this image to shape the translation evokes a powerful picture:

> The created universe is waiting with eager expectation for God's sons to be revealed. ... [T]he universe itself is to be freed from the shackles of mortality ... Up to the present, as we know, the whole created universe in all its parts groans as in the pangs of childbirth. (Rom 8:19, 21f, REB)

Dramatic and vivid as the image is, it leads to an interpretation which does not take into account a consistency in the framework of Paul's thought that the parallel passage in 2 Corinthians reveals. Although the two passages appear to have a different focus, the several common elements in the two passages invite us to consider that in each case Paul is describing the same thing.

It is necessary to recall and elaborate upon an issue involved in the translation 'the creature' or 'the creation' (*hē ktisis*). The way that the AV translates this passage gives interesting confirmation of the distinction made earlier in the chapter. In the AV, the translation usually preferred for *hē ktisis* is 'creature'. This is what is given in the first three uses in the Romans passage:

> For the earnest expectation of *the creature* waiteth for the manifestation of the sons of God. For *the creature* was made subject to vanity, not willingly, but by reason of him who hath subjected the same in hope, because *the creature* itself also shall be delivered from the bondage of corruption into the glorious liberty of the children of God. (Rom 8:19-21, AV)

For the fourth use, the consistency breaks down and the translation 'the creation' is used. The reason is that, in this fourth use, Paul qualifies the word by speaking of 'all' or 'the whole':

> For we know that *the whole creation* groaneth and travaileth in pain together until now. (Rom 8:22)

The point made at the beginning of this chapter is that the English word 'creature' is always used for a discrete part and never for the whole of creation. This is the reason why the AV translation loses its consistency at this point. To develop this point, it is important to see what the fluidity in the Greek word that Paul is using indicates about his mental conception here. This is a subtle point but very illuminating once clearly seen; it involves getting 'inside' the word in order to appreciate how it is functioning. Acknowledging that the Greek word that Paul uses (*ktisis*) needs sometimes to be rendered as 'creature' and sometimes as 'creation' in English does not indicate that the Greek work carries two different, though related, meanings. Rather there is one conception in the Greek that, because of the way English has evolved, does not have a single precisely parallel word in English. What the flexibility in the use of the Greek word indicates is that the emphasis in the word is not primarily on the form of the particular 'thing' or 'object' for which it is being used. Rather it is indicating the nature of what is being spoken of as something that is 'created'. For us, thinking in English, the words 'creation' and 'creature' both tend to evoke the image of a separate, substantial object. We do not immediately associate 'the creation' and 'the creature' with the act that creates them or the fact that they are created things. Though these nouns are both taken from the verb 'to create', we, thinking in English, have to make a gently conscious effort to associate them with the act that brought them into being; the nouns have now, as it were, a separate existence from the verb. What the fluidity of the Greek indicates is that this separation of noun from verb is not present. When the noun is used it is still directly connected with the verb. This is the sense that the clumsy translation used earlier is trying to relay. 'That which is created' places the emphasis on the action that has produced this object, whether it is the whole of creation or a discrete part of it. What Paul's Greek is referring to is not primarily a separate, substantial object but rather its *quality* as a 'thing that is created'. It is this that is particularly important in the Romans passage under examination.

One other brief point needs to be made before turning to what Paul says in Romans 8. This is a simple development of a point of interpretation from the examination of the Romans 1 account of the fall. It arises out of the clear indication in that passage of Paul's understanding of the unique place of humanity in the created order. This 'creature' shares in the dominion of God over all that is created; it carries the 'likeness' or 'image' of God. Humankind is, in Paul's conception, part of the visible creation – 'that which is created' – yet a creature given dominion over all that is created, capable of perceiving the invisible things of God and glorifying and giving thanks to God. And, we shall see that for Paul, because of the unique place of humankind, if something goes wrong with this creature – this part of what is created – then this is of consequence not simply for humanity but for the whole creation.

With these points in mind it is possible to uncover the framework of thought that Paul is working with in the Romans 8 passage. The passage will be commented upon sentence by sentence.

Through suffering to glory

> I consider that the sufferings of this present time are not worth comparing with the glory that is to be revealed to [Gk 'in'] us. (Rom 8:18, RSV)

'Sufferings' are to be associated with what is mortal and corruptible as opposed to 'glory' which is associated with what is eternal and incorruptible. The previous verse has connected suffering with being an heir with Christ. The implication is that in order to share in his glory it is necessary to share the sufferings that brought about that glory and will bring the same glory for those who follow him. Suffering with Christ is a theme that will be returned to in Chapters 11 and 12. The simple observation that the literal translation of Paul's Greek speaks of a revelation 'in' rather than 'to' us is some support for the argument to be presented that the locus of universal transformation is the human body.

The revealing of the 'sons' of God

> For the creation waits with eager longing for the revealing of the sons of God. (Rom 8:19, RSV)

By 'the creation' is meant 'all that is created' but not with that static sense evoked by the translation, 'the creation'. This is best seen in considering where the human being fits in this picture. 'The body', 'the flesh' and 'the outward person/man' are all ways of describing part of 'that which is created'. Just as in the account of the creation in

Genesis there is a progression towards the climax in the creation of humanity – 'the creature made in the image of God' – so, in this sentence, all that has been created is waiting for the climax of this new creation which is 'the revealing of the sons of God'. In the fall, humankind, made in the image of God, knowing God and active agents of God's invisible, creative power, through 'claiming to be wise' becomes identified with that which is created. In this verse Paul looks forward to the time when that image of God is restored, when there is a new climax to creation. That new climax will be when the heirs are revealed as 'sons' of God, men and women having the same relationship to God that Jesus had.

Set free from corruption

> [F]or the creation was subjected to futility, not of its own will but by the will of him who subjected it in hope; because the creation itself will be set free from its bondage to decay and obtain the glorious liberty of the children of God. (Rom 8:20f, RSV)

This is the point at which clarity over what is meant by 'creature' or 'creation' is most crucial. There is no doubt that Paul is saying something momentous here. Interpreting 'creation' as the created universe takes Paul's focus to be a transformation of the whole of creation as an event which is somehow in addition to the revelation of the 'sons' of God. Given the careful interpretation of Paul's Greek that we explored above, and, because of the unique place of humanity on the side of both Creator and created, the accurate interpretation is that, *the transformation of all that is created is to be precisely identified with the restoration of the image of God in humankind* – 'the revealing of the sons of God'. An expanded paraphrase of these verses will help make the sense clear:

> For all that is created, all of physical existence including the human body, waits with eager longing for the revealing of the sons of God, that is, humankind no longer selfishly identified with separate physical existence. For all that is created was, by its nature, always subject to decay, always subject to futility, not of its own will but by the will of God who subjected it in expectation of its eventual transformation; because once there is liberation from the bondage between physical flesh and selfishness in humankind, created stuff will itself be set free from its bondage to decay – the eternal Spirit that fills and surrounds all that is created and without which matter has no existence will be vividly perceived, still invisible but known through the very stuff of creation – and all creation will participate in the effects of humankind, God's image in creation, freely excercising God's loving dominion in all that is created. (Rom 8:19-21, author's paraphrase)

This paraphrase indicates that Paul is indeed making a momentous statement at this point, one that is totally integrated with the whole of Paul's thinking. Paul is giving here a reason for the fall. This reason is outlined in the second half of the sentence:

the creation itself will be set free from its bondage to decay and obtain the glorious liberty of the children of God.

The first half speaks of the fall:

> [F]or the creation was subjected to futility, not of its own will but by the will of him who subjected it in hope.

That which is created was, of its nature, subject to futility. Given that humanity is part of that which is created, that futility is most dramatically seen in human folly which, given the place of humanity, is of significance for the whole of creation. 'Futility' is from the same root as the word used in the Romans 1 passage:

> ... [T]hey became futile in their thinking, and their senseless minds were darkened. Claiming to be wise, they became fools ... (Rom 1:21f)

But what Paul goes on to say is that this giving up of that which is created to 'futility' – the identification of existence with what is created – was not without purpose. The subjection was in hope. It was, in a sense, 'necessary'. Paul now goes on to state what that purpose was. It was 'because the creation itself will be set free from its bondage to decay'. In Paul's understanding, 'what is created' is, as we have seen, always visible and corruptible. This is so of the flesh; it is mortal and, in its visibility and tangibility, a sign of an existence separate from other fleshly individuals and God. It is the identification of humankind with this separate fleshly existence that Paul identifies as a kind of slavery, in particular, a slavery to mortality. Paul conceives of the new act of creation as a liberation from this identification with the mortal flesh. Because of the unique place of humankind in creation – of the stuff of creation but able to exercise the loving dominion of the Creator over all that is created – this new act of creation does not only concern the reconciliation of humankind to God but also the reconciliation of all of that which is created with the Creator. The locus for this reconciliation is the human body. Once the false identification of existence with the flesh which humankind has fallen into and which is characterized by folly and a darkened understanding is at an end then there is, in humankind, a conscious integration of that which creates – 'the inner person' – and that which is created; that which is created – 'the outward person'/'the flesh' – is no longer served; existence can now be identified with the Spirit which is eternal and which, while bringing about diversity, is always itself one with God:

> That which is created will itself be set free from its bondage to decay and will obtain the freedom of the glory of the children of God.

What should also be noted in this sentence is the emphasis on freedom. The key to this 'setting free of creation from its bondage to decay' is 'the freedom of the glory of the children of God'. The 'decay' of the past is contrasted with the eternal quality of 'glory' in the future. It is not incidental that right at the beginning of this chapter of the letter to the Romans Paul also speaks of freedom:

> For the law of the Spirit of life in Christ Jesus has set me free from the law of sin
> and of death. (Rom 8:2, RSV)

There is a solid consistency in Paul's framework of thought. There is a clear line
between, on the one side, Spirit, freedom, right action and eternal life, and on the
other, flesh, law, sin and death. What Paul says in Romans 8:20f is that, in the
revealing of the children of God, there is a reconciliation of all that is created with
the Creator. The further implication is the momentous one indicated in this sentence
that this transformation could only be accomplished through the real experience of
'subjection to futility' – the real identification in humanity, the image of God, of 'that
which creates' with 'that which is created'.

The redemption of our bodies

> We know that the whole creation has been groaning in travail together until now;
> and not only the creation, but we ourselves, who have the firstfruits of the Spirit,
> groan inwardly as we wait for adoption as sons, the redemption of our bodies.
> (Rom 8:22f, RSV)

The image of childbirth that may well be contained in the opening sentence is a
vivid one for the idea of that which is created struggling to bring forth the sons
of God, the new climax of creation, echoing the way that in the book of Genesis
the whole process of creation leads up to its climax in the creation of humanity,
the image of God. The particular focus of this section is indicated by the phrase:
'but we ourselves ... groan inwardly as we wait for adoption as sons'. 'Adoption as
sons' (*huiothesia*) is the word that received attention in Chapter 7 (pp. 132-4) being
defined as 'giving of sonship'. Paul uses it on other occasions for what occurs at
baptism. Believers receive a 'giving of sonship' Spirit. Here, somewhat confusingly,
Paul uses it for something still to come, the time when that sonship will be revealed.
The two ways in which Paul uses this word indicate the source of potential confusion
for his readers, that is, the relationship between what has already begun in baptism
and its full accomplishment in the future. The point Paul is making is that those
who are baptized, while they have the firstfruits of the Spirit, are still, like the rest
of what is created, awaiting the future transformation. They have received sonship
but that sonship is still to be revealed. They are sons and heirs but are yet to inherit.
Specifically, the 'inner person/man' groans, awaiting the transformation of the
'outward man' – 'the redemption of the body'.

It is at this point that the consistency between this passage and the section of 2
Corinthians becomes most vivid:

> Here indeed we groan, and long to put on our heavenly dwelling ... For while
> we are still in this tent, we sigh with anxiety [Gk 'groan']; not that we would be
> unclothed, but that we would be further clothed, so that what is mortal may be
> swallowed up by life. (2 Cor 5:2, 4, RSV)

While the focus of Paul's thought in both these passages is different, the shape of his thinking is consistent even as it is extraordinary. What is indicated by observing the repeated pattern in his thought is that Paul's expectation for the future is not an ending of 'earthly' or 'created' or 'mortal' life, but rather its transformation – 'the redemption of our body'. Paul says that what is mortal will not come to an end – the mortal will not be 'unclothed' – but rather be 'clothed over' with what is immortal. Paul looks forward in confident hope to the future time when the separation between Creator and that which is created – between Spirit and flesh – is over. The false identification of humankind with the flesh, a life that manifests in individual self-centred striving will be at an end. But this is not the end of physical life but rather its transformation. The conscious identification of the Creator and what is created, of flesh and Spirit consciously reconciled, is the extraordinary vision of the life that Paul believes will be the adult inheritance of humankind.

Conclusion

This chapter has contained an examination of passages from 2 Corinthians and Romans 8 in both of which Paul is concerned with the way the present situation of believers relates to a future transformation. It has been argued that Paul had a view of the identification of humankind with what is created as 'necessary' in order that the whole created order might be transformed. The locus of this transformation is the human body in which Spirit and flesh – 'that which creates' and 'that which is created' – will be reconciled – 'the redemption of our body'. The pattern of Paul's thought in both passages indicates that he considered that this future inheritance would not be the end of 'earthly' or 'created' existence but rather its transformation. The perception of the invisible things of God that was lost in the fall will revive as existence is no longer identified with the mortal body but with the eternal Spirit. In this transformation in human self-understanding individual assertion is at an end.

This is the 'coming of age' when humankind comes into its 'inheritance' as adult: a life in this creation, without self-centred striving, with direct experience of the painful consequences of being at odds with the Spirit of God, having seen the true nature of what is wrong, with consequent knowledge of good and evil. This is humankind, the image of God in creation, exercising God's creative and loving dominion, fully at home in the flesh, able to enjoy mortal bodily existence, but not identified with fleshly existence, conscious of being surrounded and animated by the eternal Spirit of God. And this is a transformation that affects all creation. For matter now has at work within it a conscious utterly unselfish player in the image of God and therefore filled with the loving purposes of the creator and, being physical, able to implement that loving purpose directly.

PART FOUR
The Source of Freedom

Introduction to Part Four

In the old Birmingham Science Museum in England there was a section for children in which they could explore in a practical way certain principles of science and engineering. One display involved a scattering of large slightly odd shaped blocks with four evenly shaped blocks secured to the floor, one at each corner of a square. The task for the children was simple in principle but difficult to do in practice: to use the specially shaped bricks to build an arch between the four secure blocks. The lesson was also a simple but worthwhile one: to discover that magical moment when the keystone is placed in the middle of an arch and what has, up until that point, been a very unsteady structure suddenly becomes so strong that it provides stable elevated pathways to run across and jump from.

Earlier chapters have been carefully constructing the columns from the tops of which a final arched structure must be built. The creation of each column has proceeded with careful attention to the alignment with the other columns but now that alignment becomes still more crucial. The stage we are at is analogous to the last phase in the creation of the arch. Before it connects with the keystone each rib of the arch is useless for supporting any weight; building must proceed quickly so that this period of vulnerability is minimized. But once the keystone is in place it is as if each skinny rib is suddenly filled with strength.

Over the next three chapters a number of important topics will be presented in a relatively brief span with the deliberate intention of enabling the relatedness of one topic with another to be seen. Creating this arch of connected topics to reveal the coherence of Paul's theology is only possible because the 'columns' – the four elements of his experience that have been presented as providing the basis for his theology – have been clearly identified. The key elements of his fundamental shift in perception are the sense of being: *(a) liberated from sin felt as an empowerment to always act rightly* (Chapter 1) and *(b) directly guided by God* (Chapters 2 and 3) as a consequence of which *(c) life as it was is newly seen as having been fundamentally limited or constrained – a kind of slavery or childhood* (Chapters 4, 5 and 6). This shift in perception is further characterized as carrying *(d) a sustained sense of the corporate nature of human liberation such that the individual experience of transformation can only be understood as part of an imminent transformation for all* (Chapters 7, 8 and 9). As we move to the keystone of Paul's theological structure the importance of establishing these particular elements as the support for the whole edifice will become still clearer.

As far as we know, Paul had not been present while Jesus taught; he was not one of the group who experienced the desolation of his death in Jerusalem; he was not one of the group of close disciples who believed that they saw Jesus after his death. Yet an understanding of who Jesus was and what he did, particularly in his death, is undoubtedly the keystone of Paul's theology:

> When I came to you, brothers and sisters, I did not come proclaiming the mystery of God to you in lofty words or wisdom. For I decided to know nothing among you except Jesus Christ, and him crucified. (1 Cor 2:1f)

What will be done in these final chapters is to see how the nature of the experience that we have identified with those key elements set out above is related in Paul's thinking with the figure of Jesus. How has this keystone shaped and been shaped by the extraordinary experience that Paul and others have had? This will give us a more clear view of how he sees Jesus but also has the potential to bring further clarity to our understanding of the nature of the experience itself.

This book is concerned with human transformation, its nature and how it comes about. In Paul's mind, this transformation is indissolubly bound up with the figure of Jesus, in particular, with his death and resurrection. If we accept the genuineness of the liberation Paul speaks of, a question that legitimately concerns us today is whether, as all the New Testament writings assume, the events surrounding Jesus are essential to making this liberation possible. As with earlier stages of the book, we are concerned to see the experience that lies behind Paul's words and our primary tool for discovering this is the coherence in what Paul says in different situations. It is this experience in all its freshness and strangeness that the book seeks to reveal. To this purpose, themes that have received attention in earlier chapters now recur in particular relationship to Jesus. This both draws Jesus more firmly into this presentation of Paul's theology but it also confirms and clarifies the importance of these elements in early Christian experience.

Chapter 10

God's Outcast:
the Transformation of Jesus

Central to this chapter is the first stage of an exploration into how the theme of direct guidance relates to the figure of Jesus. We will see how it is possible to speak of Jesus as one who lives by faith, who, as expressed in the clumsy but accurate phrase identified in Chapter 2, lives in complete receptivity and obedience to 'faith's "heard thing"', the 'word of prophecy' that is an integral part of living by faith. This, in turn, opens up a new understanding of Paul's emphasis on the death of Jesus, not as something to be dogmatically asserted as the source of liberation in the past but as indissolubly bound up with the present liberation of individuals. It is the death of Jesus that Paul presents as both the catalyst for his own transformation and the means for understanding its universal theological signficance.

In order to appreciate that universal significance, at crucial points in the next three chapters, it is necessary to give some attention to the particular Jewish background of both the events surrounding the death of Jesus and the subsequent theological reflection. We will begin in this chapter to see how it is, in fact, the very particular circumstances of Jesus' death that give it the universal significance that Paul first experiences and then communicates to others.

The one right action

The title of this section will bring to mind the Romans text we explored in Chapter 6 where Paul contrasts the sin of Adam with the right action of Jesus:

> And the free gift is not like the effect of the one man's sin. For the judgement following one trespass brought condemnation, but the free gift following many trespasses brings *right action*. ... Therefore just as one man's trespass led to condemnation for all, so one man's *right action* leads to justification (absolution) and life for all. (Rom 5:16,18, adapted NRSV)

Here Paul describes in more detail the nature of the 'free gift'. Our first examination of this text established that Paul is contrasting two continuous states which follow from the actions of Adam and Jesus. The action of Adam leads to 'condemnation' for humankind with the sense of a continuous state of 'imprisonment' or 'slavery' in 'mortality'. The action of Jesus leads to a real change in which 'right action', 'doing what is right' becomes a continuous state. Now our attention will be focused on the single actions that lead to the continuous states. The 'trespass' of Adam can be simply stated: unlike faithful Abraham, Adam does not do what God asks; he disobeys the word of God.

But more needs to be said about the 'right action' of Jesus. Paul uses the same word, *dikiaiōma* ('right action'), for both the one right action, that is, the 'free gift', and continuous 'right action', the consequence of the gift. And he also says of the gift that it 'leads to justification (absolution) and life for all'. As in Chapter 6, to clarify what Paul means here by 'one right action' it is helpful to refer to the other important text where *dikiaiōma* is used. In this text, 'right action' is used to describe the continuous state:

> For what the law was unable to do in that it was weak through the flesh, God did: sending his own Son in form of sinful flesh and for sin, he condemned the sin in the flesh in order that law's *right action* might be fulfilled in us, those who do not walk according to the flesh but according to the Spirit. (Rom 8:1-4, author's translation)

It was argued earlier that Paul is here stating that those who live by the Spirit are able to fulfil the right action prescribed by the law in a way that is not possible without the empowerment of the Spirit. It was claimed that Paul can also describe the action which brought about this transformation, in other words, God's condemnation of the sin in the flesh through 'sending his own Son in form of sinful flesh and for sin', as 'the one right action'. To put this another way, the one right action of the one man, Jesus, makes possible the continuous right action of the many. The equation – one right action of the one leading to the continuous right action of the many – precisely balances the way Paul expresses the genesis of sin:

> [S]in came into the world through one man, and death through sin, and so death spread to all because all have sinned – ... (Rom 5:12)

The sin of the one man leads to the sin of humankind which means condemnation to mortality, a kind of death; the right action of the one man leads to the right action of all which means liberation into life.

One implication of Paul's talk of the one right action needs emphasizing: this is the first right action since the sin of Adam. This is to take Paul seriously when he says:

> [A]ll, both Jews and Greeks, are under the power of sin, as it is written:
> "There is no one who is righteous, not even one;
> there is no one who has understanding,
> there is no one who seeks God…" (Rom 3:9-11)

Paul goes on to quote several further texts from the Psalms and Isaiah to support this position before returning to this key point:

> For there is no distinction, since all have sinned and fall short of the glory of God;
> they are now justified by his grace as a gift ... (Rom 3:23f)

All are under the power of sin. Paul's focus here is not on individual actions but on a fundamental condition. Paul considers that this fundamental state affects and informs all human actions so that even an apparent right action, a good action prescribed by the law and carried out dutifully, is still carried out by a person under the power of sin.

To make accurate sense of this, an earlier conclusion is essential: Paul is speaking from a new sense of sin (pp. 7-11). It is the fundamental identification by humankind of life with corruptible fleshly existence – 'the sin in the flesh' – which leads Paul to speak of the impossibility of right action by anyone. This is the state that Paul describes in the central passage of the Romans letter:

> For I know that nothing good dwells within me, that is, in my flesh. I can will what is right, but I cannot do it. For I do not do the good I want, but the evil I do not want is what I do. Now if I do what I do not want, it is no longer I that do it, but sin that dwells within me. (Rom 7:18-20)

It will be remembered that this description of the struggle of humankind in the flesh ends with a plea to be rescued:

> Wretched man that I am! Who will rescue me from this body of death? (Rom 7:24)

Humankind pleads for deliverance to come from outside the closed circle of sin and death that he vividly describes.

What Paul considers to be God's response to that plea is clear:

> ... sending his own Son in the likeness of sinful flesh, and to deal with sin, he condemned sin in the flesh. (Rom 8:3)

Titles that Paul uses for Jesus – Jesus as 'God's wisdom' (1 Cor 1:24), as 'God's image' (2 Cor 4:4), as 'God's righteousness' (1 Cor 1:30) – are ways Paul indicates his understanding of Jesus as uniquely close to God. More specifically, Jesus is the only one 'who knew no sin' (2 Cor 5:21). In the understanding of sin presented earlier (pp. 92-6, 101, 103-8) this means that in Jesus there was no assertion against God. It is this condition that makes the pure right action possible. Jesus can perform an act of complete obedience to God in which there is no selfishness – a human act in which only God is the doer. As we will now see, a central theme for Paul is the new beginning for humankind opened up by 'the right action of Jesus' – an action of total faith.

The faith of Jesus

Vital for understanding the nature of faith was seeing the connection between faith and the prophetic word established in Chapter 2. Now we need to see how Paul connects faith with Jesus:

> We who are Jews by nature, and not sinners of the Gentiles, knowing that a man is not justified by the works of the law, but *by the faith of Jesus Christ*, even we have *believed* in Jesus Christ, that we might be justified *by the faith of Christ*, and not by works of the law: for by works of the law shall no flesh be justified. (Gal 2:15f, AV)

There are two important issues we need to now consider in relation to the translation of this passage. As was noted in the Introduction (pp. xiii-xiv), the English words 'faith' (*pistis*) and 'to believe' (*pisteuō*) are the noun and verb of the same Greek root. An accurate understanding of the phrase translated above 'by the faith of Jesus Christ' (*dia pisteōs Xristou Iēsou*) is obviously important for it occurs in similar form in a number of important passages. The phrase is italicized in the extracts below and the NRSV is contrasted with the AV in each case:

> ...the life I now live in the flesh I live *by faith in the Son of God*... (Gal 2:20)
> ...the life which I now live in the flesh I live *by the faith of the Son of God*... (Gal 2:20, AV)

> ...that I may gain Christ and be found in him, not having a righteousness of my own that comes from the law, but one that comes *through faith in Christ*, the righteousness from God based on faith. (Phil 3:8f)
> ...not having my own righteousness, which is of law, but that which is *through the faith of Christ.* (Phil 3:8f, AV)

> But now, irrespective of law, the righteousness of God has been disclosed, ... the righteousness of God *through faith in Jesus Christ* for all who believe. (Rom 3:21f)
> But now the righteousness of God without the law is manifested, ... even the righteousness of God which is *by faith of Jesus Christ* unto all and upon all of them that believe. (Rom 3:21f, AV)

Most modern translations replace the phrase rendered 'by the faith of Jesus Christ' in the AV translation above with the phrase 'through' or 'by faith *in* Jesus Christ' (NRSV, RSV, NIV, NJB, REB, TEV). This is a significant difference. Interpreting the phrase as 'faith *in* Jesus Christ' marks a sharp distinction between those who have faith and Jesus Christ, the one in whom they put their faith. Given Paul's description of Jesus as the Son of God and as the one 'who knew no sin' (2 Cor 5:21) and the traditional understanding of a continuing if not heightened sense of sin in those who have come to faith, this translation of the phrase supports not only a sharp distinction but a clear and qualitative separation between the person who comes to faith and Jesus, the object of that faith.

The translation 'faith *of* Jesus Christ' leads to a different interpretation. It means that those who come to faith can be understood as entering into the way of life of Jesus, sharing what we called in Chapter 1 his 'state/manner of existing'. This is an extraordinarily bold claim for the life of faith and it is this issue that has arguably distorted the plain sense in the Greek which would most straightforwardly be translated 'faith *of* Jesus' rather than 'faith *in* Jesus'. Clearly if Jesus is the one 'who knew no sin' then he is separated from all the rest who 'have sinned and fall short of the glory of God' (Rom 3:23); if living by faith is solely associated with continuing sin then it is not something that describes the way Jesus lived. However an alternative interpretation has already been offered: the life of faith can be conceived of, in Paul's understanding, as the way of liberation, crossing over the line between God and that which falls short of his glory. To live by faith is to begin living the same kind of life that Jesus lived, free from sin with all actions directly guided by God.

The beginning of faith

It is important to note alongside this interpretation that, even if there is similarity between the faith of Jesus and that of those who come after him, Paul still ascribes particular importance to the faith of Jesus; there is a significant sense in which faith has a beginning in him:

> Now *before faith came*, we were restrained under the law, protected *until faith should be revealed*. So that the law was our childminder until Christ came, that we might be justified by faith. But *now that faith has come*, we are no longer under a childminder; for in Christ Jesus you are all sons of God, through faith. (Gal 3:23-26, adapted RSV)

Note the idea that faith has a beginning: 'before faith came'; 'until faith would be revealed'; 'now that faith has come'. Clearly Paul has a specific event in mind when he speaks in this way. He could be interpreted as speaking here of the coming of faith in the individuals who come after Jesus – that once a person has come to faith he or she has no more need of the law to act as a 'childminder'; however the context of the whole passage is the discussion of the purpose of the law in human history as a whole not just on the individual scale.

Greater clarity can be found by considering what Paul means by the faith of Jesus. Paul might be referring to the actions of Jesus throughout his life as a new way of living which others can now follow. But there are very few references in the letters of Paul to the life of Jesus and those few references are very limited in content (Gal 4:4; 2 Cor 10:1, Phil 1:8; Rom 15:3; 1 Cor 11:23-26). This is a fact often noted by scholars and gives one important indication that the life of Jesus as an example of faith is not what Paul is meaning. But there is one action of Jesus to which Paul does regularly refer:

> And being found in human form, he humbled himself and became obedient to the point of death – even death on a cross. (Phil 2:8)

On many occasions, Paul refers to the death or cross or suffering of Jesus (see Rom 5-8; 1 Cor 1, 15; 2 Cor 1; Gal 6; Phil 2 and elsewhere). Further confirmation that Paul has in mind the death of Jesus when he refers to the faith of Jesus comes in a curious way.

The faith of Abraham

In order to present the primacy of faith, Paul sets out to demonstrate in the letters to the Galatians and the Romans that the response of Abraham to God was the response of faith and that, hence, since Abraham and his faith came before Moses and the law, faith does indeed have some kind of precedence over the law. For Paul to speak of the faith of Abraham would seem to undermine the idea that the faith of Jesus was some kind of beginning of faith for others. This would indeed be so if Jesus' whole life was being presented as the example of faith. It would then make no sense for Paul to use the faith of Abraham, who could not have been following the example of Jesus. However it is faith with two particular qualities which Paul is indicating when he speaks of the faith of Abraham and, by implication, the faith of Jesus: confidence in the face of death and direct guidance from God.

It can be seen in the following passage how, in describing Abraham's faith, Paul repeatedly shows how Abraham did not lose faith when faced with the power of death (this is most easily seen in the NIV translation):

> [Abraham] is our father in the sight of God, in whom he believed – *the God who gives life to the dead* and *calls things that are not as though they were*. Against all hope, Abraham in hope believed and so became the father of many nations, just as it had been said to him, 'So shall your offspring be.' Without weakening in his faith, *he faced the fact that his body was as good as dead – since he was about a hundred years old – and that Sarah's womb was also dead*. Yet he did not waver through unbelief regarding the promise of God, but was strengthened in his faith and gave glory to God, being fully persuaded that God had power to do what he had promised. (Rom 4:17-21, NIV)

Abraham's faith is referred to five times in this brief span and there are a similar number of references to death, all of which do not cause him to waver through a lack of faith. He continues to rely on God's promise.

Abraham is also for Paul the exemplary man of faith because he believes and obeys the direct word of God. His first appearance in scripture is an account of the word of God sending him away from his own country:

> Now the Lord said to Abram, 'Go from your country and your kindred and your father's house to the land that I will show you. I will make of you a great nation ... (Gen 12:1f)

Paul quotes the book of Genesis when it recounts how Abraham is promised that his descendants will be as many as the stars. The faith of Abraham is that the word spoken by God to Abraham will be fulfilled. This is the point made about Abraham in Genesis after he has been tested to the extent of having to offer his son Isaac:

> ... by your offspring shall all the nations of the earth gain blessing for themselves, *because you have obeyed my voice.* (Gen 22:18)

Abraham stays confident in and obedient to the prophetic word of God even though 'his body was as good as dead' and the womb of Sarah was dead. Even when he is asked to kill Isaac, the apparently miraculous fulfilment of God's promise that he would have descendants by Sarah, his obedience to the word of God does not falter. It is Paul's presentation of Abraham's confident obedience in the directly given word of God even in the face of death which connects the faith of Abraham with the faith of Jesus.

Faith and the liberated life

In Paul's understanding, faith enables a person to move from life under the power of sin to a life of righteousness, of right action. But there is more to faith than simply the transference to a new way of life. We need to return to the question that Paul puts to Peter, recalled in the letter to the Galatians:

> But if, in our effort to be justified ('righteoused'/'made right') in Jesus, we ourselves have been found to be sinners, is Jesus then a servant of sin? Certainly not! (Gal 2:17)

It was argued (pp. 8-9) that in this question Paul is reminding Peter that it was in coming to faith in Jesus that both he and Peter found they were sinners in a way that they had not previously been aware of. This new awareness of sinfulness is directly connected with the event of 'justification' or 'absolution', understood as a real change, the actual crossing over of the dividing line separating God and that which falls short of God's glory. The implication of the references in Paul to the 'faith of Jesus' that we have considered above is that, just as faith is an essential part of revealing what is wrong and bringing about liberation, so, after liberation, faith is the way in which life continues to be guided. 'The faith of Jesus' is continuing obedience to the word of God.

But we have highlighted one further essential dimension to faith. In presenting Abraham as an example of faith, Paul is concerned to indicate Abraham's continuing faithfulness to God's word even in the face of death. In this specific way, Abraham's faith is the faith of Jesus. The implication is that Paul is presenting Jesus as demonstrating the same faithfulness to God's directly given word even though it takes him into conflict and ultimately to his death. We will see in the next section how it is this faith – a faithful obedience to the *akoē pisteōs*, the directly given word from God, even when it leads to death – that Paul presents as being essential for liberation.

The faith of Jesus: summary sentence and discussion

Paul presents Jesus as living by faith, demonstrated pre-eminently in the way he goes to his death, obedient to God's word, just as Abraham had faith in the directly given word of God even when death seemed to undermine what he had heard.

Ziesler acknowledges in his commentaries on Galatians and Romans that there is an ambiguity in the Greek phrase, *pistis Iēsou* ('faith in' or 'faith of Jesus'). He sums up the argument for the 'faith of' interpretation in his commentary on Galatians 2:15 (*Galatians*, 24):

> It is increasingly argued that here and in 3.22 and in some other places we ought to take the genitive at its face value to mean 'of' not 'in'. If this is right, then the line of thought in this verse is that we are justified first by the faithful action of Jesus in undergoing the cross (presumably) and then by our response to, our faith in, that faithful action. This way of taking the phrase is gaining ground in scholarly circles and certainly makes good sense, but it cannot be said that the issue is settled.

Note his comment that the 'face value' of the genitive is 'of' rather than 'in'. In his commentary on Romans 3:22, 'But now, irrespective of law, the righteousness of God has been disclosed, … the righteousness of God through faith in Jesus', Ziesler acknowledges that translating the last phrase 'through the faith(fulness) of Jesus ' 'would then provide a neat contrast between Jesus's faithfulness in obeying God even as far as the cross, and human faith as response to that action …' He notes that 'the matter is not susceptible to a dogmatic answer' but is inclined to follow the traditional interpretation of 'faith in Jesus' (*Romans*, 109).

Dunn firmly rejects the 'faith of Jesus' interpretation. His essay arguing the case for 'faith in Jesus' is included as an appendix to the second edition of Richard B. Hays's influential argument in support of 'faith of', *The Faith of Jesus*. Like Ziesler, Dunn also acknowledges that attention to the Greek does not resolve this issue (*Galatians*, 138):

> The word itself can, of course, mean either 'faith' or 'faithfulness' … And the genitive construction in itself is indecisive either way …

The interpretation of this phrase is a well known and well debated example of the type of hermeneutical issue that recurs several times in this book. An assessment of which interpretation is accurate can only be made by combining judgments about the overall interpretation of Paul's theology with concern for the interpretation of individual words or phrases.

Dunn observes slightly incredulously (Hays, 258) that 'Hays's thesis vacuums up every relevant reference to "faith" in Galatians in order to defend the subjective genitive ['faith of Jesus'] reading of 2:16, 20 and 3:22. This is nothing short of astonishing.' And why so? Because, if accepted, this interpretation inevitably pulls the rug from under a traditional understanding of, what Dunn calls, 'justifying faith' (Hays, 258):

> It now appears that a text (Galatians) which has provided such a powerful charter of "justifying faith" for Jesus' self-understanding nowhere clearly speaks of that "faith".

And what does Dunn mean by that 'justifying faith'? It is 'accepting the *akoē pisteōs*', interpreted by Dunn in a way we have already seen to be inadequate as 'accepting the gospel message' (pp. 23-34). Dunn's view is that (*Galatians*, 139)

> In short, the phrase is still best taken as expressing faith in Jesus, that is, acceptance of the reliability of what was said by and about Jesus (acceptance of the gospel message – iii.2, 5) and trust in, reliance upon the Jesus of whom the gospel thus speaks …

Central to Dunn's challenge to the 'faith of Jesus' position is his argument that it significantly reduces references to 'human believing'. If the texts are speaking of the 'faith of Jesus', they are not concerned with the human response of belief. This difficulty for Dunn arises from not allowing enough flexibility in the way the phrase operates. For example, to say 'a person is justified through the faith of Jesus', while it puts the emphasis on the faith Jesus lived by does not exclude the individual who can discover and live through the faith of Jesus, in the sense that such a person can act with the same kind of faith that Jesus had. Hays makes the point that 'through the faith of Jesus' can refer to both Christ's faithfulness and the faith of the believer (Hays, 297).

As the main argument suggests, this understanding of faith makes good sense in relation to Abraham as a model of faith. Dunn presents a vivid picture of the kind of faith that Paul means by referring to Abraham as an example of faith. Dunn mentions Abraham's obedience to God's command, his confidence in God's promise and of the absolute reliance of Abraham upon God and the willingness to be obedient even in the face of death (*Theology*, 225, 375, 379). These references to Abraham are in themselves some answer to the important question that Dunn puts to Hays (Hays, 259):

> What does "the faith of Christ" mean? To what does it refer? The answer is hardly clear. The ministry of Jesus as a whole? The death of Christ in particular? The continuing ministry of the exalted Christ in heaven?

The main text answers that the death of Jesus is central: obedience to the directly given word of God even to the point of death. Hays offers a similar response to Dunn (Hays, 297):

> It should be said clearly that for Paul, *pistis Xristou* refers to Jesus' obedience to death on the cross … not on the whole ministry of Jesus of Nazareth. This narrower punctiliar sense – focused on the cross – is the only meaning supported by Paul's usage.

While there are many references to Abraham in Sanders's analysis of Paul, they do not contain any of the richness that comes through in Dunn's commentary. For Sanders, Paul uses the person of Abraham, not to throw light on the nature of faith, but, to argue that those who have faith in Jesus are the true descendants of Abraham. As we have seen in other aspects of Sanders's analysis, he considers that Paul has come to this view through revelation and then uses any means of argument at his disposal to demonstrate his case. Faith, in Sanders's assessment of Paul, is a traditional outline of the gospel message. But note that Sanders, while acknowledging that this cannot be the faith of Abraham, simply asserts this traditional view (117/138):

> Faith is not the general attitude of trusting God, but the specific commitment to Christ. Though he uses Abraham, who could not have known about Jesus, as the biblical paradigm of the faithful person, Paul thought that in his own time faith was Christian faith.

Sanders does not seriously acknowledge that Paul's use of Abraham as the paradigm of faith might provide difficulties for a traditional understanding of faith as 'commitment to Christ'.

Sanders does not open up any investigation into the experiential content of faith and it is therefore not surprising that he gives no consideration to the interpretation of *pistis Iēsou* as 'faith of Jesus'.

The accursed death of the Christ

We have now seen that there is precisely the same shape to Paul's understanding of 'faith' as for 'right action': just as the right action of the one man Jesus Christ leads to the right action of the many, so the faith of the one man Jesus Christ leads to the faith of the many. We have seen that Paul considers the 'right action' and 'faith' of the many to be real, the fruit of an effective liberation which he and others have experienced and are living. It is vital to note that although as objective events the actions of Jesus come before the liberation of Paul, in terms of the subjective appreciation of what has occurred, the transformed life *precedes* (or is simultaneous with) the understanding of the life and death of Jesus as the explanation of how this has come about. This fact is important in establishing how it was that Paul came to consider his experience of liberation as brought about by the action of Jesus. It has shaped the presentation of the book as a whole in taking time to first be clear about the nature of Paul's liberating experience before turning to this question that is central for the whole of the last part of the book.

In order to understand the universal effect that Paul is claiming for the death of Jesus, we need to return to the precise circumstances of his death. For a right understanding of the meaning of the death of Jesus can only come from understanding something of its Jewish context. An indication of this fact is the amount of effort Paul employs on the issue of the law and the Jewish people, not only, as we have seen, to convince fellow Jews (Chapter 4). It will be argued that the specific calling of the Jews and their preparation as the people from whom comes the Christ – the Messiah – is essential to Paul's understanding of liberation. It is out of this calling of a particular people, a calling mediated through Moses and the prophets, established in a covenant between God and the Jews in which the law is the central element, that the universality of God's 'righteousness', the consistent right action of God (pp. 13-15), is revealed.

To see how Paul understands the law to be crucial in bringing about the universal transforming effect of the death of Jesus it is necessary to turn to a difficult passage in Galatians where Paul speaks of the death of Jesus Christ using four texts from the Hebrew Bible:

> 'Cursed is everyone who does not observe and obey all the things written in the book of the law.' (Gal 3:10 quoting Deut 27:26)
> 'The one who is righteous will live by faith.' (Gal 3:11 quoting Habakkuk 2:4)
> 'Whoever does the works of the law will live by them.' (Gal 3:12 quoting Lev 18:5)
> 'Cursed is everyone who hangs on a tree' ... (Gal 3:13 quoting Deut 21:23)

It is not easy to follow Paul through his precise explanation of these texts. While he seems to be using an argument to demonstrate a case, it would be more appropriate to describe what he is doing as showing how his conclusion is compatible with the Hebrew scriptures. As noted above, the experience precedes the explanation. In the context of the letter to the Galatians this compatability with the Hebrew scriptures is important. Paul is arguing for both the continuity and discontinuity of his gospel in relation to Jewish law and scripture. Continuity because he is claiming obedience to the God of Abraham; discontinuity because he is advocating an abrogation of the Jewish law as the way of discerning what is right to do. If this purpose of Paul is understood, it is possible to see what Paul is seeking to express in juxtaposing these texts.

Through them, Paul is seeking to make clear something about Jesus. In Chapter 7 some preliminary observations were made about Paul's understanding of the continuing life of Jesus; we saw how Paul spoke of the second Adam becoming an 'alive-making Spirit' (pp. 127-31). We now turn to a central element of the final part of the book: to see how Paul related his experience of liberation to his conviction that this death as one cursed was not the end for Jesus. For the element which is, in effect, part of Paul's conclusion but without which his demonstration makes no sense is that the God of Abraham, the God who gave the law, brought Jesus back to life from the dead; he who appeared cursed is, in fact, blessed. What Paul is demonstrating in this sequence of texts is the consequence of this for the law and the meaning it gives to the death of Jesus.

Life and death; blessings and curses

The two texts from Deuteronomy need to be considered first. The first text is taken from an extended passage where Moses is presented as laying out the demands of the law and the curses and blessings which will be consequences of following or disregarding it. In summing up, Moses tells the people that if they obey the commandments of the Lord their God, they 'shall live'; if not, they shall 'perish', they 'shall not live' (Deut 30:16, 18). This is the conclusion:

> I call heaven and earth to witness against you today that I have set before you life
> and death, blessings and curses. Choose life so that you and your descendants
> may live ... (Deut 30:19)

What needs to be specially noted is that this extended and climactic section of Deuteronomy (Chapters 27-30) presents an absolute division between two modes of life. Follow the law and you will be blessed and live; turn away from the law and you will be cursed and die. This sharp division between blessing and curse, between life and death, is essential for Paul's argument. What needs to be remembered as we seek the explanation of Paul's meaning in these texts is the groundwork in the first part of the book (pp. 13-15, 55-61). It became possible to see the sharp dividing line in Paul's thinking between the life 'in line' with God and life that 'falls short of

God's glory'. It was noted that, for Paul, there is no blurring between these two. On the one side is the life freed from sin, doing what is right guided directly by what is heard in faith; on the other is life still under the power of sin with a consequent need for the law in order to know how to do what God requires.

This receives further emphasis when it is seen that, alongside the many specific commandments set out in the book of Deuteronomy, there is a repeated injunction which emphasizes that it is the entire law that must be obeyed (author's italics):

> This *entire commandment* that I command you today you must diligently observe, so that you may live ... (8:1)
> Keep, then, this *entire commandment* ... (11:8)
> If you will only heed his *every commandment* ... (11:13)
> If you will diligently observe this *entire commandment* ... (11:22)
> Be careful to obey *all these words* that I command you today ... (12:28)
> ... if you obey the voice of the Lord your God by keeping *all his commandments* that I am commanding you today, doing what is right in the sight of the Lord you God. (13:18)

Significantly, Paul's rendering of Deuteronomy 27:26 in the Galatians passage above includes a reference to '*all the things written* in the book of the law' that is not in the Hebrew text nor in the Septuagint. It is the law in its place at the centre of the covenant between God and Israel, providing a complete and integrated way of 'doing what is right', of obedience to 'the voice of the Lord your God', that Paul is referring to in this argument.

Still more illuminating is the fact that, just as it has been helpful in understanding Paul to posit the image of a dividing line separating two ways of life, central to the message of Deuteronomy is a literal territorial dividing line. The 'blessings' are the fruit of being in the promised land; the land is the literal 'inheritance'; the law – the entire law – is essential to 'live' in the 'land' and be 'in the right':

> He brought us out from [Egypt] in order to bring us in, to give us the land that he promised on oath to our ancestors. Then the Lord commanded us to observe all these statutes, to fear the Lord our God, for our lasting good, so as to keep us alive, as is now the case. If we diligently observe this entire commandment before the Lord our God, as he has commanded us, we will be in the right. (Deut 7:23-25)

'Curses' come as a consequence of disobeying the law; forgetting or disregarding the law leads to the loss of the land and destruction:

> See, I have set before you today life and prosperity, death and adversity. If you obey the commandments of the Lord your God that I am commanding you today, by loving the Lord your God, walking in his ways, and observing his commandments, decrees, and ordinances, then you shall live and become numerous, and the Lord your God will bless you in the land that you are entering to possess. But if your heart turns away and you do not hear, but are led astray to bow down to other gods and serve them, I declare to you today that you shall

perish; you shall not live long in the land that you are crossing the Jordan to enter and possess. (Deut 30:15-18)

This sharp division in Paul's thought, parallel to the separation in Deuteronomy between life in the land and the destruction that comes with expulsion from the land, is essential for understanding the significance of the second curse text in Paul's argument:

> When someone is convicted of a crime punishable by death and is executed, and you hang him on a tree, his corpse must not remain all night upon the tree; you shall bury him that same day, for anyone hung on a tree is under God's curse. You must not defile the land that the Lord your God is giving you for possession. (Deut 21:22f)

Paul is presenting a text that highlights an essential element of his understanding of Jesus' death:

> For our sake he made him to be sin who knew no sin ... (2 Cor 5:21)

Deuteronomy provides a text from 'the law' that confirms and sharpens Paul's understanding of the nature of Jesus' death. He is one who was 'hung on a tree'; in his death, he 'is under God's curse'. The law, as interpreted by Paul, therefore specifically identifies Jesus as one who was accursed by God. In terms of the sharp dividing lines in Paul's thought we have identified at earlier points in the text, to say that he was, in his death, 'under God's curse' is a powerful way of saying that he dies as one who was apparently completely over against God. Although he 'knew no sin', that is, in him there was no assertion against God, he was made 'to be sin'.

A faith beyond human logic

Earlier in the chapter, consideration was given to how Paul can present the faith of Abraham as the faith of Jesus. It was argued that it was Abraham's faithfulness in the face of death that connected the two. One further vital connection needs to be drawn out at this point. *Abraham is absolutely faithful to God's directly given word even when it is, by any human logic, in conflict with God's purposes*. This additional element is clear in his story. Abraham was absolutely faithful to the directly given word of God even when that word appeared to contradict itself. Consider the promise to Abraham. He, at 100 years old, is told that his wife, Sarah, at 90 years old, will be blessed and have a son. Not only that but, as a consequence, Sarah 'shall give rise to nations; kings of peoples shall come from her'. And despite Abraham's disbelieving reaction at that point, they are given a son, Isaac, with whom, God says, a covenant will be established include his offspring and last for ever (Gen 17:15-19). Once Isaac has grown, the word of God comes to Abraham again. Abraham is tested and told 'Take your son, your only son Isaac, whom you love, and go to the land of Moriah, and offer him there as a burnt-offering on one of the mountains that I shall show you'

(Gen 22:1f). Abraham is obedient to this word (Gen 22:3-10) but, of course, as the story goes, just before he is about to kill Isaac, the angel of the Lord calls to him from heaven and stops him (Gen 22:11f). Abraham's faith in the word of God remains even when God's own promises appear to be contradicted: in an extraordinary way, he has been given a son; he is promised that God will make an everlasting covenant with his offspring; yet Abraham is told to take his son and kill him. Even though this contradicts the promise made by God, Abraham is faithful to the same directly given word that carried the promise in the first place.

How does this connect with the faith of Jesus? As we have seen, Paul is not concerned to present the way Jesus was faithful in the events of his life but, rather, connects the faith of Jesus to his death. And just as with the faith of Abraham, it is not simply a faith that goes beyond death which Paul presents as the faith of Jesus but a faith that perseveres even when God's promises appear to be contradicted. For Paul, there is no question that Jesus is the Christ, whose life and death is bound up with the fulfilment of the covenant promises of God to Israel. Yet, far from fulfilling the will of God revealed to the people of Israel in the law of that covenant, in Paul's assessment of what happened, the obedience of Jesus to God leads him to the apparent contradiction of it. Jesus is put to death at the behest of Jewish authorities believing that they are acting to defend the law. Putting this in the most powerful way that he can, Paul suggests that Jesus was obedient to God's directly given word, even though it took him into contradiction to that word revealed in the law:

> Let the same mind be in you that was in Christ Jesus,
> who ... humbled himself
> and became obedient to the point of death –
> even death on a cross. (Phil 2:5,8)

The word 'cross' here is translating the Greek word, *stauros*, meaning 'a spiked wooden stake' (pp. 41-3). The significance of the phrase, 'even death on a wooden stake', directly connects the death of Jesus with the curse text of Deuteronomy 21:22f. It is not simply going to death in obedience to God that expresses Paul's understanding of the faith of Jesus; it is not even going to the particularly horrific and despised death of Roman crucifixion; it is, very particularly, death on a tree – death as one accursed by God. It is this 'mind that was in Christ Jesus'. It is this obedience to what God directly reveals, even when it contradicts God's written law and therefore, from the perspective of the law, brings the consistency and faithfulness, in other words, the righteousness of God into question.

Faith, according to Paul, is an obedience to the word of God in each moment, even when it seemingly contradicts what God has promised. For Abraham, that faith meant being prepared to kill Isaac, even though Isaac's very existence was the vindication of God's promise to Abraham that, while he was 'as good as dead', he would have a child and be the father of a great nation blessed by God. For Jesus, that faith meant accepting a death at the behest of the guardians of the law, and cursed by the law, even though it had seemed in his ministry of word and healing that the inauguration of God's kingdom – God's vindication of Israel and the promises of

God's covenant law – was at hand. This is the faith of Abraham and Jesus and, as we shall see in the next chapter, the faith of Paul and his fellow apostles.

Conclusion

Paul's use of texts from Deuteronomy is significant (21:22f; 27:26). Deuteronomy offers a vision of life in the land given by God to Israel to possess. Life in the land is sustained and nourished by faithfully following the commandments given by God. Any deviation from these is equivalent to idolatry, to the worship of alien gods (30:15-18). The consequence of such deviation from the whole law is the loss of the land and destruction.

Paul is seized by a new way of living. With complete confidence that he is guided by God, particularly in his call to move into the Gentile world, he is indeed led outside of this all-embracing framework of the law. It is an extraordinary step, hardly conceivable for a Jew by any process of thought, but just understandable in the context of a radical experience of what Paul believes is the Spirit of God, the Spirit of prophecy, guiding him and others outside the world that has formed them.

Confirmation for this extraordinary step which otherwise from within a Jewish perspective can only be seen as a denial of God's blessings and opposition to what God requires lies in Paul's understanding of Jesus himself. Just as Paul's experience of new life is bound up with a sense that this life comes from Jesus, so he comes to the view that Jesus, acting under the same Spirit, guided directly by God, goes to his death cursed under the law but completely faithful to the direct living guidance from God. Central to this transformed view of the cursed death of Jesus is the experience of a vivid and new source of guidance that comes to Paul and others. They are absolutely confident that the Spirit has come upon them, liberating them from the struggle between right and wrong – guiding and empowering them to do what is right. In this experience they recognize the experience of Jesus – that just as they are now living by faith and not law, so Jesus was guided and empowered in the same way; just as they are now able to do what is right, so Jesus did what was right, most particularly in the right action of going to his death as one cursed by God.

What makes sense of what Jesus did is the present experience of those like Paul who have had revealed to them a new life of faith, in which they are guided in how to act and a new empowerment to act rightly, liberated from the struggle with sin. It is being faithful to these experiences that takes them outside the framework of the law and enables them to understand the faith of Jesus to the same direct guidance in all that he did and his climactic right action in accepting the nature of his death as one apparently rejected by God. So Jesus is no longer seen as cursed but as one who, through his complete faith in his direct relationship with God, has been the instrument through which a new intimacy has been opened up between God and humankind.

Paul presents the one sin of Adam as bringing about the universal spread of sin; he presents Jesus as performing one right act through which doing what is right will become universal. Just as the right action of the one man Jesus leads to the right action of the many, so the faith of the one man Jesus leads to the faith of the many. The Spirit of prophecy that was previously only experienced by a very few in Israel's history, is now being experienced by many and is meant for the whole world. That intimate knowledge of God's Spirit means that the law is no longer needed. The inheritance is no longer the land given to Israel as a possession bounded by the keeping of the entire law but the intimate relationship between God and the whole of humankind which has no boundary but rather the complete freedom of living empowered and guided by God's own Spirit as Jesus was.

Chapter 11

God's Fools:
the Transformation of a Few

Abraham is absolutely faithful to God's directly given word even when it is, by any human logic, in conflict with God's purposes. (see p. 187)

This is the 'mind that was in Christ Jesus' that, as was shown in the last chapter, was demonstrated most clearly in his death. This is obedience to what God directly reveals, even when it contradicts God's written law and therefore brings the consistency and faithfulness, in other words, the righteousness of God into question. Faith, according to Paul, is obedience to the living word of God in each moment. There is no way of 'fixing' God's guidance, of capturing God's word in written form, 'the letter'. The most extreme demonstration of this claim is that, as demonstrated in the way Jesus goes to his death and in the way Abraham is prepared to sacrifice Isaac, faithfulness demands following this living word even when it seemingly contradicts what God has promised. For Abraham, that faith meant being prepared to kill Isaac, even though Isaac's very existence was the vindication of God's promise to Abraham that, even though he was old, he would have a child and be the father of a great nation blessed by God. For Jesus, that faith meant accepting a death at the hands of the guardians of the law, and cursed by the law, even though it had seemed in his ministry of word and healing that the inauguration of God's kingdom – God's vindication of Israel and the promises of God's covenant law – was at hand. This is the faith of Abraham and Jesus; further clarification about the nature of this faith is to be found in this chapter by considering how Paul presents the faith of himself and his fellow apostles.

This chapter explores several elements that illuminate Paul's understanding of faith. Paul clearly acknowledges that what he and his fellow apostles have been through gives them a place of leadership in the early Christian communities. But this chapter will present two ways in which Paul describes the basis of this authority both of which reveal how this is no straightforward assertion of power and clarify his understanding of faith. The first concerns time: Paul speaks of what he has experienced as a foretaste of what is to come for all. The second concerns the nature of the experience that brings authority: it involves a deep change in self-perception that Paul describes as a kind of death, accepting the appearance of a fool, ready to accept ridicule and hostility from others as essential to the task he has been called to do.

Arriving early at adulthood

Transforming encounters with Jesus

The word 'apostle' has acquired such a weight of significance during the history of the church that it is particularly important to note it derives from the Greek word, *apostellō*, which simply means 'to send'. The straightforward meaning of the word 'apostle' is 'one who is sent'. We saw in Chapter 2 (pp. 19-20) how this idea of 'one who is sent' is explicitly associated in Paul's mind with the call of the Hebrew prophets: in speaking of himself in Galatians, he deliberately draws on words from the call of the prophet Jeremiah to indicate that his own call is from God (Gal 1:15f). The majority of his letters begin with a reference to his apostleship and its source in God:

> Paul, a servant of Jesus Christ, called to be an apostle ... (Rom 1:1)
> Paul, called to be an apostle of Christ Jesus by the will of God ... (1 Cor 1:1)
> Paul, an apostle of Christ Jesus by the will of God ... (2 Cor 1:1)
> Paul an apostle – sent neither by human commission nor from human authorities,
> but through Jesus Christ and God the Father, who raised him from the dead ...
> (Gal 1:1)

This last reference to God who raised Jesus from the dead indicates a further element of apostleship which is central for Paul and which we now need to turn to: integral to his understanding of the experience of being 'one who is sent' is an encounter with Jesus risen from the dead. Both these aspects are involved in an exclamation Paul makes when he is defending his apostleship to the Corinthians:

> Am I not an apostle? Have I not seen Jesus our Lord? Are you not my work in the
> Lord? If I am not an apostle to others, at least I am to you; for you are the seal of
> my apostleship in the Lord. (1 Cor 9:1f)

Paul's sense of himself as an apostle, 'one sent by God', is bound up with his experience of having seen Jesus.

That Paul believes that he had an encounter with Jesus risen from the dead in which something transformative happened to him that gave him his sense of 'being sent' is clear. Paul himself refers to it in Galatians, how God 'was pleased to reveal his Son to [Gk 'in'] me, so that I might proclaim him among the Gentiles' (Gal 1:15f). In the following section Paul is affirming the central importance to his gospel of the resurrection of Christ. He begins by outlining the resurrection appearances that have occurred. He does this with concern to express exactly the sequence in which they took place emphasizing in this way that these appearances are real historical events:

> For I handed on to you as of first importance what I in turn had received: that
> Christ died for our sins in accordance with the scriptures, and that he was buried,
> and that he was raised on the third day in accordance with the scriptures, and that

he appeared to Cephas, then to the twelve. Then he appeared to more than five hundred brothers and sisters at one time, most of whom are still alive, though some have died. Then he appeared to James, then to all the apostles. Last of all, as to someone untimely born, he appeared also to me. (1 Cor 15:3-8)

That last sentence gives a further indication that Paul is speaking of a particular sequence of historical events. The phrase, 'last of all', indicates that Paul believes that this sequence has come to an end. The resurrection appearances which began with Peter finished with Paul himself. In this sequence, Paul is identifying a particular group of a limited number who, in his understanding, have had this encounter with Jesus risen from the dead. After Paul has listed the resurrection appearances in the passage quoted above he then goes on to defend, not belief in the resurrection of Christ, but, belief in the resurrection of the dead. This is important. Paul is integrally connecting the past resurrection appearances of Jesus Christ to a transformation that is to come for others:

Now if Christ is proclaimed as raised from the dead, how can some of you say there is no resurrection of the dead? If there is no resurrection of the dead, then Christ has not been raised; and if Christ has not been raised, then our proclamation has been in vain and your faith has been in vain. (1 Cor 15:12-14)

Paul moves on to speak of the kind of transformation that is to come: the clothing over of the mortal body with immortality that has already been examined (pp. 128-31). After a passage where Paul explores the nature of transformation by comparing the figures of Adam and Christ, Paul speaks of the sounding of the trumpet in connection with the future transformation of human kind:

Listen, I will tell you a mystery! We shall not all die, but we will all be changed, in a moment, in the twinkling of an eye, at the last trumpet. For the trumpet will sound, and the dead will be raised imperishable, and we will be changed. (1 Cor 15:51f)

In this important section, Paul's thought has moved from an affirmation of the small number of resurrection appearances of which his is the last to look forward to a time 'when the trumpet shall sound' and many, if not all people, will encounter the risen Jesus. This same idea of 'the day of the Lord', a future transformation in which the appearance or 'revealing' of Jesus is central, occurs at other points in Paul's letters:

For this we declare to you by the word of the Lord, that we who are alive, who are left until the coming of the Lord, will by no means precede those who have died. For the Lord himself, with a cry of command, with the archangel's call and the sound of God's trumpet, will descend from heaven, and the dead in Christ will rise first. (1 Thess 4:15f)

> ... so that you are not lacking in any spiritual gift as you wait for the revealing of our Lord Jesus Christ. He will also strengthen you to the end, so that you may be blameless on the day of our Lord Jesus Christ. (1 Cor 1:7f)

> I am confident of this, that the one who began a good work among you will bring it to completion by the day of Jesus Christ. (Phil 1:6)

From this consistent link between transformation and encountering Jesus risen from the dead, we need to look further at the significance of the claim that a relatively small group have already had that encounter. For just as Paul considers the future transformation of humankind to be tied together with the future revealing of the risen Lord Jesus, so also the apostles, who have witnessed the risen Lord, are already, to some extent, transformed by that experience. We need to see the way in which, for Paul, the apostles are already participating in the change that will only come about for others in the future 'day of the Lord'. The shift in perception and self-understanding that is to come to all is already taking place in them.

Parent in Christ

It is not hard to show that Paul considers there to be a significant division between himself, as one of the apostles, and the members of the communities to which he writes. Look again at the 'infants in Christ' passage considered in Chapter 7 (p. 138):

> And so, brothers and sisters, I could not speak to you as spiritual people, but rather as people of the flesh, as infants in Christ. I fed you with milk, not solid food, for you were not ready for solid food. Even now you are still not ready, for you are still of the flesh. (1 Cor 3:1f)

While the first point is obvious, it is important to make it: Paul does not consider himself to be an 'infant in Christ'. He is the one feeding the community, making the decision about what it is or is not ready for. Paul writes in a way that demonstrates a clear authority over the communities. Three examples out of many possible ones will make the point clearly. Paul has been writing about the disgrace suffered by him and his fellow apostles as evidence for the genuineness of their apostleship:

> I am not writing this to make you ashamed, but to admonish you as my beloved children. For though you might have ten thousand guardians in Christ, you do not have many fathers. Indeed, in Christ Jesus I became your father through the gospel. I appeal to you, then, be imitators of me. (1 Cor 4:14-16)

Shortly after this he continues to speak as a parent:

> What would you prefer? Am I to come to you with a stick, or with love in a spirit of gentleness? (1 Cor 4:21)

In the second letter to the Corinthians his tone is just as firm:

> So, I write these things while I am away from you, so that when I come, I may not
> have to be severe in using the authority that the Lord has given me for building
> up and not for tearing down. (2 Cor 13:10)

Paul writes as a parent berating his children, implying both a confidence in his own maturity and a relative immaturity on the part of the communities he has formed. But a brief examination of one Greek word in a passage from Philippians will suggest that, in Paul's mind, this contrast between the apostles and the communities is temporary and that he sees the lives of the apostles as an anticipation of a transformation into maturity that is to come for all humankind.

The translation of phthanō

Leading up to the following passage from the letter to the Philippians, Paul has been speaking of perseverance in the life of faith:

> ... [O]ne thing I do: forgetting what lies behind and straining forward to what
> lies ahead, I press on toward the goal for the prize of the heavenly call of God in
> Christ Jesus. Let those of us then who are mature be of the same mind; and if you
> think differently about anything, this too God will reveal to you. Only let us hold
> fast to what we have attained. (Phil 3:13-16)

Before making the main point; it is worth noting the way in which Paul advises 'the mature' that they can expect guidance from God: 'this too God will reveal to you'. This echoes his comments in the first letter to the Corinthians where 'the mature' comprehend 'the thoughts of God' (1 Cor 2:11) and are 'taught by the Spirit' (1 Cor 2:13) and are equivalent to the spiritual person who 'judges all things, but is himself to be judged by no-one' (1 Cor 2:15). However the main thing to be examined here is the word at the end of the passage translated above as 'attained' (*phthanō*).

There is a vital element present in the word that is missing in this translation. The NIV tries to capture it by inserting 'already' into the phrase:

> Only let us live up to what we have already attained. (Phil 3:16, NIV)

This missing element is that of time. There are a number of ways of translating this word and it is perhaps better to replace 'attained' with 'reached' but what is most important is that it contains the sense of arriving or attaining beforehand, in other words, 'to come before, precede' (BAGD), so, 'to reach early' or 'to reach before others'.

It is not a word that occurs often in the New Testament but there is one use in the same story recorded in the gospels of both Matthew and Luke which demonstrates this sense extremely well. Jesus has been accused of casting out devils by the power of the devil himself. This is part of his answer:

> But if it is by the Spirit of God that I cast out demons, then the kingdom of God
> *has come* to you. (Matt 12:28)

The translation of *phthanō* as 'to come early' or 'to reach early' sharpens the
picture:

> But if it is by the Spirit of God that I cast out demons, then the kingdom of God
> *has come early* to you *[has reached* you *before others]*. (Matt 12:28, adapted
> NRSV)

With this additional element of time in the word, *phthanō*, we can draw closer to a
very significant observation:

> Let those of us then who are mature be of the same mind; and if you think
> differently about anything, this too God will reveal to you. Only let us hold fast to
> what *we have attained [reached] before others*. (Phil 3:13-16, adapted NRSV)

In Chapters 8 and 9 we examined Paul's sense of a 'coming of age' and 'inheritance'
for all. His meaning here is that those who are mature have reached that adulthood
early, before others.

The foolishness of the apostles

This section builds on the work on 'liberation from sin' where we have seen that
Paul can make the extraordinary claim that those who live by the Spirit definitely
will not sin (pp. 11-12, 38-40, 108-14). This confidence is particularly marked in the
way Paul speaks about the work of the apostles. The end of the self-centred life is
presented by Paul as investing them with a new kind of authority, not rooted in any
cleverness of their own, leading them to forcefully challenge others.

Stewards of God's mysteries

In the first letter to the Corinthians, Paul is concerned to establish that his authority
is not based on any worldly achievement at the same time as he affirms that there is a
new way of seeing things – a new 'wisdom' – not available to those who are 'infants
in Christ' but only to those who are 'mature' or 'adult':

> Yet among the mature we do speak wisdom, though it is not a wisdom of this
> age or of the rulers of this age, who are doomed to perish. But we speak God's
> wisdom, secret and hidden, which God decreed before the ages for our glory. (1
> Cor 2:6f)

Paul speaks in a very similar way of apostles:

> Think of us in this way, as servants of Christ and stewards of God's mysteries.
> (1 Cor 4:1)

In this section we will pursue what Paul is meaning by this new wisdom that the apostles have to impart. Of particular value in this examination are the letters to the Corinthians, in both of which Paul speaks about apostleship. It is clear from these letters that he is having to defend his role as apostle because it is under attack from what he calls 'false apostles' or 'super-apostles'. Why this is of particular help in understanding Paul is that the dispute pushes him to make a defence of himself and thus to expose the paradox at the heart of his understanding of what it is to be 'mature in Christ'.

Treasure in clay jars

In a section on these false apostles, Paul states one thing that indicates they are false:

> We do not dare to classify or compare ourselves with some of those who commend themselves. But when they measure themselves by one another, and compare themselves with one another, they do not show good sense [or RSV 'are without understanding']. (2 Cor 10:12)

What indicates their falsehood is the fact that they 'measure themselves by one another'; however, shortly after this, we find Paul comparing himself with these other apostles:

> But whatever anyone dares to boast of – I am speaking as a fool – I also dare to boast of that. Are they Hebrews? So am I. Are they Israelites? So am I. Are they descendants of Abraham? So am I. Are they ministers of Christ? I am talking like a madman – I am a better one ... (2 Cor 11:21-23)

But there then follows a list of the calamities that have befallen him as an apostle and at the end of the list, he gives what he regards as the only grounds for comparing himself with others:

> If I must boast, I will boast of the things that show my weakness. (2 Cor 11:30)

A few verses later the paradox underlying this boasting in weakness is bluntly stated:

> Therefore I am content with weaknesses, insults, hardships, persecutions, and calamities for the sake of Christ; for whenever I am weak, then I am strong. (2 Cor 12:10)

Other examples from Paul's letters expressing this same sense of 'boasting in weakness' are not hard to find. The following emphasizes the separation between the apostles and the rest of the community:

> For I think that God has exhibited us apostles as last of all, as though sentenced to death, because we have become a spectacle to the world, to angels and to mortals.

> We are fools for the sake of Christ, but you are wise in Christ. We are weak,
> but you are strong. You are held in honour, but we in disrepute. To the present
> hour we are hungry and thirsty, we are poorly clothed and beaten and homeless,
> and we grow weary from the work of our hands. ... [W]e have become like the
> rubbish of the world, the dregs of all things to this very day. (1 Cor 4:9-13)

So apostles have and impart the wisdom of 'the mature' – 'God's mysteries', 'secret
and hidden' – yet Paul connects this exalted calling with being weak and being
fools.

In order to get a clear idea of the importance of what Paul is saying here it is
worth recalling a phrase from the Romans 1 account of the 'exchange' or 'fall':

> Claiming to be wise, they became fools ... (Rom 1:22)

Repeatedly in speaking of the role of the apostle Paul describes himself as a fool
and what he preaches as foolishness. The opening section of the first letter to the
Corinthians returns to this theme again and again:

> For the message about the cross is foolishness to those who are perishing, but to
> us who are being saved it is the power of God. For it is written, 'I will destroy
> the wisdom of the wise, and the discernment of the discerning I will thwart.' ...
> Has not God made foolish the wisdom of the world? For since, in the wisdom
> of God, the world did not know God through wisdom, God decided, through the
> foolishness of our proclamation, to save those who believe. (1 Cor 1:18-21)

What this amounts to, when set alongside several other texts from this section of
the letter, is Paul's understanding that what has been done by God is to invert the
worldly perception of wisdom. It is the 'foolishness' of the apostles that Paul is keen
to profess. Clearly this 'foolishness' is closely linked with the cross and this will
be investigated in the final chapter but it is important to see how consistent Paul's
thinking is on this. He is saying that the wisdom of the world, that is, human wisdom,
is foolishness to God but with a very particular sense: *human wisdom is an actual
obstacle to perceiving the things of God*. Just as in the account of the 'exchange' or
'fall', the assertion of human wisdom leads to the loss of perception of the invisible
things of God, so, says Paul, in order to become wise in the things of God, it is
necessary to become a fool in the terms of the world. The clear implication is that
human wisdom simply cannot perceive the things of God:

> Do not deceive yourselves. If you think that you are wise in this age, you should
> become fools so that you may become wise. For the wisdom of this world is
> foolishness with God. (1 Cor 3:18f)

It is worth pausing at this point for a moment. This book has been proceeding on the
assumption that, while what Paul says may be extraordinary, it is not incoherent and
if the connections between the various aspects of his thought are rigorously pursued
a remarkably sharp and integrated picture appears. For this reason it is important to

establish what Paul is meaning here in this inversion of wisdom and foolishness. The element that makes sense of what he is saying is his understanding of 'the flesh'. It is easy to think of the flesh solely as the motivation for sexual sins. That this is one side of Paul's understanding of the flesh is not in doubt; it is these sins that the list in the letter to the Galatians begins with:

> Now the works of the flesh are obvious: fornication, impurity, licentiousness ... (Gal 5:19)

However, when Paul speaks of the flesh he is not simply referring to the source of sexual sins but also to a category of sins that can be described as 'selfish assertiveness'. This is how the Galatians list continues:

> ... enmities, strife, jealousy, anger, quarrels, dissensions, factions, envy ... (Gal 5:20f)

It has been argued (pp. 158-62) that Paul understands the 'fall' to involve an 'exchange': the identification of humankind with what is created over against the Creator. In Paul's account of the 'fall', humanity comes to be identified with the flesh, that is, with what can be seen and what, of its nature, perishes over time and the assertion of human wisdom – 'claiming to be wise' – is integrally linked with this state of affairs. What confirms this picture is the view that Paul takes of human wisdom and the flesh that can be found in the letters to the Corinthians. Any kind of divisive assertiveness is an indication of continuing fleshliness.

This is the point of the quotation with which this section started: an apostle who is concerned to compare himself with another must, Paul says, be false. Paul himself does this but always with the qualification that the only grounds for boasting is in weakness and even then such boasting is 'foolishness':

> I have been a fool! You forced me to it. Indeed you should have been the ones commending me ... (2 Cor 12:11)

The reason Paul gives for boasting in the weakness of the apostles is that it is because this weakness is so clearly evident that it can be known without doubt that it is God's power at work and not that of any individual apostle:

> But we have this treasure in clay jars, so that it may be made clear that this extraordinary power belongs to God and does not come from us. (2 Cor 4:7)

The momentous fact claimed in this understanding of Paul is his view that in the weakness and foolishness of the apostles, the false identification of humankind with fleshly existence is genuinely reversed. The wisdom and power of God is seen at work in human flesh.

In the first letter to the Corinthians Paul expresses this same sense but with more detail:

> When I came to you, brothers and sisters, I did not come proclaiming the mystery
> of God to you in lofty words or wisdom. For I decided to know nothing among
> you except Jesus Christ, and him crucified. And I came to you in weakness and
> in fear and in much trembling. My speech and my proclamation were not with
> plausible words of wisdom, but with a demonstration of the Spirit and of power,
> so that your faith might rest not on human wisdom but on the power of God. (1
> Cor 2:1-5)

What Paul is claiming is not simply that, as might be said today, he and his fellow
apostles are inspired by God, but rather that the work that they do is truly God's
activity. This claim has to be set alongside the understanding of the Spirit of God
that has been presented as Paul's consistent view, that it is a motivating source from
'outside of' the individual believer. Just as it has been argued that it is necessary to
acknowledge that the way Paul speaks of the coming of the Spirit indicates that he is
speaking of a clearly recognizable event, so, similarly, the way he speaks about the
power of God working through him in his weakness indicates that he experiences
this as an objective power.

The last quotation above is one of the reminders to the community about what
happened when he preached, incompetent though his preaching might have been.
What he says makes no sense unless his listeners recognize what he means when he
reminds them of the 'demonstration of the Spirit and of power'. What sense does it
make to boast in weakness and folly unless it is known with absolute certainty by the
one who boasts that it is through this very weakness that God's power is effective?
This is where the paradox in what Paul says is revealing. In the human order of
things it is wisdom and strength that are effective; what Paul is proclaiming is truly
an inversion of this order. Something happens when Paul preaches; he can remind
those to whom he preached of the objective reality of what happened to them; but
he also affirms that whatever happens arises even though he is subjectively aware of
his weakness and folly; it is this combination of real power and real weakness that
affirm that the power that is at work comes from beyond the individual preacher.
Paul is saying that his work is not any individual activity, that is, it is not 'according
to the flesh' but it is truly from God.

An end to 'boasting'

In Paul's affirmation that he has come to maturity early there is a claim that is central
to the argument of this book: that the theological picture that he presents is founded
in a real experience of liberation. Paul is stating that he has no concern with fleshly
achievement and reputation; liberation is a real ending to identification with concern
for the achievement of the separate self identified with a particular fleshly existence;
the death of self-interest has already happened in him. His complete confidence that
his outward ability is not what is effective in bringing about change in others is his
primary evidence that he is called and sent by God, that he is an apostle. Far from
being a limitation to God working through him, his awareness and acceptance of
his limitations are necessary for the powerful and effective transformative work of

God to operate through him. He, like those others called to be apostles, is thus a forerunner of a way of living that human beings were created for and that will come eventually to all: living free from any selfishness, filled with the Spirit, living by faith understood as guided by the prophetic word.

This is the nature of the clear separation between the community and the apostles in that they are living early a life that is to come for all. From the perspective of the old life, characterized by identification with separate existence, the power of the apostles is misunderstood as human authority and wisdom. What Paul expresses is that it is only with an end to identification with separate fleshly existence that the authority and wisdom of God can work. What he says of himself is that he lives no longer (Gal 2:20). It is this end of the separate self that is essential for the authority and wisdom of God to operate through the apostle. That is why those who 'boast' in any achievement cannot be true apostles.

The ministry of reconciliation

In 2 Corinthians Paul describes the task with which he believes he has been commissioned by God – the 'ministry of reconciliation':

> [I]n Christ God was reconciling the world to himself, not counting their trespasses against them, and entrusting the message of reconciliation to us. So we are ambassadors for Christ, since God is making his appeal through us; we entreat you on behalf of Christ, be reconciled to God. (2 Cor 5:19f)

A simple but important matter of translation needs tackling in this passage to show how it clearly connects with the *akoē pisteōs*, faith's prophetic word. This is another section where the lack of a literal translation obscures the simple clarity of what is being said. We are particularly concerned with the phrase rendered in the NRSV above 'entrusting the message of reconciliation to us'. Other translations (RSV, NEB, REB, JB, NJB, NIV) adopt almost identical translations.

In Chapter 2 the translation of *hrēma* and *akoē* as 'the message that is preached' was firmly challenged as obscuring their interpretation as the directly given word of prophecy (pp. 23-34). There is precisely the same issue here; the sense of the Greek words when translated literally is very clear: not 'entrusting the message of reconciliation to us' but *'placing the word (logos) of reconciliation in us'*. The simple but extraordinary idea being presented here is that those who receive the word of reconciliation in them become quite literally 'ambassadors for Christ'; they speak the words of Christ. God appeals through them just as God appealed through Christ. And the implication is that they suffer as a consequence just as Jesus suffered.

This commission is not for all. Many times in the chapters running up to and following 2 Corinthians 5:19f, Paul speaks of what 'we' (those who are sent to proclaim the gospel) are doing for the benefit of 'you' (those who are ordinary members of the community):

If *we* are being afflicted, it is for *your* consolation and salvation ... (1:6)

I do not mean to imply that *we lord it over your faith*; rather, *we are workers with you for your joy*, because you stand firm in the faith. (1:24)

[Y]ou show that you are a letter of Christ, prepared by *us*, written not with ink but with the Spirit of the living God, not on tablets of stone but on tablets of human hearts. (3:3)

For *we do not proclaim ourselves*; we proclaim Jesus Christ as Lord and *ourselves as your slaves* for Jesus' sake. (4:5)

We are not commending ourselves to you again, but giving you an opportunity to boast about us, so that you may be able to answer those who boast in outward appearance and not in the heart. (5:12)

[W]e entreat you on behalf of Christ, be reconciled to God. (5:20)

As we work together with him, *we urge you* also not to accept the grace of God in vain. (6;1)

We have spoken frankly to you, Corinthians; our heart is wide open to you. ... In return – *I speak as to children* – open wide your hearts also. (6:11, 13)

The 'we' here are those who have already been reconciled to God; they have been specifically called and sent by God. Those 'in Christ' in Corinth are the object of their appeal: '*we* entreat *you* on behalf of Christ, be reconciled to God' (5:20).

More needs saying about the nature of this work that Paul feels he is called to. The designation of his task as the 'ministry of reconciliation' evokes an activity that is completely oriented to peace; however, it is clear that his work is anything but peaceful. There is a passage later in this same letter which vividly reveals this paradox; Paul begins by speaking of the peaceful source of his ministry:

> I myself, Paul, appeal to you, by the meekness and gentleness of Christ... (2 Cor 10:1)

He then goes on to describe what is involved in 'the ministry of reconciliation' in terms of warfare in a way that further indicates his belief that the power that he exercises is from God, that fleshly assertion has gone and now God can work powerfully in Paul and others. In this power from God, Paul is quite prepared to boast. The following translation from the NRSV utilizes the footnotes which translate *sarx* as 'flesh' and *sarkika* as 'fleshly' enabling us to see Paul's clear understanding that, although he is engaged in conflict, he is not acting 'according to the flesh':

> I myself, Paul, appeal to you by the meekness and gentleness of Christ – I who am humble when face to face with you, but bold towards you when I am away! – I ask that when I am present I need not show boldness by daring to oppose

those who think we are acting *according to the flesh*. Indeed, we live *in the flesh*, but we do not wage war *according to the flesh*; for the weapons of our warfare are not *fleshly*, but they have divine power to destroy strongholds. We destroy arguments and every proud obstacle raised up against the knowledge of God, and we take every thought captive to obey Christ. (2 Cor 10:1-5 incorporating text in footnotes)

So the paradox is that the ministry of reconciliation involves a kind of warfare. What needs to be seen is that essential to the ministry of reconciliation is not only the peace making task of liberating or absolving from sin. Along with this goes another task that was also referred to in Chapter 1: bringing people to a new perception of sin, a recognition that they are sinners in a way that they had not previously been aware of. It is not difficult to see that such a task – exercising what Paul calls 'divine power' to oppose any 'fleshly' human assertion against the knowledge of God – has the potential to bring strong resistance and acute conflict. What follows is further evidence that this is indeed what Paul is speaking of.

Exposing what is wrong

In the course of 1 Corinthians 12-14, Paul presents a unique description of the effect of a Spirit-led community upon someone coming in from outside:

If, therefore, the whole church assembles and all speak in tongues, and outsiders or unbelievers enter, will they not say that you are mad? But if all prophesy, and an unbeliever or outsider enters, he is convicted by all, he is called to account by all, the secrets of his heart are disclosed; and so, falling on his face, he will worship God and declare that God is really among you. (1 Cor 14:23-25, RSV)

There are two Greek words here that are difficult to put into English: *elegchō* ('to reprove') and *anakrinō* ('to call to account'). One reason for the difficulty is that what Paul would seem to be describing here is not something commonly known in the church today. Recent translations evoke a scene closer to some contemporary Christian experience:

But if all are uttering prophecies, the visitor, when he enters, hears from everyone something that searches his conscience and brings conviction...(1 Cor 14:24, REB)

Paul is considered to be recalling a picture of an unbeliever entering a Christian gathering and hearing inspired words which that person then applies to him or herself, just as someone might enter a church today and apply the words of scripture or preaching that are heard to him or herself bringing some kind of change of heart. This changes the sense in the Greek in a subtle way.

Anakrinō, is used in five passages by Paul, all of them in this letter. It always carries the sense of 'close examination' and is used by Paul in the context of examination in a law court or by conscience; it can aptly and consistently be translated, 'to scrutinize'.

Elegchō, is more interesting and more difficult to translate. It will be argued that, as with *stoicheia* and *stoicheō*, this word does have a precise and relatively simple meaning, but one that is not carried by a single English word. The proposed definition is 'to expose the wrongness of someone or something'. There is no other use of this word in any writing definitely attributed to Paul but it is used in other parts of the New Testament and in the case of this particular word this is helpful. It turns up in several different contexts but, in all of them, the proposed definition brings greater clarity, sharpening the sense of the passages in which it is used.

One translation given in the RSV is very close to what is proposed:

> If your brother sins against you, go and *tell him his fault*, between you and him alone. (Matt 18:15, RSV)

Two uses of the word in John's gospel show the value of the more precise definition. John is presenting words of Jesus about the coming of the Spirit or 'Counsellor':

> And when he comes, he will *convince* the world of sin and of righteousness and of judgment ... (John 16:8, RSV)

This translation is somewhat obscure. The pronoun translated 'of' is more usually translated 'about' or 'concerning'. A revised translation then reads:

> And when he comes, he will *expose the wrongness* of the world concerning sin and concerning righteousness and concerning judgment ... (John 16:8; adapted RSV)

The three verses which then follow confirm the aptness of this translation in that they go on to describe the wrongness of the world concerning sin, righteousness and judgment. The NRSV has moved close to that interpretation:

> And when he comes, he will prove the world wrong about sin and righteousness and judgement. (John 16:8)

Earlier in the gospel is this section:

> For every one who does evil hates the light, and does not come to the light, lest his deeds should be *exposed*. (John 3:20, RSV)

Once again the proposed definition is entirely apt in the context and brings a greater sharpness:

> For every one who does evil hates the light, and does not come to the light, lest *the wrongness of his deeds should be exposed*. (John 3:20, adapted RSV)

An essential part of the meaning proposed is that it is the nature of something as 'wrong' that is exposed to an individual; this exposure leads to a judgement that a thing (a deed or an idea for example) not previously seen as wrong is so and is, by implication, seen by that individual to be in need of change.

This brief examination enables us to return to the passage in Paul's letter with the possibility of gaining a clearer idea of what he is describing. Replacing 'to convict' with 'to expose the wrongness of' is a very appropriate change and evokes a vivid scene:

> But if all prophesy, and an unbeliever or outsider enters, his wrongness is exposed by all, he is scrutinized by all, the secrets of his heart are disclosed, and so, falling on his face, he will worship God and declare that God is really among you. (1 Cor 14:24f, adapted RSV)

Paul is presenting here a description of how, through the mouths of others, the prophetic word of God exposes, scrutinizes and discloses the secret wrong of the individual, in other words, reveals the personal state of sin of the unbeliever or outsider. As a consequence of this extraordinary activity of the community, 'the secrets of his heart are disclosed' and the unbeliever is convinced that it is not by any human ability that the truth about himself is revealed but that it is God who is speaking to him through the word of prophecy and hence he declares that 'God is really [Gk 'living', 'existing'] among you' (1 Cor 14:25). In this unique passage, Paul is describing the effect of a community led by the Spirit, actively guided by the prophetic word of God, upon unbelievers, that is, those on the outside. Something previously hidden and painful for the individual to see is revealed as an essential part of the experience of liberation.

This provides further support for the view that central to the experience of transformation as explored in this book is a revelation about the old life as essential to entry into the new. That old life is now newly revealed as a form of slavery or death. What Paul speaks of is liberation from a fundamental state of sin that stays unexposed until it is revealed in the process of liberation; only its consequences in 'sins', in small or great acts of wrongdoing are seen. It is this that explains why he can be both strongly positive and negative about the law. Within the old life it is an extraordinary blessing, providing guidance from God in a state of blindness; once blindness is revealed in the coming of the new life, the law is no longer necessary, indeed it is a temptation to pull back from demands of the adult life of faith.

Courage to speak the word

In Chapter 2, Paul's account of the coming of the word to the Thessalonians was discussed:

> [W]hen ye received from us the word of that which is heard of God, ye accepted not the word of men, but, as it is in truth, the word of God, which also worketh in you that believe. ... [F]or ye also suffered the same things ... (1 Thess 2:13f, adapted RV)

One important aim of this chapter is to make a connection between the suffering of which these verses speak and obedience to the prophetic word of God. While the prophetic word is a word of reconciliation, it has been argued here that it is also a word which exposes what is wrong and which, therefore, leads to conflict. There is real connection here with the experience of the prophets relayed in the Hebrew scriptures.

> I have become a laughing-stock all day long; everyone mocks me. For whenever I speak, I must cry out, I must shout, 'Violence and destruction!' For the word of the Lord has become for me a reproach and derision all day long. (Jer 20:7f)

Paul expresses his determination not to compromise the word of God that he has received:

> For we are not peddlers of God's word like so many; but as men of sincerity, as commissioned by God, in the sight of God, *we speak in Christ*. (2 Cor 2:17, RSV)

The Greek word which, in the following verses, is translated 'to tamper' is evoking the image of the 'adulteration' of wine – a good image for diluting the word of God. The sense of the passage is even clearer if 'we do not lose heart' is understood to mean 'we are not cowardly':

> Therefore, having this ministry by the mercy of God, we do not lose heart. We have renounced disgraceful, underhanded ways; *we refuse* to practise cunning or *to tamper with God's word*, but by the open statement of the truth we would commend ourselves to every man's conscience in the sight of God. (2 Cor 4:1f, RSV)

In the final section of the same letter, Paul returns to state his commitment to speaking God's word even if it brings distress to members of the community:

> I warned those who sinned previously and all the others, and I warn them now while absent, as I did when present on my second visit, that if I come again, I will not be lenient – since you desire proof that *Christ is speaking in me*. (2 Cor 13:2f)

When the unbeliever or outsider enters the community at Corinth and finds himself scrutinized and his wrongness exposed this leads to the individual concerned worshipping the living God dwelling and speaking among the community. The several New Testament quotations used above to clarify the translation of *elegchō* also provide an indication that a completely different reaction might not have been uncommon to the 'exposure of wrongness'.

The words of Jesus from the Gospel of Matthew imply that, if you go and expose the wrongness of another privately, what you say may not be accepted and so you will then have to take witnesses; if what you say is still not accepted you may eventually have to separate from that person. John's Gospel speaks of the hate of those who do evil towards the light because it leads to the exposure of their wrongness. Here we have the beginnings of an explanation as to why obedience to the prophetic word of God may have led directly into conflict with both Jew and Gentile. If what was being spoken confronted directly and threatened to expose the sin – 'the secrets of the heart' – of those preached to, then the reactions described above, whether of acceptance bringing transformation or of resistance and hatred become understandable.

The ministry of reconciliation: summary sentence and discussion

> **For the apostles, being ambassadors for Christ meant speaking God's word without compromise, engaging in what Paul could call a kind of warfare which, as an essential part of the process of liberation, involved exposing the wrongness of the common condition in others not previously perceived by them to be wrong.**

> Paul did not become a Christian because he had come to the end of his tether as a Jew.

The point Ziesler makes here (24) has now become a commonplace amongst scholars. He speaks of it in other places (107):

> Paul encountered Christ before he saw anything wrong in contemporary Judaism, and it is because he believes that Christ exposes and then solves the human dilemma that he can dismiss all other ways that claim to lead to life.

Note how Ziesler affirms that something is both exposed and solved through his encounter with Christ. The main text has sought to establish that through Christ, Paul experiences a liberation which he did not know that he needed. Taking this seriously involves affirming the possibility that Paul goes through a transformation to a life that is unmistakably more desirable and worthwhile than the life he had previously led but that he only knows this because of his experience of liberation. Prior to this change he had not come, as Ziesler put it, 'to the end of his tether as a Jew' nor, as far as we can tell, was he even mildly dissatisfied with his lot as a Jew. The weakness of Ziesler's presentation here is in the neutral term 'human dilemma' for the state that Christ exposes. As we have already seen (pp. 111-14), Paul describes his previous state as a form of slavery or condemnation or death. It is not a 'dilemma' that needs a solution but an imprisonment from which release is required.

Dunn acknowledges the importance of the revelatory nature of Paul's 'conversion' and how this affected how Paul saw his past (181):

> [I]n some sense at least Paul did reconstruct his theology "from solution to plight." That is to say, it is an unavoidable conclusion that from his conversion onwards Paul theologized in the light of the fundamental "revelation of Jesus Christ" given him on the Damascus road. It does not mean, however, that in order to rationalize his solution he had to invent a plight. All it need mean is that as a believer in Jesus Messiah he now recognized serious faults in his previous theology, that the gospel of Jesus Christ showed up the flaws in his previous "zeal for his ancestral traditions" (Gal 1:14). ...

Even though Dunn rejects the idea that Paul 'invents a plight', he still sees this change primarily in intellectual terms. The 'wrongness that is exposed' according to Dunn is in Paul's 'previous theology' where he now recognizes 'serious faults'. This does not remotely catch the sense of seeing one's condition in a way that brings one to one's knees. In a later section Dunn captures more powerfully the experiential nature of the change (388f):

> ... Paul experienced his coming to faith in Christ as one of liberation. The practice of the law, which had previously been his delight, he now regarded as a kind of slavery, the slavery of the spiritually immature (Gal 4:1-3). This, of course, is the language of hindsight. But if his language resonated in any degree with his Galatian converts, they too must have experienced justification by faith as a liberation, initially at least. ... Not least of Paul's delights in justification by faith was that it had liberated from what he now recognized to have been a spirit of slavery, whose motivation was fundamentally one of fear (Rom 8:15).

In this section we sense that the reappraisal that Dunn indicates Paul has made of his past is rooted in more than intellectual insight. A state that had not previously been seen as such is, from the new experience of liberation, perceived to have been a state of slavery in which the motivation was fear. It is important to keep the clarity that we have established in previous chapters that it is not, as Dunn believes, 'the practice of the law' that is 'a kind of slavery' but that there is a state of slavery, for which Dunn's description is apt – 'the slavery of the spiritually immature' – which, according to Paul, is the universal state of humankind, because of which the practice of the law is necessary. With the maturity of freedom, the law is no longer required. It is worth noting that Dunn observes that the sense of liberation must have been felt by the Gentiles who came to faith as well as the Jews and this rather undermines his view that it is 'the practice of the law' that is, in itself, the 'slavery'.

A more serious reservation about Dunn's position comes when he comments on Romans 7. On the one hand he expresses very clearly the emotional power of coming to an awareness of sinfulness not previously perceived but on the other he believes that this awareness of the struggle with sinfulness is the continuing reality of the Christian life as understood by Paul (*Romans 1-8*, 407):

> Evidently conversion for Paul meant becoming aware as never before of the power of sin in his own life ..., not just as a power now broken insofar as he had died with Christ, but as a power still in play insofar as he was still a man of flesh ....

In Part One we explored why this will not do as an assessment of Paul's position.

The tremendously valuable insight that Paul's thought moved 'from solution to plight' can be found at many points in Sanders's analysis (41/48f):

> [Paul] thought 'backwards' from the revealed solution – that God sent Christ to save the world – to the plight from which he saved it – that all things were 'under Sin'. ... But since God, in Paul's new insight, had sent Christ to save the world, both everybody and everything, it was necessary to conclude that he had not previously provided for its salvation. Thus the lead-up to universal salvation was negative: the world previously must have been condemned, and whatever preceded Christ must have served to put it in that condition.

There are also many places where Sanders elaborates on the thought processes of Paul that follow from this basic view, the way in which, according to Sanders, rationalization follows on rather crudely from revelation (38/45):

> If the considerations put forward in Romans 1-2 and 5 do not explain the origin of Paul's conception of Sin, can we say where it came from? There are two principal possibilities. One is that Paul did not come to Christianity with a pre-formed conception of humanity's sinful plight, but rather deduced the plight from the solution. Once he accepted it as revelation that God intended to save the entire world by sending his Son, he naturally had to think that the entire world needed saving, and thus that is was wholly bound over to Sin. His soteriology is more consistent and straightforward than are his conceptions of the human plight. It seems that his fixed view of salvation forced him to go in search of arguments in favour of universal sin. This explains why Romans 1-2 and 5 are so weak as reasoned arguments but lead to such a definite conclusion. The conclusion that all need to be saved through Christ, since Paul received it as revelation, could not be questioned; the arguments in favour of universal bondage to Sin, then, are efforts at rationalization.

At no point that I am aware of has Sanders seen the possibility presented in this chapter: that awareness of the human 'plight' – a real, emotionally felt and intellectually apprehended experience of the everyday experience of humankind as 'slavery' – might be an essential part of the experience of the liberation that is the solution. Sanders has seen that Paul's emphasis is on the 'solution' provided by the revelation that Christ has been sent by God to redeem humankind; what he has not seen is that the descriptions of the 'plight', while not based on sociological or psychological assessments of humankind in general, can be understood as based upon Paul's encounters with an experience of revelation or liberation in himself and others that has a common and consistent form: individuals have a dramatic experience of liberation which has at its centre a perception of their previous existence as a state of slavery they had previously been unaware of.

Given that the nature of the transformation that Paul is describing is not seen, none of the three scholars has an appreciation of the cause of the conflict that Paul and the other apostles bring about in their engagement with others.

Conclusion

This chapter takes seriously the sharp distinction in what and how Paul writes between the apostles, those who have encountered the risen Jesus and sent out to the world and those who are baptized but have not experienced such a transforming encounter. One important way of understanding this experience of the risen Jesus is that it enables those who have been through it to live with one foot already in the liberated world to come. This gives Paul a distinctive perspective on the topics he deals with. On the one hand he can affirm very strongly what has happened, the new things that God is doing – the reality of the liberated life. At the same time, he can offer appropriate guidance to those who do not share this state as they wait for their own encounter with Jesus 'when he returns'.

So Paul is able to talk with complete conviction about the reality of liberation from sin and how the completely unselfish life looks like complete folly to the eyes of the world. What blocks others coming to an experience of selflessness is their experience of sin, often unperceived. The task of Paul and other apostles in exposing what is wrong is a direct cause of suffering to them and very clearly connects them with the suffering that came on Jesus as he gave the same witness.

The material of this chapter provides us with a way of seeing how Paul could look back on his Jewish past – and indeed the past of his fellow Jews and also Gentiles who have come to faith – and make observations about it that he would never have made while living wholeheartedly within it. If a common, if not universal, part of the experience of transformation was a heartfelt, painful realization that one's previous life had indeed been a kind of slavery, but had not been perceived of as such, this can significantly aid us in coming to an understanding of what Paul is saying and how his thought moves from solution to plight. Paul could indeed observe the way in which unbelievers broke down as the wrongness of their previous lives was exposed and thus he could speak confidently of the way in which, without faith, all are under the power of sin.

Far from being a caricature of life before faith, Romans 7 (see Chapter 5) can be regarded as an attempt to describe a universal enthralment which is no less real for being unperceived. Taking Paul's view of the sinful nature of the human condition seriously has enabled us to go further with him into a deeper understanding of the nature of the entrapment and the way of liberation to which he is pointing.

In the case of Paul and the apostles, this faith in the face of the contradiction of God's will is most evident in the resistance to the gospel of their fellow Jews. The apostles claim that in what God has done in Jesus, there is the fulfilment of all God's promises to the Jewish people yet their word receives violent opposition. In facing this contradiction, Paul boldly states the faith that lies behind the title of this book: that the disobedience of all humankind, Jew and Gentile, comes within God's plan – it is 'the necessary sin'.

Chapter 12

Seeing is Becoming:
the Transformation of All

In one major section of 2 Corinthians, Paul describes the process of transformation with which this book has been concerned. This verse is at the heart of the passage (2:14-5:21):

> And all of us, with unveiled faces, seeing the glory of the Lord as though reflected in a mirror, are being transformed into the same image from one degree of glory to another; for this comes from the Lord, the Spirit. (2 Cor 3:18)

'All of us ... seeing the glory of the Lord ... are being changed into the same image ...' We have examined earlier (pp. 158-9) how 'glory' is associated with God's immortality. It is a quality of the invisible God that can be 'seen' or perceived by humankind. It is the loss of this perception that characterizes the fall according to Paul (Rom 1:23). Central to Paul's description of transformation is revelation (*apokalupsis*) which means literally, in both English and Greek, 'the lifting of a veil or curtain'. It is the removing of this veil that enables the glory of God to be seen.

In this section of 2 Corinthians, where he focuses on transformation, Paul's thought has a striking internal consistency, enabling us to draw together all the themes that we have already explored. Losing perception of the glory of God is what leads into darkness, death and sin, or, in other terms that we have considered in detail (pp. 101-4), to an identification of existence with what is created, the flesh that dies. This chapter will show how Paul presents the lifting of the veil as something that happens within people, yet, in a way that transforms everything. People see and simultaneously come to participate in the glory that is seen; they become what they see.

The new covenant

Vital for understanding what Paul is saying about the new covenant is the contrast he makes with what went before. In the story of Moses and the Exodus, after Moses has encountered God, his face shines with glory, so much so, that the people cannot bear to look at it and, as a consequence, he has to wear a veil (Ex 34:29-35). Paul does not deny that the glory on Moses' face is the glory of God. God's glory, God's eternal quality is 'seen' in the face of Moses. But Paul says that this glory has now been 'set aside'; it had the nature of impermanence from the beginning. The much greater glory belongs to 'the permanent' (2 Cor 3:11). The law which Moses brought did reflect the glory of God and kept God's glory in sight. In terms we have explored, it served as a 'childminder' but here again we encounter Paul's consistent conclusion: it was 'impermanent', for a limited time. Whereas the people could not bear to look upon Moses' face, they now 'with great boldness' look 'with unveiled faces' at 'the glory of the Lord as though reflected in a mirror' (3:18).

> ... [W]hen one turns to the Lord, the veil is removed. Now the Lord is the Spirit, and where the Spirit of the Lord is, there is freedom. (2 Cor 3:16f)

And in Paul's mind the Spirit and Jesus Christ are bound together (p. 131). In 1 Corinthians Paul says that 'the last Adam', that is, Jesus Christ, 'became an "alive-making" Spirit' (15:45); similarly, here in 2 Corinthians, Paul, having made clear that he has is speaking of Christ as Lord (3:14-16), says that 'the Lord is the Spirit' (3:17). For Paul, 'turning to the Lord' is 'turning to the Spirit'; can we get closer to what he means by this?

Several themes come together here to illuminate the experience that Paul is speaking of. There is no question that this text from the prophet Jeremiah is in Paul's mind as he writes the words of 2 Corinthians 3.

> The days are surely coming, says the Lord, when I will make a *new covenant* with the house of Israel and the house of Judah. ... *I will put my law within them*, and *I will write it on their hearts*; and I will be their God, and they shall be my people. No longer shall they teach one another, or say to each other, "Know the Lord", for they shall all know me, from the least of them to the greatest, says the Lord; for I will forgive their iniquity, and remember their sin no more. (Jer 31:31, 33f)

Paul speaks in 2 Corinthians of 'a new covenant (3:6), of 'a letter of Christ' written 'not on tablets of stone but on tablets of human hearts' (3:3). When a few verses later he speaks of Moses coming down from the mountain (3:7), it is absolutely clear that 'the tablets of stone' are the words of the law. What has replaced what Paul calls the 'ministry of death' are letters 'written not with ink but with the Spirit of the living God' (3:3). We have seen how the Spirit is bound up with the idea of prophecy – words from God (pp. 18-23); in the new covenant, according to Jeremiah and Paul, words of prophecy, words from God, are written on each heart. Completely in line with what we have seen throughout this book, for Paul, turning to the Lord, the Spirit, is turning to the living word of God.

Confirmation for the centrality of the living word comes through relating this section of 2 Corinthians with Romans 3:21-26, one of the most important passages in all of Paul's writing and one we have referred to at key points (pp. 8, 11, 177, 178). We might note the importance of liberation in both passages. In Romans 3:21-26 Paul speaks of 'the redemption that is in Christ Jesus' (3:24). 'Redemption' could read 'freedom' but it has the additional connotation of freeing a slave, one who was clearly not free before. This fits the focus of the first part of Romans in establishing that all are 'slaves' and in need of the liberation that is in Christ. We will return later in the chapter to the central concern of each passage with 'the righteousness of God' (Rom 3:21f, 25; 2 Cor 5:21) but there is a different but vital point of connection between these two passages that needs making now.

For while the translation and lack of context for the contemporary reader might obscure the fact, the Romans 3 passage is also concerned with a contrast between Moses and his encounters with God and the situation in the new covenant. For right at the centre of the passage is the rare word *hilastērion*, which the NRSV renders as 'a sacrifice of atonement' (3:25). This is not easy to translate: 'the means of expiating sin' (REB); 'the means by which people's sins are forgiven' (TEV); 'sacrifice to win reconciliation' (JB); 'sacrifice for reconciliation' (NJB); 'the means of expiating sin by his sacrificial death' (NEB); 'sacrifice of atonement' (NIV); 'a propitiation' (AV, RV). What is being referred to here is something quite specific from the story of the Exodus and temple ritual set out in the Torah.

Encountering God: the hilastērion

All the above translations of *hilastērion* emphasize sacrifice and the forgiveness of sin. Central to the argument of the book has been the idea that Paul presents the directly given prophetic word of God, manifest in the early Christian communities, as a new and superior way to receive guidance from God. Despite its absence from the above translations, this same issue of God's communication with humankind is involved in the understanding of the purpose of the *hilastērion* and in the whole of the scriptural presentation of the establishment of the covenant between God and the people of Israel when the law is given at Sinai.

The central figure in the giving of the law of the old covenant is, of course, Moses. He receives his commission to lead Abraham's ancestors out of Egypt when he hears God speak to him at the burning bush (Ex 3:1-4:17). An important concern for Moses in this passage is how he will demonstrate for the people to whom he is sent that the words he speaks are from God and his fear that his word will not be accepted:

> But Moses said to the Lord, "Oh, my Lord, I have never been eloquent, neither in the past nor even now that you have spoken to your servant; but I am slow of speech and slow of tongue." Then the Lord said to him, "Who gives speech to mortals? ... Is it not I, the Lord? Now go, and I will be with your mouth and teach you what you are to speak." But he said, "Oh, my Lord, please send someone else." Then the anger of the Lord was kindled against Moses and he said, "What of your brother Aaron, the Levite? I know that he can speak fluently ... *You shall speak to him and put the words in his mouth; and I will be with your mouth and with his mouth, and will teach you what you shall do. ...*" (Ex 4:10-15)

Moses is called as a prophet who, despite his human reluctance, is given words from God which Aaron takes to the people for him.

After the miracles by which Moses leads the people out of Egypt, culminating in the Passover, the issue of God's communication is present in the giving of the law at Sinai. At the giving of the ten commandments, all the people are to hear God's voice:

> Then the Lord said to Moses, "I am going to come to you in a dense cloud, in order that *the people may hear when I speak with you* and so trust you ever after." (Ex 19:9)

But, when it comes to the moment, fear overtakes them:

> When all the people witnessed the thunder and lightning, the sound of the trumpet, and the mountain smoking, they were afraid and trembled and stood at a distance, and said to Moses, *"You speak to us, and we will listen; but do not let God speak to us, or we will die."* (Ex 20:18f)

The story presents the understanding that, because of the awesome nature of God's presence, the people are not able to receive the word of God directly. So, in the giving of the 'old' covenant, God's word comes through his chosen servant, Moses, and is channelled into a written form in the commandments.

This sets the scene for understanding *hilastērion*, the word Paul uses in Romans:

> For there is no distinction; since all have sinned and fall short of the glory of God; they are now justified (liberated/absolved) by his grace as a gift, through the redemption that is in Christ Jesus, whom God put forward as a *hilastērion* by his blood, effective through faith. (Rom 3:22-25)

Hilastērion is only used on one other occasion in the whole of the New Testament (Heb 9:5). What illuminates its use is the Septuagint, the Greek translation of the Hebrew Scriptures known to Paul. It is used there to refer to a particular part of the ark of the covenant – the 'mercy-seat':

> The Lord said to Moses: ... And have them make me a sanctuary, so that I may dwell among them. ... They shall make me an ark of acacia wood ... You shall put into the ark the covenant that I shall give you. Then you shall make a mercy-seat (*hilastērion*) of pure gold ... You shall put the mercy-seat on the top of the ark; and in the ark you shall put the covenant that I shall give you. *There I will meet with you*, and from above the mercy-seat, from between the two cherubim that are on the ark of the covenant, *I will deliver to you all my commands* for the Israelites. (Ex 25:1, 8, 10, 16f, 21f)

Central to the Romans passage are the themes of forgiveness and sacrifice; both are integral to the 'mercy-seat':

> The Lord said to Moses: Tell your brother Aaron not to come just at any time into the sanctuary inside the curtain before the mercy-seat that is upon the ark, or he will die; for I appear in the cloud upon the mercy-seat. ... He shall slaughter the goat of the sin-offering that is for the people and bring its blood inside the

curtain, and do with its blood as he did with the blood of the bull, sprinkling it upon the mercy-seat and before the mercy-seat. Thus he shall make atonement for the sanctuary, because of the uncleanesses of the people of Israel, and because of their transgressions, all their sins ... (Lev 16:2, 15f)

The mercy-seat is the place where the sin-offerings for the people of Israel are made and forgiveness is received. The conventional translations and interpretation are clear about this element. What also needs seeing is that, located directly above where the tablets of the covenant, God's essential communication with the people of Israel, are stored, is the *hilastērion* – the 'mercy-seat' – the place of 'meeting', of communication, between God and Moses. The awesome presence of God, the thought of which is able to terrify the people, is channelled through a particular holy place and through a specially chosen individual.

The illumination this provides for Paul's understanding of the death of Jesus is vital. Identifying Jesus with the sacrificial sin offering is not adequate for understanding how Paul is thinking about the death of Jesus. Clearly, the idea of sacrifice is present, in connection with forgiveness for sin, but understanding the mercy-seat as the location of God's special communication with Moses connects Jesus with that major theme of this book: God's communication with humankind.

Sacrifice, forgiveness and God's communication with humankind are all involved in the giving of the first covenant to the people of Israel. In Paul's understanding, they are equally involved in the giving of the new covenant but whereas, in the first covenant, forgiveness is for the people of Israel, now, forgiveness is for 'all', as everyone has sinned and fallen short of the glory of God. Whereas the *hilastērion* is the special place of communication with one chosen individual, now, the faith of Jesus has opened up a new intimacy of communication between God and humankind.

This combination of sacrifice evoking powerful associations with forgiveness and a new covenant carrying the implications of an intimate communication between God and humankind are also involved in the most often repeated passage of Paul:

> For I received from the Lord what I also handed on to you, that the Lord Jesus on the night when he was betrayed took a loaf of bread, and when he had given thanks, he broke it, and said, 'This is my body that is for you. Do this in remembrance of me.' In the same way he took the cup also, after supper, saying, 'This cup is *the new covenant* in my blood. Do this, as often as you drink it, in remembrance of me.' For as often as you eat this bread and drink the cup, you proclaim the Lord's death until he comes. (1 Cor 11:23-26)

These words echo the Passover meal in which the Exodus, the liberation from Egypt, is recalled but with Jesus himself in the place of the Passover lamb, the sacrifice through which the people are set free from slavery. Here again there is reference to blood and sacrifice and to eating and drinking in the presence of the Lord (see Ex 24:7-11), a powerful evocation of intimacy between God and humankind. That intimacy is vividly confirmed in the use of the phrase Paul presents as the words of

Jesus: 'the new covenant', evoking the famous passage from the prophet Jeremiah with which this section began.

It is important that the sacrificial dimension to Paul's words on the death of Jesus – his death as a liberation from sin which will be explored in more detail in the next section – does not obscure the equally prominent theme of Jesus as the *hilastērion*, the place of God's forgiveness, but also of God's communication with humankind. And whereas in the old covenant only Moses can enter, now Paul refers to 'all of us, with unveiled faces, seeing the glory of the Lord' (2 Cor 3:18) and, as we have seen, hearing the word of the Lord.

A new creation; the image of God

While sharpening Paul's picture of the new covenant is essential, more revealing of the scale of Paul's conception is his talk of a new creation. Our exploration of Paul's thought has already been helped by seeing how ideas of humankind's entrapment and liberation are central to Paul's thought (Chapters 5 and 6). As we see now how his ideas are coherently interlocked we need to return to that extraordinary conception that the whole of creation is being transformed as a consequence of what God has done in the action of Jesus.

The way Paul refers to aspects of Genesis in 2 Corinthians 3-5 confirms the view presented earlier in the book (Chapter 9) that his sense of how God is transforming creation is primarily a drama taking place in the human sense of self. Something shifted in human perception which brought the enslavement of darkened human consciousness in the fall; something is now shifting to bring liberation. It is hinted at when Paul speaks of transformed human existence as 'a new creation':

> So if anyone is in Christ, there is a new creation: everything old has passed away;
> see, everything has become new! (2 Cor 5:17)

This follows a section where Paul discusses the death of Jesus and there is the same pattern of human transformation connected with the death of Jesus when Paul refers to 'a new creation' in Galatians:

> May I never boast of anything except the cross of our Lord Jesus Christ, by which
> the world has been crucified to me, and I to the world. For neither circumcision
> nor uncircumcision is anything; but a new creation is everything. (Gal 6:14f)

Here Paul indicates the effect that the death of Christ has had on him: it has shifted the ground for all his activity. No longer is it his zeal as a Jew that provides the motivation for what he does. But the related, if larger, issue is how he can conceive of the cross of Christ as having a universal effect, way beyond his own life or even the issue of circumcision and the Jewish law – an effect he can describe as a 'new creation'. In order to make sense of this a major issue is how the phrase 'Christ died for me' or 'Christ died for us' is interpreted.

'Christ died in place of us'

The Greek word, *hyper* in the phrase 'Christ died for (*hyper*) me', can be used, like 'for' in English, in a number of ways. Paul speaks of praising or thanking or praying to God 'for' something or more usually, someone. It can be used with the sense of doing something 'for' someone, in other words, doing something 'for the sake of' someone. The purpose of discussing it here is not to establish that these interpretations are inaccurate and that there is an alternative, precise, consistent use of this word by Paul. Rather it is to suggest a certain prominence to a meaning within the word which, though present in English, tends to recede into the background when reading Paul because of the strangeness of what he is saying. The root of the English phrase, 'on behalf of' is 'on the side of'. If we talk about 'acting for' or 'speaking for' or 'standing for' someone it can have and often does have this sense. But the English can be expressing a more concrete connection between 'one acting' and the 'one who is acted for'. It is the connection contained in the concept of being an 'ambassador' – the image Paul himself uses in 2 Cor 5:20 – for someone or some cause, even in modern usage. The SOED defines 'ambassador' as, 'a minister of the highest rank who permanently represents his sovereign or country at a foreign court'. On a day to day basis a British ambassador deals with issues involving Britain in a foreign country 'on behalf of' the sovereign and his or her government. The ambassador acts with a certain independence but always, in that role, 'on the side of' the British sovereign and government being represented. But there are times when 'on the side of' is an inadequate way of expressing this role. On certain occasions, especially ceremonial ones, the ambassador actually 'embodies' the British sovereign, that is, he or she is the presence of the monarch at the event. There is the same logic in the idea that the embassy where the ambassador lives, is actually part of Britain and under British law and not part of the surrounding 'foreign' country. The ambassador is, in a certain similar sense, an extension of the presence of the monarch. The purpose of pursuing this analogy is to establish the possibility in the reader's mind that, when Paul uses the preposition 'for' or 'on behalf of' in the phrase 'Christ died for me', the weighting of its meaning can be understood as towards the sense examined above, that, when a British ambassador acts and speaks 'for' the monarch this can be not just, 'on the side of', but also, 'in the place of', or more clumsily, 'as an extension of the presence of'. Clarity is important here as will become obvious.

To examine the aptness of this interpretation it is necessary now to turn to an important and famous phrase:

> But God proves his love for us in that while we still were sinners Christ died for us. (Rom 5:8)

In other passages the way Paul describes the ones for whom Christ died varies in expression but not in substance. He speaks, for example, of Christ dying for 'the ungodly' (Rom 5:6) or of 'one for whom Christ died' (Rom 14:15). There is a more substantial and interesting variation in the fact that Paul can replace the phrase, 'Christ died for us', with

> ... Christ died for our sins ... (1 Cor 15:3)

Paul can also vary the way in which he speaks of the death of Christ while using the same preposition in exactly the same way:

> ... [T]he Son of God ... gave himself for me. (Gal 2:20)
> ... [T]he Lord Jesus Christ ... gave himself for our sins ... (Gal 1:4)

The importance of the interpretation of these phrases for understanding Paul can be easily seen and therefore the need for correctly understanding the weight that this simple word 'for' carries. To consistently replace 'for' with 'in the place of' in some of the above phrases makes an interesting sense:

> ... [W]hile we were still sinners Christ died in the place of us. (Rom 5:8, adapted NRSV)
> ... [T]he Son of God ... gave himself in the place of me. (Gal 2:20, adapted NRSV)

Where it does not seem to make sense is in the phrases where Paul speaks of Christ dying for our sins:

> ... Christ died in the place of our sins ... (1 Cor 15:3, adapted NRSV)
> ... [T]he Lord Jesus Christ ... gave himself in the place of our sins. (Gal 1:4, adapted NRSV)

However, before looking for an alternative for these phrases, it is worth remembering that Paul's thought at this point is operating in an unusual way. We have seen (p. 187) that he can say of Jesus that, 'God made him to be sin', (2 Cor 5:21). It is clear that such a statement moves outside any common way of thinking. The examination can be taken a stage further.

Support for interpreting 'Christ died for us' as 'Christ died in the place of us' comes before an important section of 2 Cor 5 which will shortly be examined. Once again what Paul says is strange:

> [W]e are convinced that one has died for all; therefore all have died. (2 Cor 5:14)

If Paul is interpreted quite loosely, as if his meaning were 'Christ has died for the sake of all', then there is no sense in his conclusion 'therefore all have died'. For the second half of the sentence to make more sense, Paul has to mean that Christ died in the place of all, that instead of all dying literally, Christ died in their place. With this interpretation, it is possible for Paul to go on to say that because this was a death in the place of all, the consequences are as if all have died. Obviously, all have not died but it is at this point that a consideration of the two phrases we have been examining together is illuminating:

> Christ died in place of us.
> Christ died in place of our sins.

The essential effect that Paul gives for the death of Christ is that, through it, God 'condemned sin in the flesh'. It is the sin in the flesh that has to die. Yet, as has been argued, the sin in the flesh is an identification that all humankind has made with the separate and mortal flesh. All are under the power of sin:

> ... [A]ll have sinned and fall short of the glory of God ... (Rom 3:23)

In Chapter 6 (pp. 101-4) it was argued that, as a consequence of this identification with the flesh, there is always in humankind an infirmity of purpose and that it is for this reason that even the most committed attempts to live by the law of Moses will never put an end to the struggle in the flesh. Indeed, the continued use of the law is itself an indication that the struggle in the flesh goes on otherwise there would be no need for the law, for external instructions for behaviour. It is argued in what follows that, when Paul speaks of the death of Christ as a death 'for' or, better, 'in place of' all, this is a further indication of how radical is the nature of what has gone wrong in humankind. From within the closed circle of sin, death, law and flesh that Paul so vividly describes in Romans 7 there is no escape (Chapter 6); the actions of humankind are always veiled with selfishness. Paul's words imply that it is only the death of humankind and a new creation that is adequate to transform this situation. But somehow through the death of Christ, Paul claims that the situation is saved and a new beginning comes about without the destruction of the old. How can this be?

In the last chapter, an effort was made to introduce the idea of a continuity of experience between Jesus and the apostles who Paul presents as witnesses to his resurrection. In particular, they come to share his faith and come to no longer identify their existence with the individual flesh. It was claimed that because of this God can work through them as he worked through Jesus. As we saw in the last chapter, in the following text from 2 Cor 5, Paul is speaking of the role of the apostles. For its accuracy in some important details of translation the *Revised Version* is used here:

> But all things are of God, who reconciled us to himself through Christ, and gave unto us the ministry of reconciliation; to wit, that God was in Christ reconciling the world unto himself, not reckoning unto them their trespasses; and having committed unto us [alternative in margin – 'placed in us'] the word of reconciliation. We are ambassadors therefore on behalf of Christ, as though God were entreating by us: we beseech you on behalf of Christ, be ye reconciled to God. Him who knew no sin he made to be sin on our behalf; that we might become the righteousness of God in him. (2 Cor 5:18-21, RV)

The useful contribution of the RV translation to an accurate understanding is in its consistency in translating *hyper*, 'on behalf of', which occurs three times in the last two sentences. This is the same word that can be helpfully understood as having the meaning, 'in the place of':

> [God] placed in us the word of reconciliation. We are ambassadors therefore in the place of Christ, as though God were entreating by us: we beseech you in the place of Christ, be ye reconciled to God. Him who knew no sin he made to be sin in the place of us; that we might become the righteousness of God in him. (2 Cor 5:19-21, adapted RV)

A cluster of ideas come together in this passage. There is the idea of Christ as the one 'who knew no sin' – the one in whom there was no identification of existence with the flesh and therefore no assertion against God – and yet he is 'made to be sin in place of us', that is, as we saw in Chapter 10 (p. 187), he comes to be wholly identified with assertion against God, the fundamental sin of all humankind. There is the idea of the apostles speaking now in the place of Christ. The word of reconciliation that was his is now placed in them; there is a continuity of ministry between him and them. The word which exposes what is wrong in the condition of humankind is now being spoken through them. And the purpose of this is that God's righteousness, God's 'way of doing what is right', might now be manifested in the world. God's purpose in making humankind is now coming to its fulfilment. Here is a creature – a part of creation – that can act as God acts. But so complete has been the identification of humankind with separate fleshly existence that there is a consequent blindness affecting all human perception and colouring all human actions. Working from within this identification with what is created there is no way out. Human life without sin is inconceivable; sin will only end with the destruction of humankind. What Paul does is present Jesus as one who is sent from outside this circle of selfishness whose death is essential to bringing about a shift in human perception such that this new creation can happen. This shift in perception is so powerful according to Paul that it enables humankind to consistently do what is right but now in full knowledge of good and evil – now truly the image of God.

Becoming the revelation of God

Paul makes extraordinarily bold claims for his ministry and that of his fellow apostles in 2 Corinthians 3-5. As we saw in the last chapter (pp. 195-6), Paul's sense is that they have arrived early at experiences that will be universal in the future. As we have already suggested (pp. 192-4), it is his own lived experience which gives him the confidence to speak of the transformation to come to all. This section of 2 Corinthians gives the clearest indications of the nature of the ministry exercised by the apostles. Central to that ministry is 'God's word' and it has been a major aspect of the presentation of Paul's ideas in this book that this is not a message or a collection of ideas about Jesus but a ministry of speaking words from God, words which primarily have the purpose of revealing what is wrong, that is, what needs reconciling with God. This is a ministry which is bound together with faith – a faith in the living word of God rather than an external, already given, word – even the word of the law. It is also the same ministry as Jesus exercised; this is his ministry of reconciliation. This is not an easy ministry and this passage affirms both the nature of that ministry and the cost of it.

So Paul states at the beginning of this section:

> For we are not peddlers of God's word like so many; but in Christ we speak as persons of sincerity, as persons sent from God and standing in his presence. (2 Cor 2:17)

He goes on to speak of his ministry among the Corinthians in terms of writing on human hearts:

> [Y]ou show that you are a letter of Christ, prepared by us, written not with ink but with the Spirit of the living God, not on tablets of stone but on tablets of human hearts. (2 Cor 3:3)

The link between faith/belief (see pp. xiii-xiv) and speaking the word receives one of its most powerful expressions in Paul::

> But just as we have the same spirit of faith that is in accordance with scripture – 'I believed, and so I spoke' – we also believe, and so we speak ... (2 Cor 4:13)

These themes come together in the most powerful way in the section that we have already referred to above:

> All this is from God, who ... has given us the ministry of reconciliation; ... entrusting the message of reconciliation to us [Gk 'placing in us the word of reconciliation']. (2 Cor 5:18f)

A subtle indication of the centrality of the work of exposing what is wrong for Paul lies in how he links this work together with the idea of new creation and the Genesis story:

> For it is the God who said, 'Let light shine out of darkness', who has shone in our hearts to give the light of the knowledge of the glory of God in the face of Jesus Christ. (2 Cor 4:6)

'Let light shine out of darkness' evokes the Genesis story of the creation of light (Gen 1:3). What Paul's words, 'who has shone in our hearts', point to is that central claim of this work that the drama of the new creation is one going on in the heart of each human being. Paul then goes on to indicate the demanding nature of this calling, the personal cost that it carries:

> But we have this treasure in clay jars, so that it may be made clear that this extraordinary power belongs to God and does not come from us. We are afflicted in every way, but not crushed; perplexed, but not driven to despair; persecuted,

but not forsaken; struck down, but not destroyed; always carrying in the body the
death of Jesus, so that the life of Jesus may also be made visible in our bodies.
(2 Cor 4:7-10)

It is important to see the paradoxical way that the glorious outcome of transformation
is being expressed in these last two sections. The invisible things of God are being
made visible, first, in the face of Jesus Christ, so that then, 'the life of Jesus' is made
visible in 'our bodies'. A few verses later Paul puts this paradox in a different but no
less vivid way:

For while we live, we are always being given up to death for Jesus' sake, so that
the life of Jesus may be made visible in our mortal flesh. (2 Cor 4:11)

Is the life of Jesus that Paul is speaking of here 'visible' and 'mortal'? Surely, it
has to be one of the invisible, imperishable things of God? Yet through the death to
self that Paul is claiming that he and others have gone through, the invisible 'life of
Jesus' becomes visible in mortal flesh. The life of God, incarnated first in Jesus, now
becomes incarnated in those who accept his ministry, which involves 'being given
up to death for Jesus' sake'.

All of this is powerfully integrated with what we have seen earlier of the
framework of Paul's thought and the extraordinary claim he is making. If to live
according to the flesh is to be identified with what is created – that which is seen and
mortal – and, as we have seen, Paul states that all have made this identification, then,
when Paul claims that the apostles no longer act 'according to the flesh', he is clearly
claiming that they are living by the Spirit. They are already 'on the side of God' in a
way that others in Christ will only be in the future. In them, the inversion of the place
of humanity in the created order which occurred in the fall is being reversed. The
flesh – 'that which is created' – is no longer worshipped and served; it is no longer
the source of motivation. It is 'the life of Jesus' that is now at work in him. This is
precisely what Paul says of himself:

I have been crucified with Christ; and it is no longer I who live, but it is Christ
who lives in me. And the life I now live in the flesh I live by the faith of the
Son of God, who loved me and gave himself for me. (Gal 2:19f, incorporating
alternative translation in footnote)

'You will be like God'

It would be easy to stop at this point and be satisfied with the connections that have
been made between Paul's understanding and the Genesis account of the creation
and fall of humankind but there is one further point to be made. Given that, for
Paul, God did not make some sort of mistake in the process of creating humankind
then the fall has to have a purpose. Some effort has been taken in earlier chapters to
demonstrate that Paul does indeed attempt to show this to be the case. Through the
identification of existence with the flesh, humankind experiences evil and, through

the gift of the law, comes to know good and evil through the struggle in the flesh. This is the knowledge of good and evil that both God and the serpent said would come to humankind through eating from the tree. God says that along with this knowledge will come death. This is the precise consequence of identifying existence with the flesh. What the serpent says is this:

> 'You will not die; for God knows that when you eat of it your eyes will be opened, and you will be like God, knowing good and evil.' (Gen 3:4)

It has been argued that what Paul claims for those who come to faith is that they are set free from the law of sin and death, enabled to do what is right without need of the law.

To fully appreciate what Paul is claiming is to take seriously the idea that the fall was for a purpose – it was 'necessary'. For this to be so, Paul must consider there to be something added to the human situation which was not there in Adam. This is why Paul talks of coming to 'maturity' or 'adulthood'. How Paul understands the extra dimension of adult life recurs over and over again in his gospel: it is 'freedom' or 'liberation':

> For freedom Christ has set us free. Stand firm, therefore and do not submit again to a yoke of slavery. (Gal 5:1)

Now, having the intimate knowledge of good and evil, humankind can freely choose to do God's will, no longer a child needing the guidance of the law, truly adult, sharing God's responsibility for the whole of what is created. This is the 'inheritance' to which Paul looks forward. This is an important counter to the picture of suffering that needed attention in the last chapter and above (pp. 205-7, 220-22). The centrality of suffering has its place in the time of transition, a time in which for freedom to come, it is essential for the unperceived slavery to sin to be exposed. However, the transformed life is one of complete freedom. Humankind, made in the image of God, with no hostility to God, delights only in doing what is right. Human action and God's action are aligned; human delight and God's delight are one and the same. Living in God's dominion is a life of complete freedom.

Inheriting the dominion of God: God's way of acting in the world

There is still one more point to draw from Paul's conception of the nature of human transformation in terms which are directly connected with the account of the fall in Genesis. As we have seen, towards the end of the first letter to the Corinthians, Paul speaks of the image of Adam alongside the image of Christ confirming that when he uses the word 'image' he is deliberately recalling the Genesis account of the creation of humankind in 'the image of God' (1 Cor 15:49). At the centre of the 2 Corinthians 3-5 passage Paul speaks of transformation into the 'image' of the Lord (3:18). These uses echo the Genesis account of the creation of humankind:

> Then God said, 'Let us make humankind in our image, according to our likeness; and let them have dominion ...' (Gen 1:26)

In Genesis, being created in the image of God and sharing God's dominion over all that is created are directly related. What should not be missed is the similar way in which Paul also relates the restoration of the image of God in humankind through Christ to a renewed dominion over all that is created. To see this it is necessary to be aware that one of the first lessons of New Testament studies is that the word translated 'kingdom' in Greek, *basileia,* is more properly understood, not as a 'state', but, as the 'activity of ruling', that is, as 'sovereignty', 'royal power' or 'dominion':

> Just as we have borne the image of the man of dust, we will also bear the image of the man of heaven. What I am saying, brothers and sisters, is this: flesh and blood cannot inherit the kingdom (*basileian*) of God ['God's dominion'], nor does the perishable inherit the imperishable. Listen, I will tell you a mystery! We shall not all die, but we will all be changed, in a moment, in the twinkling of an eye, at the last trumpet. For the trumpet will sound, and the dead will be raised imperishable, and we will be changed. (1 Cor 15:49-52)

What cannot be 'inherited' by flesh and blood here is a way of acting like God, exercising God's dominion. 'Flesh and blood' is a phrase which characterizes humankind still identified with separate, fleshly existence. But with humankind no longer identified with mortal flesh and blood but rather with the eternal Spirit of God, what becomes possible is a new humanity, no longer trapped in a self-centred life, now bearing the image of God and exercising God's dominion over all that is created. After this transformation, the very existence and activity of humankind, now guided by the Spirit of God, reveals God's righteousness – God's 'way of doing what is right'. Once the identification of existence with the separate individual mortal flesh is at an end then the pointlessness of individual assertion is evident. Humankind is set free – 'absolved' – from sin and the dominion of death is over.

There is precisely the same mixture of ideas at the climax of the section of Romans 5 that we considered in Chapter 6 (pp. 108-14). There we were reviewing how Paul contrasts the one trespass of Adam and the grace of God and the free gift in the grace of the one man, Jesus Christ. Paul goes on to present the significance of this gracious act that brings about a new creation:

> If, because of the one man's trespass, death exercised dominion (*ebasileusen*) through that one, much more surely will those who receive the abundance of grace and the free gift of righteousness exercise dominion (*basileusousin*) in life through the one man, Jesus Christ. ... [W]here sin increased, grace abounded all the more, so that, just as sin exercised dominion (*ebasileusen*) in death, so grace might also exercised dominion (*basileusē*) through justification ('righteousness') leading to eternal life through Jesus Christ our Lord. (Rom 5:17, 21)

The old 'dominion' or 'kingdom' of death is ending, the 'dominion' in life is coming. This is nothing other than the 'dominion' or 'kingdom of God'. Not a place but rather the activity that humankind was created for: doing what is right, God's grace-filled, right action in the midst of all that is created, consciously aware of the nature of life as eternal, no longer identified with the passing mortal body, but rather delighting in its God-given place in creation.

Disclosing the righteousness of God: God's way of acting in the world

Returning one last time to Romans 3:21-26, we note how it opens with the statement that 'the righteousness of God has been disclosed'. The passage that we have been specially referring to in this chapter, 2 Corinthians 3-5, ends by describing those who are 'in Christ' as 'the righteousness of God'. Both passages are concerned with reconciliation and with freedom; both passages present the death of Christ as the source of reconciliation and freedom. It is important to return to the first stage of our presentation of Paul's thought. A very simple observation was made there:

> The free gift of absolution from God is a real and effective liberation from sin …
> (p. 12)

Everything that has followed in this work has built on this observation and the last stages confirm it as much as the first steps. Paul writes out of a conviction based in experience that what has happened to him and others is a real and effective liberation, once for all, for good. Any attempt to modify this fundamental element of Paul's theological picture leads to distortion and complication. His central affirmations about the righteousness of God confirm it: the righteousness of God is disclosed in the faith of Jesus, specifically in how he goes to his death. The death of Jesus only discloses the righteousness of God to the extent to which those who witness it do so in the light of an experience of the continuing life of Jesus, the 'alive-making Spirit'. As they encounter that 'alive-making Spirit' which fully illuminates their hearts revealing what was wrong as well as the way to act rightly, they are themselves transformed and become ministers of the same transformation for others: they become 'the righteousness of God', God's way of acting rightly, God's dominion, and speakers of God's revealing and reconciling word as Jesus was. Paul's understanding of the law needs to be understood in this context. It is from and only from this radical experience of liberation that the law is seen to be no longer needed. The law is God's gift to bring humankind safely to this destination. Once the living word is established, the need for the written word falls away.

The first chapter ended with a further question about 'the righteousness of God' (p. 15):

> Given God the creator's righteousness – give that God's state/manner of existing always subsists in doing what is right, why did sin occur at all? Why was it necessary that sin entered the world? How can it be that the existence of sin contributes to the 'disclosure' of God's righteousness?

The answers to these questions have been emerging in the course of the book and have been reprised above. The first is liberation, true freedom. Humankind aligned with what God requires with no choice in the matter is not free. Humankind aligned with what God requires, knowing the serious consequences of action, any action, knowing the reality of good and evil, is in a position of freedom. This is the adulthood of humankind we have discovered in Paul's thought. And it is also the life of faith. Faith as listening to words from God, entering a place of communication with the divine. Confident that although it might not always appear to be the case to the perception of reason, although there may be serious contrary signs, all that is created reveals the righteousness of God. Once human life trapped in sin is truly seen in all its emptiness and horror, a way opens which is literally inconceivable before the change takes place. Being trapped in sin involves a blindness which has to shift; a veil has to be lifted. Only the gift of revelation can do this. The consequence of this seeing is true liberation into the glory for which humankind was created. Living in that glory, constantly and without struggle, awake to the Spirit, knowing the cost of selfishness, there is true freedom … with nothing to be gained from getting lost once again in darkness.

Becoming the revelation of God: summary sentence and discussion

It is in the nature of turning to the Lord, the Spirit, that the only way in which the veil can be lifted between the Lord and the beholder transforms the one who sees, who then, in turn, embodies the righteousness of God, God's way of acting rightly, God's dominion, and becomes a speaker of God's revealing and reconciling word as Jesus was.

Ziesler well expresses a view that Christians and scholars are comfortable with (43f):

[F]or Paul 'God was in Christ, reconciling the world to himself' (2 Cor. 5:19). This accurately reflects Paul's belief that Christ's activity conveys God's activity ...

What is not accepted is the argument of the main text that when Paul talks about the righteousness of God being revealed, he is referring to the fact that, it is not just Christ but those who are *in* Christ, living by the Spirit, effectively liberated from sin, who convey God's activity – God's right way of acting.

As part of establishing Paul's view of the humanity of Jesus, Dunn quotes Irenaeus – 'Christ became what we are in order that we might become what he is' (Adversus Haereses 5 preface) – and Athanasius – 'He became man that we might become divine' (De Incarnatione 54) (204) and he talks of how 'the divine programme for humankind had failed to achieve its goal: humankind was not exercising the intended dominion over the rest of creation' (201), but the change achieved by the 'second Adam' remains limited to one man (201):

But in Jesus God had "run the programme through again." And in him it had achieved its goal: all things were at last under the feet of God's man.

The goal for humankind remains unachieved in the present, even in the experience of the apostles. For example, Dunn says (229):

> If Christ is the representative of God in effecting the reconciliation ("God was in Christ"), the apostles are the representatives of God in proclaiming it ("God makes his appeal through us").

While a very positive interpretation of the role of the apostles, this distinction between 'effecting' and 'proclaiming' downplays the closeness of the relationship between God and the apostles. According to Paul, both Christ and the apostles are effective ministers of reconciliation. Just as the apostles now share the faith of Jesus, so they speak the same effective reconciling word that Jesus spoke, with the same willingness to suffer for it as he did. Despite investigating in depth the importance for Paul of the figure of Adam and the importance of associated ideas of 'glory' and 'image' (468), Dunn does not connect dominion as mentioned above with the 'kingdom of God' (492).

Sanders, as we have seen in earlier sections, is clear that Paul is speaking of a real change when he talks of people being 'righteoused' by God (73/86):

> As a result of this change the new person found that good deeds flowed out naturally and that everything which the law had required was 'fulfilled' in his or her life (Rom. 8:4).

But, despite his understanding that this change involves being 'transferred to another sphere' where what God requires flows naturally, he does not identify this activity with the 'righteousness' or 'dominion' of God.

Conclusion

Paul's sense of transformation involves a radical shift in the centre of human consciousness to a new way of seeing the things of God and the relationship between God and humankind. He expresses this first as a new covenant. This covenant replaces religious law, including the sacrificial system of the Jewish law and the widespread use of sacrifices in the pagan world, with the faithful death of Jesus, which marks a radical break with the old. This is presented by Paul as establishing a new beginning in which there is a once for all release from sin and a new way of communication with God.

The phrase 'Christ died for us' has for Paul a very specific meaning. The nature of our identification with separate fleshly existence means that a change cannot be effected from within. An external act is needed. Paul's conception is that God has acted in the person of Christ to reveal and, in revealing, break the identification of humankind with fleshly existence and its consequent selfishness, isolation and mortality. To describe this as a shift in perception is inadequate; describing it as a shift to a new sense of identity from which things all things look different gets closer. Elements that we have already considered are thus central to Paul's conception of what, based on his experience and that of others, needs to be 'seen' to bring about an effective and definitive liberation. First is the death of Jesus, understood with the essential link with faith that we have discovered. Second is the continuing life of Jesus enfleshed in the life of another who speaks living words from God as Jesus spoke living words from God, words that are for a particular person, revealing what is wrong for him or her. For the person so transformed, the closed circle of sin, law and death is at an end but with the corollary that the unselfish nature of the Spirit-led life inevitably means that that person is drawn into the continuing revelation and challenge to everything that is not Spirit-led, all that is still enslaved in sin: 'the ministry of reconciliation'. This is the new way of acting opened up by the death of Jesus. And Paul's confidence is that it is for all. As the individual separate self dies, issues of self interest die too. What is left is a living sense of the life of all in God. This becomes the reality, bringing with it the sense of an imminent change for all.

While the new covenant expresses this change in Jewish categories, Paul's talk of a new creation opens a broader view to embrace all humankind. The new creation is not a transformation out in the world but rather a transformation through a complete break with the old way of being human, the false identification all have made with the separate, mortal flesh. Once the death of this old sense of self occurs, the invisible life of God becomes visible in human flesh. This is the same reconciliation of Spirit and flesh that was examined in Chapter 9. Seeing this life in others is itself transformative; it can only be seen by one in whom the death of the old self, the shift in consciousness is actually happening. Without awareness of this alive-making Spirit, the living connection with the things of God is lost. With the connection, humankind cannot help but act as the image of God in creation. And central to that 'acting as God's image' is becoming the means by which others encounter the same revealing word of God. As individuals become agents of God's Spirit as Jesus was, they cannot help but expose what is wrong in others, themselves becoming ministers of reconciliation.

For a remarkable and illuminating consistency has emerged in which both 'inheriting the kingdom of God' (1 Cor 15:50) and 'becoming the righteousness of God' (2 Cor 5:21) can be understood as expressions for humankind sharing in God's way of acting rightly. No longer identified with fleshly existence and hence free from mortality, aware of right and wrong, good and evil, open to God and God's creation, humankind can freely do what is right without any need for law, becoming the conscious instrument of God's love in creation.

Conclusion

This book has clarified the nature of the experience that led to the radical change of direction in Paul's life and which he believed was to bring transformation for all humankind. A sustained focus has been applied to the interrelationships between similar words and concepts used at different points in Paul's letters. This, combined with an openness to explore conclusions previously excluded by scholarly and church presuppositions, has enabled the nature of the experience at the heart of Paul's theology to be clearly perceived in a way not previously possible. In the introduction to the final part of the book, that content was outlined in terms of key elements in a fundamental shift in perception to a sense of being: (a) *liberated from sin felt as an empowerment to always act rightly* (Chapter 1) and (b) *directly guided by God* (Chapters 2 and 3) as a consequence of which (c) *life as it was is newly seen as having been fundamentally limited or constrained – a kind of slavery or childhood* (Chapters 4, 5 and 6). This shift in perception is further characterized as carrying (d) *a vivid and sustained sense of the corporate nature of existence such that, from this new perception, the individual experience of transformation can only be understood as part of an imminent transformation for all* (Chapters 7, 8 and 9). The final part of the book has explored further the interrelationships between these different themes and shown how they relate in Paul's understanding to the figure of Jesus and, in particular, the death of Jesus as a focus for transformation. Both aspects of the final part have added further evidence to support the coherent picture that has emerged.

Several key factors in understanding Paul have been offered which do not figure with the same or any prominence in the work of the scholars who have provided material for discussion alongside the main text. The transition from childhood and immaturity to adulthood and maturity has been shown to be a particularly useful one that Paul offers. It is especially helpful in showing how that change involves both steady development, as in the growth of understanding of the child, and a dramatic transition to a new stage, as in the rapid change of adolescence, after which everything is different. From the perspective of the new life, the things of childhood – specifically, in this case, the law need to be left behind. They were good for childhood but destructive of the maturity of adult life.

A new perspective has been offered on what has become known as the way Paul's thought moves 'from solution to plight'. This is the view that Paul did not feel himself in desperate need of being saved from his situation as a law-abiding Jew but nevertheless experienced God 'saving him' and concluded that all needed the salvation God was offering. What we have seen as an alternative is Paul experiencing a transformation which is just as much a revelation about his former state as an introduction into a new way of life. The new reveals the old as a kind of slavery which was even more enslaving because it was not perceived of as such. Exposing what is wrong about the human condition is a major part of the transformation Paul speaks of.

As a consequence of seeing this fact clearly, it has been possible to see a good deal more of the nature of the enslavement. Through examination of what Paul means by 'mind set on the flesh', we have seen how the slavery of the old life can be helpfully conceived of as a false identification with the flesh, understood not as sinful in itself but, as the location of separate individuality. This individuality we found was part of the God-given diversity in creation but we saw how Paul describes humankind created able to perceive the invisible things of God being taken in by what he calls 'the lie', each person coming to identify with separate, fleshly existence. This Paul presents as 'the sin', a fundamental self-centredness from which all wrongdoing arises. For with that identification with the flesh which is mortal comes death to humankind. It is this fundamental state of sin for which Paul believes the remedy has been given.

It has been shown how the opposition in Paul's thought between faith and law arises because both give guidance on what to do. Paul presents the law as God-given but unnecessary once there is release from this identification with the flesh. Identified instead with God's eternal Spirit, good actions flow naturally. Just as the prophets of old were seized by the Spirit and heard words from God which guided them in all their actions and words, so, the new life is characterized by guidance from God. A new insight has been offered into how faith and the prophetic word are directly connected. Central to the revelation that Paul describes as bringing a once for all liberation is the recent scholarly insight that Paul speaks on several occasions of 'the faith of Jesus' (pp. 178-84). Where that faith is most in evidence is in the way Jesus goes to his death. His complete confidence in what God asks of him transcends the logical thought that in going to his death the extraordinary creative possibilities of his ministry die with him. He is obedient to the same word that led his teaching and healing even though it takes him to his death as one apparently cursed by God. Paul uses this idea of the curse as a way of demonstrating his experience that, in encountering Jesus risen from the dead, it is clear that Jesus is blessed by God and the curse falls instead on sin, the law and death.

Paul's subtle view of the way transformation occurs is that something is seen only as there is a radical shift in the ones seeing. As their old sense of self dies they come to see from a new place. Real understanding of what Paul speaks of can only occur as transformation happens. The understanding of transformation presented in the book is described by Paul in the most exalted terms. This is humankind as 'new creation', as 'the image of God', instruments of God, sharing God's dominion, and God's righteousness or 'right way of acting'. Specifically, this is humankind now with God's 'knowledge of good and evil'. In the flesh of humankind, God the creator has been truly united with the creation.

All that we have seen of Paul points to an extraordinary observation: the necessity of sin. At one point Paul speaks of how both Jew and Gentile have been imprisoned in disobedience *by God* (Rom 11:32). Only this way can humankind genuinely have come to knowledge of evil. Just as real understanding of what Paul says cannot happen without the transformation into the life he speaks of, so becoming the image of God, knowing both good and evil could not come without losing the consciousness of the things of God and entering the blind slavery of sin.

Consequences

Taking the conclusions of this present work forward offers potential new understandings in five key areas:

1. If Paul's dramatic transformative experience is central to early Christian life as suggested, then evidence of it will be clear in other early Christian writings. The rest of books of the New Testament need to be approached open to discovering signs of the same kind of experience. To what extent is there evidence of a similar experience behind Luke's focus on the guidance of the Spirit or John's emphasis on the voice of the shepherd that the sheep recognize? What can be discerned from this enquiry about Jesus and how he understood himself and was understood by others? We are at the point where placing what we have seen Paul says about various particular topics such as the nature of Christ, the resurrection, the return of Christ, the kingdom of God is best studied alongside the other early Christian writings.

2. The context in which Paul is articulating this universal shift is that of the specific relationship between the emerging Christian movement and what becomes the established Jewish rabbinic tradition. This situation is marked by conflict and those who faithfully hold to their traditional commitment to the Jewish law are identified by Paul as 'still in the flesh' with all the negative connotations that carries. 'Circumcision', the mark of being a Jewish man, is characterized as 'fleshly' in contrast to the 'spiritual' transformation bought about by faith. This conflict, which exists both within and outside the early Christian communities, marks, to a greater or lesser extent, all the texts of the New Testament. As mentioned in the introduction, it has been helpful to put this issue to one side in order to see with clarity the fundamental experience that underlies Paul's theology. Having done that, the nature of this conflict needs to be tackled afresh by approaching all the texts of the New Testament and other non-biblical sources in the light of the new clarity about early Christian experience that has emerged in the current work. This task is as important for Jewish-Christian relationships today as it is for historical clarity and insight.

3. Almost every topic of Pauline scholarly debate is touched by the reinterpretation of Paul in the main argument. The accuracy of that reinterpretation needs to be brought into relationship with other scholarly work on Paul to both test and be tested by other approaches. More work on aspects and details of Paul's letters not included in the present work need

to be brought into relationship with the new framework for understanding Paul offered in the main argument. This will, no doubt, lead to some reshaping of the big picture at various points but, if that picture is right, other aspects of Paul's thought will be seen with more clarity.

4. The work raises questions about religious experience and the points of connection and difference between the understandings of different faiths. The relationship between body and spirit, the physical and the spiritual; spiritual guidance and how to determine what it is right to do; the nature of surrender and spiritual transformation; good and evil; spiritual authority and leadership: the way early Christian experience and reflection related to these universal religious questions now emerges with more clarity in a way that has the potential to illuminate points of connection and difference between different religious traditions.

5. The work raises questions about the nature of Christian faith today. Its view of the centrality of the 'prophetic word' in Pauline Christianity challenges contemporary Christians to look again at what is meant by 'the word of God' and how to discern its direction for today. Contemporary Christian communities all recognize the need for this but have various different ways of framing the task. Catholic and Orthodox communities, while recognizing that any individual can be the recipient of spiritual gifts, tend to see the church hierarchy as the trained and tested medium for discerning what God requires. Protestant communities prioritize the word of God in scripture; the living word today is tested by what is found there. Quaker, Pentecostal and charismatic communities place great value on the living word sounding today. In the Quaker tradition, in particular, there have developed ways in which guidance is recognized through a subtle interplay between individuals who feel a sense of calling and the community which tests the truth of the inspiration and may come to support or embrace that call as something that demands action from others.

This work points to the importance of the tasks of listening and discernment in Christian communities but also highlights the fact that, for Paul, the empowerment from the word of God only came alive once individuals had gone through a life-changing transformation. Central to that transformation was an experience that, according to Paul, not only revealed a life so different that it could only be understood as part of a new creation but also revealed the necessity of what had gone before as the only way to bring an understanding of good and evil essential to the adult life of humankind. This work raises vital but uncomfortable questions: are Christians today familiar with the life-changing experience at the heart of Paul's theology and able, therefore, to understand and communicate to others what he is talking about? How do we discover today an experience of the Spirit so vivid that the preoccupations of our separate existences recede to be replaced by a hunger which will refuse to be satisfied by anything less than the transformation of all humankind?

Even though there are many examples of heroic service, day-by-day generosity and self-sacrifice, it would be hard to find someone who does not believe that the propensity of humankind to self-centredness is so deeply woven into us that discovering that quality is always something of a struggle involving some kind of discipline. It is precisely this situation that Paul is both realistic about but is completely confident is being brought to an end. He would subscribe to the view that human self-centredness can only end with the death of humankind, a reality that humankind is now actually faced with in its most acute form: unless there is transformation, human selfishness will bring an end to human life. What he claims is that the death of Christ is the God-given means of revealing something essential about the human condition and the nature of human enslavement, a revelation that transforms as it is seen. What places that revelation in the hearts of people is encountering 'the alive-making Spirit', the power that Paul and others identified with Jesus risen. This is not something that it is in any individual's power to bring about, but, according to Paul, that Spirit is 'made visible' in the bodies of those who have gone through the transformation he speaks of and have become effective ministers of reconciliation.

Through individuals in the early church that powerful and effective ministry of reconciliation changed the world irrevocably. Two thousand years later that extraordinary explosion of the Spirit still impacts upon us today, still raising the question: how do we come to that place of transformative self-sacrifice now? And what are we waiting for that will change the situation where the transformation of a few inspirational individuals and the glimpses of transformation of the many becomes the irrevocable and effective transformation of all humankind expected by Paul?

Index of Greek words discussed

Key passages discussed

Subject Index